THE ARTS IN THE MIDDLE ENGLISH ROMANCES

MARVIN ALPHEUS OWINGS

the arts
in the
middle
english
romances

BOOKMAN ASSOCIATES   NEW YORK

TO MY FAMILY

ƒOREWORÐ

THIS STUDY OF the fine and applied arts in the English metrical romances, primarily of the thirteenth and fourteenth centuries, is pursued with the hope of shedding more light on the nature of and attitude toward the arts in the English accounts, regardless of their origin. Because the distinctly English quality in the English romances has for the most part been overlooked by scholars and because the very fine study of Miss Harris on the *Mural as a Decorative Device in Medieval Literature*[1] showed that the English romances made an important contribution to literature, the writer feels that further investigation in the field may be profitable; therefore this study.

As a result of a comparison of the romance depictions of the fine and applied arts—with the exception of mural decoration, which has already been treated by Miss Harris—with the fine and applied arts of historical certainty, we have found that the two are strikingly similar, and that the English romance representations in most cases are highly realistic.

At this point it seems advisable to define, *romance, romantic,* and *realistic* or *realism* as used in this study. The word *romance* is used as a historical term without any critical significance. It represents a type of narrative work produced during the Middle Ages and featured by certain formal conventions, such as adventure, feudal society, the order of chivalry, courtly love, idealized knighthood, etc. When we speak of the English romances, therefore, we shall refer to a formal classification of literature, not matter which is merely unrealistic. However, within the romances is found the *romantic;* that is to say, the unattainable, the "notion of mystery and fantasy," the spell of everything that is characterized by the magical touch, by the sort of imagination that possesses the mystery of the "remote and unattainable."[2] Thus, when this definition is applied to the romances, we find them to be largely romantic. That part of the romances dealing with the arts, which may be called romantic, is the creation of the imagination. Nevertheless, I am interested in showing that in the English romances the portrayal of the arts is for the most part *realistic*. By realistic art representations we mean depictions that are transcripts from contemporary life, depictions that reflect the historical facts as we know them. For example, I have found that the structure of the feudal castle as represented in the romances, insofar as it is presented, corresponds with the historical facts about castles in England. Also, representations in the romances of interior decoration reproduce the interior decoration of the time. On the other hand in the representation of the arts the English romances, like all others of the period, produce pure art works of the imagination, such as fabulous gardens with jewelled gold and silver trees in the branches of which sat marvelous metal singing birds. But, comparatively speaking, the purely romantic in the arts is not nearly so vitally important as the realistic. In fact, in the English romances we find that the purely romantic element tends to be slighted. Where art representations in the English and French romances are compared, we do not find a single instance in which the fantastic has been amplified from the French, but we do find several in which it is minimized or omitted altogether. This difference in treatment would seem to indicate that sometimes, in the representation of the romantic in the arts, the English romances tend to become less romantic.

Granting that the English romances are translations of the Old French, we may come to the conclusion that in respect to the fine and applied arts the English romances are for the most part realistic—are largely transcripts of contemporary civilization and taste.

In conclusion, I take this opportunity to acknowledge my indebtedness to the Vanderbilt University Library staff for the many courtesies extended me during the preparation of this study,

Foreword

and to both the Clemson College Library staff and Mr. W. W. Smiley, Librarian of Eastern Carolina Teachers College, for assistance in acquiring materials.

To members of the staff of the English Department of Vanderbilt University I express appreciation for assistance, especially to Professor Claude Lee Finney, who read this manuscript and offered valuable suggestions. A debt of inestimable gratitude I owe to Professor Walter Clyde Curry, who suggested this field of study and whose enthusiastic inspiration and painstaking correction brought this work to fruition; an even greater debt I owe him for his direction and encouragement of my previous studies.

Also, to my colleague, Professor C. Hugh Watson, I am indebted for critical assistance that has been a gift of time and energy. Finally, the courtesies of the Trustees of the British Museum and of Mr. Sidney Toy in permitting the reproduction of illustrative materials are gratefully noted here and specifically acknowledged later.

M. A. O.

Clemson, S. C.

contents

ILLUSTRATIONS

THE ARTS IN THE MIDDLE ENGLISH ROMANCES

CHAPTER ONE

realism and romance

THE LITERATURE OF any period is the product, directly or indirectly, of the age which produced it. The circumstances and material concepts portrayed in literature are conditioned by those which have been experienced by the writer himself. There must be a basis in fact. And this basis in fact is found, by the writer, in the culture of which he is a part and in the material surroundings through which he moves. Thus, believing that there is in all creative art a basis in fact—a reflection of reality—I purpose to show that there is realism in romance, that the metrical romances are part of the life of the time, and that the life of the twelfth, thirteenth, and fourteenth centuries is reproduced in these romances. In furtherance of this belief, I shall compare the romance accounts of the fine and applied arts with the historical descriptions that are recorded in authentic records of the period; furthermore, I shall compare the romance accounts with the conclusions of recognized authorities, and with illuminated manuscripts which were current at the time of the romances and which are supposed to be realistic. Let us, then, examine these romance accounts in order to reconstruct a composite picture of the fine and applied arts. Architecture, because of its detailed treatment, will occupy most of our attention. We shall begin with city architecture in general, and then particularize.

The medieval town, when viewed from a distance, gave an impression of a closely encircled forest of spires of varying heights and shapes—all reaching skyward, all pressed together in the protecting embrace of the city wall; when viewed close at hand, this forest proved to be the superstructure of proud palaces, lofty castles, imposing halls, and majestic churches. But such a display of human aspiration and craftmanship was not created without a comparable display of protective measures; in fact, protection might well have been the watchword of medieval peoples. This pressing need for protection determined in many instances the very existence of the cities and villages. In England, the villages and towns had one of four origins, all of which were associated with the problem of defense. Some of the towns were of ancient Roman foundation. Others grew up in the neighborhood of monasteries, which offered refuge as well as work to artisans, travelers, and pilgrims. In some cases the sheltering walls of the castle of a powerful lord drew a population together; later, commerce was the motivating factor, but defense was never forgotten. For example, King Edward I, returning from Scotland, observed a site with exceptional possibilities for a fortress for the security of his kingdom, and for a port for extension of commerce. Questioning a shepherd, he learned the height to which the tides rose, the owner of the place, etc. Then he acquired the land and issued a proclamation offering freedom and commercial privileges to all merchants who would build and inhabit there. The king erected a manor house for himself in the town, which was incorporated as a free borough in 1299. By 1312 the great church was built, and by 1322 the town was fortified with a wall and towers.[1]

The site of the towns was determined by the conformation of the terrain or by the direction of the river courses—in short, by the conditions of nature. A site highly favored for its natural advantages was the seashore; consequently, numerous cities were constructed there so that their outer wall was continually washed by the waves.[2] In the romance of Alexander, the conquering king described a town so protected by the sea and the difficulty he experienced in surmounting such an obstacle.[3] Likewise, the city of Troy seems to have been equally strong although its walls were surrounded by water only at high tide.[4] In lieu of sea protection, a favorite city site was a riverbank. Like London and many others, the romance town of Ile d'Or was built by the side of a river.[5] Particularly formidable as well as especially desirable was the dual natural defense of a river and a marshland. Godeffroy of Bologne, in his adventurous wandering, came to a town in the Balkans which was built on the peninsula formed by the confluence of the Danube and the Lintans. This site was defensively ideal, because the landward side of the town was defended naturally by a great marsh.[6] In the event that there were no water barriers available, the next most desirable natural site was a hilltop or a mountain summit, such as that upon which Old Edinburgh was built. King Alexander of romance, in selecting a location for the city which was ever to be a monument to him, chose a similar elevated knoll.[7] In the event that a town grew up on a plain or in any area which lacked the contour bulwarks of terrain, it had the difficult but necessary task of constructing more formidable defenses.[8] In short, the towns of the Middle Ages were a phenomenon determined as much by physical environment as the course of rivers is determined by the conformation of the mountains and valleys.

The need for protection, as I have already indicated, occasioned the rise of some cities; this is particularly true of those which curled around the sheltering walls of a castle. To begin with, the castle with its outlying buildings was nothing more than a fortress which came to be known as a *burg*. These burgs, the walls of which enclosed a strictly limited area, were so small within that there was no room for the gradual influx of merchants, etc.; consequently, a suburb or "outside burg" grew up. This "new burg," as it was called by contemporary texts,[9] attached itself to the burg (the fortress) in a number of ways. For instance, the castle was often held in a full embrace by the suburb; thus, the castle was completely surrounded by the growing town. Partonope of Blois visited a romance town of this nature:

> Ther stode a towne, wythowten dowte,

Ryghte welle I-walled 'rounde a-bowte.
A-myddes the towne, wyth-in the walle,
There stode a castelle þat was ryalle.[10]

A variation of this general plan is found in the location of the castle at the end of the "new burg": "A toure she did to be made betwixt the Fortresse and the tounne."[11] In both variations of this general plan the town was doubly defended. The suburb with its wall served as the first line of defense, and in the event that it fell, the people could withdraw into the impregnable fortress which was in the nature of a donjon. Occasionally the castle was joined to a corner of the town, thereby making the intervening section of the wall serve both fortress and town; however, this economy weakened the defensibility of both units. A romance town was rendered impotent because it was constructed according to this plan:

Florence and Sorbare went before them and sessyd not tyll they were entred into the towne, for ther enter coude not be defended, for the castell ioyned to a corner of the towne.[12]

Rather than hazard in this manner the existence of both units, the medieval city-builder often separated the two entirely, but placed them sufficiently close that the one could augment the other in time of peril. Very often the suburb was built at the foot of a knoll or rock which had precipitous sides, and on the summit stood the burg.[13] A castle so located possessed tremendous defensive advantages and served as an almost impregnable rendezvous for the suburbans. A variation of the plan of mutual augmentation for defense by the burg and suburb is found in the building of burg and suburb as entirely separate units but within one locality; both were on the same elevation.[14] Such a plan made it necessary for an attacking force to envelop both units before a decisive action could be undertaken; otherwise, an attack on only one unit would expose the attacker's flank to harassment by the other unit. Thanks to these and similar defenses, the towns could almost always victoriously oppose the assaults of the invaders.

Security, in an age when private war was the custom, was a dire necessity; therefore, it is almost impossible to imagine a town existing during the Middle Ages without a wall. In fact, the most obvious external feature of a medieval town always was its wall.[15] Until the twelfth century the walls of even the larger cities had been simple enough. The old Roman walls, or their equivalent, had given sufficient protection until they were destroyed by the assault of the enemy or were sacrificed to the internal need for more building space. Then simple walls of earth, crowned by palisades, with fortifications at the gate, had sufficed.[16] This earthen wall, with it solid palisade of wood, pierced with gates and surrounded by a moat, constituted a security against bandits; it could not have withstood a regular siege, so that by the twelfth century the burghers made their security somewhat more certain by building ramparts of more durable material.[17] Sometimes these old walls were searched to their very roots for a substantial foundation for the new ones:

> And first þe grounde roots he made to be souzt,
> Ful depe and lowe, þat it faille nouzt
> To make sure þe foundacioun; . . .
> And when þe soille, defouled with ruyne
> Of walles olde, was made pleyn as lyne,
> Þe werkmen gan þis cite for to dounde.[18]

Sometimes from the old earthen wall rose arch upon arch, and these arches supported the new walls.[19]

The material used in the new ramparts was stone, and occasionally brick. A fifteenth-century illumination, "Battle of Alexander under the Walls of Ephesus against the Hindus and Persians," from *Histoire d'Alexandre* shows a fair city protected by a strong brick wall which is fortified by towers that are of stone.[20] The romance descriptions were probably a bit florid, referring to the material as stone,[21] lime and stone,[22] marble,[23] white marble,[24] or black marble;[25] however, by far the most common was stone.

The height of the wall often reached the respectable elevation of twenty-five to thirty feet. The wall surrounding medieval London was twenty-two feet high.[26] The romance accounts go from the extreme of sixty cubits for Troy[27] down to that of London's wall, which may be considered as approximating the norm.[28] Interestingly enough, another writer more realistically describes this same wall of Troy as being twenty cubits.[29] In another romance the measure of the wall was taken by a twenty-two foot giant who could scarcely lean over it.[30] Still another writer told of the embarrassment that the low walls of Berwick occasioned the inhabitants:

> At great myschef defendit thai
> Thair toune; for, gif we suth sall say,
> The vallis of the toune than wer
> Sa law, that a man with a sper
> Micht strik ane othir vp in the face.[31]

The prodigious task of building and keeping in good repair a construction as huge as a city wall naturally limited the extent of the town itself. At London, the wall extended all the way around the town except along the river-front. Its total length even in the fifteenth century, after several extensions had been made, was two miles and six hundred and five feet, and it enclosed a space of less than a square mile.[32] The romance accounts are far from realistic in this regard, for the city of Alexander is described as being sixty-six miles in circumference and Troy's perimeter as being a journey of three days.[33]

The wall had to be made thick enough, as well as high enough, to afford a sense of security, if not absolute security, to the townsmen who dwelt within its encircling shelter. Some city walls were wide enough to drive a team and wagon along the top.[34] A writer of the period, in giving instructions for the erection of a city wall which would withstand any assault, advocated the erection of two parallel stone walls which were to have an inside measurement of twenty feet apart; no directions were given for the thickness of the two stone walls. The twenty-foot interval was to be filled with dirt, which was to be packed and tramped until it was almost as hard as rock.[35] In general the town walls of romance were not presented so definitely in this respect, but the town of Lusynen was surrounded by a barrier of twenty-foot thickness.[36]

In contradistinction to this earth-filled double wall is the true double wall, which may be described as a building of walls in depth, or in series; the walls were built parallel to each other but without any material filling the interval. The device was merely an expedient of added protection. In the event that an enemy might tear down or gain possession of the outer wall the citizens were still protected by the inner wall. A fifteenth-century illumination in the *Poems* of Charles Duke of Orleans (Royal MS 16 F ii) presents a picture of the Tower of London which stands impregnable behind its defenses of triple walls.[37]

The crown of each wall, on the outside, was the parapet, or solid barrier raised along the top of the body of the wall. A more effective crown was a battlement, which was a parapet with open spaces, along the top line. The battlement consisted of the open spaces, called embrasures, and the solid intervals between, called merlons. Normally, the merlons were from six and a half to nine feet high and five feet to six feet wide; the embrasures, which had a breast wall of about three feet, were from two to three feet wide. About the thirteenth century the merlons were often pierced in the middle with loopholes. [38] William of Palerne, in his adventuring, saw the crenelated walls of a city: "a cite nobul/ enclosed comeliche a-boute wiþ fyn castelwerk" and "þat þe komli kerneles were to-clatered wiþ engines."[39]

In time, all city walls, whether single, double, or triple, supported a promenade known as the wall walk. During earlier periods a few guards were posted along the city wall. It was their duty to make the rounds of the walls regularly, especially during the night; for this service a path was made just inside the wall. This arrangement was very unsatisfactory because the guards, on their rounds, could see little or nothing of what occurred outside the walls; consequently, the builders placed the walk on the wall. For this reason they either made the wall broad enough to have a path behind the battlements which crowned it, or else built a wooden walk on supports at the top of the wall.[40] The wall of London was provided with battlements on the outside and a walk or standing place within, two feet or three feet wide, for the defenders. There may have been some kind of rail for protection on the inside; the railing, however, sometimes found on old walls still existing, such as at Chester, is modern; also, the walls of York, Avignon, and other places are without any railing along the wall walk.[41] Moreover, a contemporary writer of the period suggested, in the building of the earth-filled double wall, that the inner wall be made lower than the outer so that it may be easier of access to defenders of the town. A dirt ramp or any easy flight of stairs was the means of ascending to the wall walk.[42] Although the romance pictures are not so clear cut, the essential features are the same. To illustrate, the citizens of Thebes maintained constant vigil on the wall walk when there was danger of attack. Also the citizens of another town rushed, in typical fashion, to the wall walk to observe and to fight, if need be:

> Thanne entreden they the town anon,
> these zonge Bacheleris everychon,
> drowen vpe here brygge & Schet here zates faste
> And vp onto þe wallis they wenten in haste.[43]

A wall such as I have just been describing is technically known as the "curtain" in the complete wall fortifications. This curtain, twenty-five to thirty feet in height and twenty feet thick, served simply as a stone barrier; it had no great defensive purpose other than holding the enemy at bay while lethal missiles were hurled from the towers. The truly defensive element in the wall fortifications was the towers which pierced the curtain at such intervals that each section of the wall could be covered by the archers in two adjacent towers. At London, towers were built every two hundred and fifty feet.[44] Charles the Great, in his romance town of Onsea, had ten strong towers in the city walls; there is no account given of the circumference of the wall.[45] The usual height of the towers was approximately twice that of the curtain wall. The wall around London was twenty-two feet high and the towers forty feet.[46] In the romances, the height of towers is given by inference; for example, a king of Sicily, who was in possession of a tower, was "so hy a-lofte that nedid to drede neither gonne shot ne stone cast nor no hurt they might do him."[47] Very often these towers were built with no wall at the back and frequently had scarcely any roof. Some of them were open in the rear from the ground to the summit, where there was a platform of timber; others had a stone arch crossing them at the level of the wall. Usually the towers were so placed within the curtain that the inside face of the wall was smooth; sometimes the tower marred this regularity by projecting slightly on the inside. But regardless of the inside surface, the tower projected principally on the outside; this expedient permitted the defenders to shoot at the flank of an enemy attempting to attack the curtain. Towers such as I have just described are seen in the thirteenth-century fortifications of Conway, Visby, and Avignon. Often the tower was entered from the wall walk by a doorway on one side only, and in order to pass from one side of the tower to the other it was necessary to ascend to its battlements. This was done so that if one section of the curtain were taken by the enemy, that section could be isolated by removing the timber stairways in the tower at either end of the conquered section. In the town walls of Conway there was a doorway from the wall walk to the timber floor of a tower, but there was no doorway on the other side. In order to reach the walk on that side it was necessary to climb to the tower battlements by means of a wooden stairway within the tower and then descend by a flight of stone steps built against the tower wall, on the outside. The romance tower occupied by a king was of this design. Although he alone occupied the tower, no one could approach near enough to dislodge him: "than toke they i j a laddir, and drew them toward the toure . . . thies i j knyghtes of Scotland

did all their payne to come vp."[48] At Avignon there are doors to
the wall walk on both sides of the towers, and a stone bridge
spans the gorge from one doorway to the other. In this wall fortification, the open-backed towers are closed all around at strategic
points particularly liable to attack. The tower at the west angle
of the town is closed at the back to the height of the wall walk
of the curtain, but the tower at the north angle is closed to its
full height.[49] The romance of Alexander and Soredamour describes
the storming of an ill-fortified tower. Some of the besiegers having mounted the wall, the count took his stand beside the door-
post of the tower and defended himself with an axe, cleaving all
he struck, while his friends were ranged behind.[50]

In order to protect the curtain between the wall towers, the
architect often added turrets, or smaller towers. A city of magnificence is pictured in the illustration of the emperor at Constantinople, from an early fifteenth-century plate in *Mandeville's Travels*
(Add. Ms 24189, f. ii). A thick, irregular wall is reenforced by
means of cylindrical towers built in two stages, the second of which
is reduced in diameter. Many of these tile-roofed towers are further strengthened at their summits by a halo of bartizans, or overhanging turrets.[51] These turrets were constructed from the ground
up or corbelled out from the wall. At Visby may be seen corbelled
turrets which sit like a saddle upon the curtain. These turrets are
also open at the back. At Avignon the two turrets between each
pair of towers rest, on the outside, upon buttresses rising from
the ground; the turrets are flush with the inside face of the wall.[52]
The romancers refer, without comment, to these turrets as watch
towers. Upon one occasion, when Valentine entered a city, all
the citizens "mounted vpon the walles toures & garettes."[53]

To augment further the defensibility of walls and towers, there
were constructed in those fortifications loopholes, or meurtrieres.
In the earlier form these loopholes were, as seen on the outside
of the wall, simple vertical slots about six feet in length. In the
late twelfth century the bottom of the slot was often shaped into
a triangle; others were made with a horizontal slot added, thus

giving the loophole the shape of a cross. During the thirteenth century the terminations of these slots were slightly enlarged and made circular in order to give the cross-bow greater play from side to side. The thirteenth-century loopholes of Kenilworth were, as viewed from the outside, vertical slots from one-half inch to an inch wide and from five and a half feet to six and a half feet long. When the loophole was viewed from within, it showed deeply splayed jambs; the splayed side of the hole enabled the archer to direct his fire towards the flank as well as the front. Also there was a recess in the wall behind the loophole for the accommodation of the archer. These recesses, which contained stone seats built across the inner angles of the recesses, were about five feet wide by seven feet high.[54] Regarding this phase of the defenses, the romancers were not specific. A woman who built a town was very careful to see

> At louers and lowpes, Archers had plente,
> To cast, draw, and shete, the diffence to be.[55]

A supplement to the wall fortification was the moat, or ditch, which was dug outside the wall, unless there was some natural defense, such as a river. A contemporary writer of the period, in his notes of instruction for builders, advocated that the ditch or ditches be made so deep and broad everywhere that they might not be filled under any circumstances.[56] The moat around Troy was so large that barges could sail therein.[57] The sultan of Babylon bore witness to the nuisance value of the moat: "The Diches were so develye depe/ Thai helde hem selfe chek-mate."[58] In contradistinction to this protection, the Germans in one of their escapades found their efforts greatly aided by a moat which was dry.[59] Moreover, entrance was made into Perth by a daring soldier who forded the moat in a shallow place, which was neck deep: "Bot till his throt the vattir stude."[60]

In order to pass over the outer fortifications of the wall, one had to cross a bridge, either a drawbridge or a fortified bridge. If an encircling river formed part of the city defenses, it was important that the bridge across it should be fortified and protected on the far side by a barbican, a strongly fortified gateway. The fortified Ponte Castel Vecchio, Verona, was defended by the great square tower of the castle on the town side of the bridge, and by two drawbridges on the far side. The Pont Valentre of Cahors is a medieval bridge of six spans and is defended by a tower at each end, as well as by a third tower in the middle of the bridge. All three towers stand across the road; each tower, which possesses a fortified gateway, is defended by an embattled parapet. In addition to this, the two end-towers have machicolations placed immediately below the parapets.[61] In general, the romance accounts of bridges were not so specific, but the fortified bridge of Mantrible was carefully delineated:

þar is a brigge of grete fertee,/ A Citee ys sett þer-bye:/ Mantrible þe Citee ys y-called,/ Wuþ marbre fyn ys he walled, & abatayed with toures hye./ Vnder þe brigge flet flagot, On him ne may dure schip ne bot. . . ./ Of brede ys he a gret bozeschot, & thre spere-shaftes deþ ech grot. . . ./ A þhys syde þe toun þat ryuer rend, & þe brigge þar ouer stent. . . ./ Oþer passage ne ys þar non bote by þat brigge y-mad of ston. . . ./ Amydde þe brigge þar stent a tour y-buld aboze wyþ gret honour/ Wyþ brytaskes [battlements] many & fale:/ In þar dwelleþ þe briggeward. . . ./ Vnder þe tour buþ zeates two, whar þorz men mote nedes go/ at wolleþ pacye þere:/ þar stondeþ algates an hundred kniztes, þat passage to kepe.[62]

Just as this passage indicates, the customary material used in bridges was stone; however, the romance *Libeaus Desconus* refers to one of wood.[63]

In the event that the city was protected by a man-made moat, this ditch was spanned by a drawbridge or drawbridges. The causeway into Caerphilly was strengthened by two drawbridges.[64] In realistic fashion, each gate into the romance city of Troy was secure behind two such bridges.[65]

The last unit in the wall fortifications was the city gate,[66] which was considered the most dangerous point in the fortification; therefore, it was made very strong. Although the number of gates was an indication of the importance of a city, they were added only because of necessity. Fifteenth-century London could boast of only eight.[67] In general, the romance references are realistic on this point. Babylon had four, Jerusalem four, Thebes twelve, and Troy six, although this last city was credited with seven by another author.[68] The gate was customarily built with a pointed arch, flanked on each side by a strong tower of some three stories in height.[69] The late twelfth-century gates of Cairo have a wide gateway, defended by a powerful two-leaved door and by two towers, the towers projecting boldly out on either side of the passage to the door. Between the door and the inner arch there is a large hall with vaulted recesses on either side. The towers are square on the outer face. Other gate towers in this wall fortification are round on the outer face. One of the most scientifically designed gateways was the Burg Ez-Zefer of Cairo. This gateway projected entirely on the outside of the wall and had its entrance on the flank, and not on the front face; thus a person seeking entrance had to approach in a line parallel with the city wall until he entered the gateway. Then he was forced to make a right-angle turn before he could pass through the gateway. Close to the gateway, on the entrance side, there was a wall tower, and immediately on the other side of the tower there was a sally port. The gateway was approached by a bridge of two spans; the first span reached from the outer bank to a pier in the moat, and the second, from the pier to a broad stone platform which filled the space between the gateway and the tower. The second span of the bridge was probably a drawbridge which would be raised or drawn back on the platform. Even if an enemy gained the platform, he had no important advantage; in fact, he was in a confined space. To his left was the round tower; to his front was the curtain; to his right was the gateway. Deadly fire from the meutrieres and battlements of these units would fall from three sides. The gateway was defended by a machicolation, which spanned the entire width of the opening, and by a two-leaved door secured by long timber bolts. The gateway and curtain were

built of strong concrete faced with ashlar.[70] Even though no romancer gave such a detailed description, a composite picture,
based on essential details, shows that the writers were governed
by reality. Let me be more specific. One romancer insisted that the
side posts of the gate be made strong: "The yates Iumelles, mighty
and strong."[71] Another told of a gate of wood which was burned.[72]
Troy had gates made of beaten brass.[73] Another described the destruction of a gateway, even down to the boards and beams: "A
prystour stood ovyr the gate/ He bent hys engynes and threw
therate/ A great stone that harde droff,/ That the tour al to-roff,/
The barre, and the burdys:/ The gate burste and the portecolys./
Therto he gaff another strok,/ To brek the bemes al off rok."[74]
Still others depicted the gates which always hung from hinges
placed on the jambs of the gateway, and which always swung outward:

to þe Citee þaye gunne flee,/ þe zeates wern opened azen hem wyde,
& þay floze in & nold nozt & sperede hem faste azee/ Boþe brigge and
baly in-to þe toun-zeate,[75]

and

> thereto the zates Ful clos they ben
> With joyntes of yrne þat men mown sen;
> an on euery zate vil hynges wel gode
> as any on this half the Salte Flode.[76]

Others referred to the locks or to the iron bolts that barred the
gates. Troy had great, thick, broad locks in addition to the strong
iron bars, both round and square, which reinforced the gate.[77]

Following out the principle of providing obstacles to access, the
city dwellers might add to the usual gateway a barras or a portcullis, or both. The barras was a low inclosure, generally of timber,
erected before the gate. Round the barras occurred the preliminary
struggle in an attack on a city.[78] The romance of Bruce pictures
the destruction of a barras, as well as the burning of a drawbridge.[79] The barras was sometimes used, but the portcullis came
to be an accepted part of every gateway. Portcullises were gener-

ally made of oak, plated and shod with iron; these barriers were moved up and down in stone grooves. Portcullises were usually operated from a chamber over the gateway by means of ropes or chains, and pulleys. Sometimes a winding drum was also used. The thirteenth-century gateway at Parthenay was defended by a portcullis, in addition to other devices.[80] Aldgate, in the wall of London, had a double gate with two portcullises.[81] On this point the writers are sufficiently detailed, one writer referring to the pointed lower ends of the uprights of the portcullis which were set to the ground:

Louken þe gates,/ Barren hem bigly with boltes of yren,/ Brayden vp brigges with brouden [interlinked] chaynes/ & portecolis with pile picchen to grounde.[82]

In contradistinction to the regular gate was the postern, which was a subterranean or hidden passage, closed by a door or gate which led inward from the moat. Frequently it was referred to as a sally port. Usually posterns were built on the side of wall towers to facilitate the making of sorties. The gateway Burg Ez-Zefer, Cairo, was re-enforced by a postern hidden behind the great defense tower. Also, two of London's eight gates were really posterns, afterwards converted into real gateways.[83] The romancers paid tribute to the effectiveness of escape or sortie through the postern, but they did not particularize. To illustrate, Ancean "yssued out at a posterne out of the toun."[84]

Another device for protecting the gateway of a city was the wicket, a small door in one of the two leaves of the great gate. In time of impending danger, the great, cumbersome leaves could be securely fastened and still there could be communication from without the city by means of the easily defended wicket. In 1321 the Aldermen of London decreed that the great gates should be closed every night at sunset, and the wickets of the gates should be kept open until curfew rang.[85] The wicket foiled some Saracen tricksters who "knokkyd at the wycket;/ He leet it stande stylle y-shet."[86] When Huon knocked at a closed gate, the guardian "opened a wycket."[87]

31

The gateways to a town were placed in the curtain, usually according to the situation of the highways on which they opened. Naturally, from each of these gates a street led into the heart of the city. In general, where the site permitted, the town was rectangular; consequently, there were always parallel streets running through the town from end to end, and others cutting them at right angles and dividing the area into rectangular blocks.[88] In London there were three or four principal streets; the apparent labyrinth of winding lanes was pierced by parallel thoroughfares and by others at right angles. However, in towns which grew without any planning, there were, in the early centuries, no attempts to make the streets straight. For example, Elstow contains houses which were built without regard to line; consequently, the streets follow the winding, twisting line of houses rather than the reverse.[89] The romancers took cognizance of the two types of streets, but the emphasis was placed on the broad thoroughfare. The streets of Troy were well laid out:

And of þis toun þe stretis large & wyde/ Wer by crafte so prudently prouided,/ And by werkmen sette so and deuided,/ þat holsom eyr amyddis myzt enspire/ Erly on morwe to hem þat it desyre;/ And Zephirus, þat is so comfortable/ Forto norysche þinges vegetable.[90]

Also, from each of the twelve gates of Thebes ran "hyghe" streets.[91] In one romance, Richard the Lion's men defeated the enemy in streets and lanes; another king in search of recruits sent his men into every street and sty. Also Duke Huon entered Burdeux and was led "by preuy darke lanes to the palayes."[92]

The condition of the streets of a town depended somewhat upon the local government. As a rule, sufficient enactments were passed to keep the streets in good repair; lack of enforcement accounted for their deplorable state. A boon to street maintenance was the practice of paving with stones. The paving of London's streets did not become general until the fourteenth century. Then paving was required of every burgher before his house, but the paving of the middle of the street was financed by means of income from a tax levied on carts.[93] In the time of Edward I there were four surveyors of pavement for each ward. The duties of these dignitaries were "to preserve, lower, and raise the pavements, and to remove all nuisances of filth and to take distresses, or else four pence, from those who placed them there, the same being removed at their cost."[94] Moreover, paving must have been a trade of some importance at this time, for there was a guild of pavers. For the most part, the romancers seem reticent on the subject of the surface of streets, but a few did mention that the streets were paved. Partonope rode down a long city street that was paved, and Alexander noticed the decorations along a broad paved street. Troy's streets were paved their entire length and breadth with white and red stones placed checker-wise.[95]

A panoramic view of a medieval city, viewed from a principal street, would show a great variety of buildings and many of the same type. Among them would be palaces, towers, a castle or castles, halls, houses, churches, and shops, as well as miscellaneous structures. Later on I shall treat these in some detail. A city like London, which was a city of palaces, possessed many monastic houses and churches, surmounted with spires and towers. These religious houses circled London as with a chain fortress to keep out the hosts of hell. The domestic houses, which were for the most part of three stories, were gabled and tile-roofed, and the windows were glazed. In some towns these houses of wood and plaster stood side by side in line, but in London the houses were unattached and stood each according to the will of the builder. Some of these served only as private dwellings whereas others were both shop and dwelling.[96] A late fifteenth-century miniature from the Book of Hours of Bona Sforza, Duchess of Milan, shows a background generously filled with towers, castles, palaces, and other arresting structures.[97] Also a woodcut from the Royal MS. 16, E. I., f. 436 presents a view of a rich, battlemented city which contains spired churches, imposing dwellings, and arresting houses of religion.[98] Likewise the miniature of an early sixteenth-century Flemish Horae (British Mus. Add., 24098) gives an interior city scene of a hall and palace backed by countless gabled houses lining the sides of a broad, straight street which leads to a church.[99] The romance pictures of a general view of a city are strikingly parallel. Perceval visited a city which was deserted. The streets were desolate, the houses in ruin, the abbeys and monasteries destroyed, the castle gates open, the mills silent, and the ovens cold.[100] Another described the destruction done in a town to the monasteries, hospitals, churches, chapels, houses, and inns:

> Mynsteris and masondewew they malle to erthe,
> Chirches and chappelles chakle-whitte blanchede,
> Stone steppelles fulle styffe in the strete ligges,
> Chawmbyrs with chymes, and many cheefe inns,
> Passede and pelid downe playsterede walles.[101]

In the walls of lancet-like houses flanking the streets were the shops, which stood open on the ground floor and which had windows, glazed at the top or not at all. The goods were displayed on the counter. A penthouse, or pentice, projecting from the front of the house, protected the goods displayed on the counter. In France, hangings on either side sheltered them further from wind, rain, and sun; a curtain suspended from the pentice afforded further protection. The severer climate of England required greater precautions; consequently, the upper half of the window was covered in and glazed, and the lower half, in very cold weather, was closed by means of a shutter. In summer the window was always open and the shutters were removed. Specifications found in a manuscript belonging to the Dean of St. Paul and condensed in the *9th Report of the Royal Historical Commission,* page 20, call for the erection of three shops in Friday Street, London, with one cellar below. The three shops are to have three "stalles" and three "entreclos" on the ground floor. On the second floor each house is to be divided into "une principal chambre, une drawying chamber, et une forein." Also, the first floor is to be nine feet from floor to ceiling. Each house is to have a gable towards the street.[102] Unfortunately the romancers seem to have had no interest in the interior of these shop-houses.[103]

Riley, explaining Fitz-Aylwin's Assize, made a distinction between stalls and shops. The stalls, of wooden framework, were projections from the gable facing the street and were used as shops to display articles for sale. London's city council ordered that these stalls should not be more than two and a half feet in depth, movable and flexible, according as the streets or lanes were wide or narrow. The shops were probably mere open rooms on the ground floor, with wide windows, closed with shutters but destitute of stanchions. Extra space in some instances was afforded by the projecting and movable walls just described. The pentices were projections on a larger scale than the stalls, for the aldermen decreed that they must be at least nine feet in height "so as to allow of people riding beneath."[104] This statement implies that the pentices must have extended beyond the portion of the street reserved for a footpath. A plate in Le Croix and Sere's *Moyen Age*, vol. "Corporations et Métiers," Plate 8, gives an interesting street and shop scene. On the right we see a row of very tall frame houses with gables turned to the street. Portions of the sides are decorated with patterns in timber framework, raised plaster ornamentation, or painted panels. The ground floor, which is protected by the overhanging penthouse, is comprised of a row of shops under arches which are not glazed. The shops have open fronts and have display benches spanning the lower part of the arches.[105] Two street scenes in the *Alchemy Book* (Plut 3469—Brit. Mus.) of the early sixteenth century show medieval shops similar to those just described.[106] Regarding this aspect of the city, the romancers were almost as realistic as the historians. The city of Troy had shops and penthouses in the best medieval tradition:

By the sydes [of the streets] for sothe of sotell deuyse,/ Was archet full Abilly for aylyng of shoures,/ Pight vþ with pilers all of playne marbill,/ Weghis into walke for wetyng of rayn. There were stallis by þe strete stondyng for peopull,/ Werkmen into won, and þaire wares shewe,/ Bothe to selle and to se as þaim selfe lyked,/ Of all þe craftes to ken as þere course askit.[107]

Another romancer described thus the penthouses:

Of pulsched marbil vy-on strong pilleris,/ Deuised wern, long, large, and wyde,/ In þe frountel of euery stretis syde,/ Fresche alures with lusty hiȝe pynacles,/ And moustryng outward riche tabernacles,/ Vowted a-boue like reclinatories,/ þat called werne deambulatories,/ Men to walke to-gydre tweine & tweine,/ To kepe hem drie whan it dide reyne.[108]

The realistic eye of the romancer has caused him to record an interesting observation about a certain type of shop. The barber shops were all situated at the corners of the streets. A woodcut of Old Edinburgh shows a barber's shop in a quasi-corner of a street, which is filled with lofty houses.[109] The romancer accurately described this custom thus: "With barburs bigget in bourders of the stretes."[110]

Some of the buildings flanking the streets were flats, or apartment houses. The interesting feature about these flats was that there was one stairway for all floors and all tenants. This was a circular stairway enclosed in a round tower affixed to one end or to a corner of the tenement. Because of the nature of the stairway, it was commonly called turnpike stairs; these were in general use in England and Scotland. [111] A number of woodcuts of Scotland show a common entrance to the stairs that lead upward to the several flats.[112] Very realistically has the romancer recorded this interesting feature: "With all maister men þat on molde dwellis,/ Onestly enabit in entris Aboute."[113]

Others of the buildings along the streets were inns, which were primarily houses in which a person could obtain lodging. A fourteenth-century illumination from the *Quatre Fils d'Aymon,* in the French National Library, pictures the interior of a hostelry and shows the beds arranged in the apartment in separate berths, similar to those of a ship's cabin. A woodcut from the Royal MS 18 D. II shows the interior of an inn. In the common dormitory there appear travellers tucked into their trundle beds and fast asleep. On the bench in the room are the staves and scrips of those travellers who are pilgrims.[114] The romance of Valentine and Orson illustrates a medieval inn in which the pair were refused admittance because of the wild man, Orson:

Valentyne cryed vnto them, byddyng them haue no dreade and that they should open their gates, for he woulde haue lodging. . . . Orson . . . made him sygne that he should smyte against the gate of a great place, in the which was holden hostry. . . . When they that were within sawe that the wilde man was entered they ran all out at the backe dore. Valentine went toward the stable and dressed his horse. After that he and Orson went to the kechyn. . . . And then he toke a pot and ledde Orson into the seller that was open.[115]

Contrary to the usual custom, Beves was carried to an inn where he was given "mete and drynke" as well as a bed.[116]

Just as there are today degrees of elegance in hotels, so there was similar distinction in inns. Many of them, and especially those patronized by the poor and by traders, were located outside the city wall. Just outside of one of London's gates stood certain inns for the convenience of travellers; among them the Nun's Inn. Also, just outside Newgate was one of the great inns.[117] Sir Ewain and his maiden, in their romantic wandering, spent the night outside the wall, in an inn little and low, for he did not wish to be known.[118]

In the very center of a town was usually found the open market space, which was often bordered by a church and a town hall. The town hall, a large hall in which to transact business and to hold feasts, was often built over one of the gates of a city; that was true at Lincoln and Southampton. Sometimes it was a separate building—a large oblong hall of stone or timber, supported on pillars; the open colonnade beneath served for a market place. Sometimes the town hall was not municipally owned. In the heyday of guilds, the guild was obliged to possess a hall for meetings and other business. Because of the fact that the town was often in debt to a wealthy guild, and that not infrequently the same burgesses served both guild and borough, it was found convenient to transact the municipal affairs there also, so that in many towns the guild hall became the town hall.[119] The town hall of

Leominster, which was probably of this origin, was a rectangular building of three stories, the first of which was entirely open and was supported in the market space by fourteen cylindrical, pedestaled columns connected with arches. At this height a projecting penthouse surrounded the building. The upper stories, which were reached by an inner stair, were covered with plaster and timber and arranged in simple framework patterns; one of these was filled with a clock. The dormer, ridge roof was surmounted by a belfry cupola.[120] The romance writers referred often to the market place, but without elaboration; for example, "the turkes drewe them to the market place, sore disconfit." [121] Moreover, the guild halls seem hardly to have interested the writers ("Azein to þe zild-halle þe gomes vn-greiþ"),[122] and the town hall rarely. But the open, arched market place of the town hall served as a place of shelter to one hapless knight who arrived too late to be entertained in the palace:

And in the porche bilt of square stonys,/ Ful myghtely enarched anvyroun,/ Wher the domys and pleis of the toun weren execut and lawes of the kyng,/ And ther this knyght without more tarying/ Wery maat from his stede alight.[123]

One other item concerning the city was the water supply and the sewerage system, if such existed. The usual source of water was wells. Jean Fouquet's fifteenth-century miniature of the presentation of a book to the author's patron depicts a populous paved street, in the center of which is a well.[124] Quite often these wells had to be supplemented by water brought in by means of conduits. In 1236 a conduit of stone was erected at Marleybone to bring water to London from Tyburn. Such a constant flow of water not only served to provide water for personal and commercial needs, but also provided a steady stream to flush away the sewage. In the event that a town was surrounded by a river, this stream served as a conveyance for the removal of garbage and sewage; devoid of this, a city had to rely on cesspools, which were not particularly satisfactory. The sewerage system had its source in the public and private latrines. Quite generally there was a public latrine outside each city gate; such was true in London. Also along the Walbrook in London, every house had its latrine built out over the bed of the stream, and for each a yearly rent of twelvepence was paid. In fact, thirteenth-century London's sewerage system consisted of the Walbrook, which flowed down through the center of the city, and Fleet stream on the west side. An adjunct to this system was the open sewers, large and small, flowing down through the streets. If the thoroughfare were wide, it would be flanked on either side by a ditch which separated it from the walks or footpaths next the houses; if this were not the case, down the center ran one gutter through which flowed refuse, slops, and drainage water from the streets and roofs. The city fathers allowed drains for the liquid filth from the households, but each householder was supposed to provide a grate so as to prevent solid matter from dropping through into the open sewers.[125] Even this most unromantic of subjects received the attention of the romancers. Vespasian, in besieging a city, stopped up every conduit and every stream that ran into the city, and then he filled these as well as the moat with carrion and decomposing bodies.[126] Another presented a stream, flowing through the midst of the town, which acted as a simplified sewerage system, because it flowed through gutters and conduits, carrying away contamination.[127] The system of Troy consisted of a stream deflected into conduits which dispersed the water into the city gutters, etc.:

Þat in his course þe stremys myzt atteyn/ For to areche. . ./ By archis strong his cours for to reflecte/ þoruz condut pipis, large & wyde with-al,/ By certeyn meatis artificial,/ þat it made a full purgacioun/ Of al ordure & fylþes in þe toun,/ Waschyng þe stretys as þei stod a rowe,/ And þe goteris in þe erþe lowe,/ þat in þe cite was no filþe sene;/ For the c nel [gutters] skoured was so clene,/ And deuoyed in so secre wyse,/ þat no man myzt espien nor deuyse/ By what engyn þe filþes, fer nor ner,/ Wern born a-wey by cours of the ryuer-/ So couertly euery þing was cured.[128]

Moreover, before each house was an iron grate over the open sewer; the holes in it were round.[129]

CHAPTER TWO

castles

THE CASTLE, WHICH was the most characteristic structure of the Middle Ages, dominates the landscape of medieval literature. The castle, a private residence openly equipped for defense, had so many variations of form that it is difficult to present a typical example; however, in its evolution there were certain distinct plans which we shall consider. Probably the earliest plan used in England was the mote-bailey. Johannes de Collemedio in *Vita S. Joannis Morinorum Episcopi*, 1130, referred to the noblemen who spent their time in private war and who, in order to protect themselves,

heap up a mound of earth as high as they can and surround it with a wide ditch of great depth. The crest of this mound they surround in the manner of a wall with a strong, close stockade of squared timbers with as many towers as possible in its circuit. Within this stockade they build at its center a house or citadel which overlooks everything. In this way the entrance to the place can be reached only by a bridge, which, starting from the outer edge of the ditch, rises by degrees on posts set at equal distances two or three together. Thus at an easy slope it rises above the ditch till it reaches the surface of the mound, where it meets and rests upon a threshold.[1]

William the Conqueror's castle at Hastings, as depicted in the Bayeux tapestry, was simply a great mound with a wooden stockade round its flattened summit, standing in a levelled courtyard or bailey. The dirt dug from the deep moat which encircled the bailey was used in building up the mound. An outer ditch, with a fenced bank, enclosed the whole. Within the fence, or bailey, were wooden sheds for garrison and horses; and upon the mound itself stood the timbered tower. An inclined plane of timber, half bridge and half ladder thrown across the inner moat, gave access to the mound from the bailey. The drawbridge over the outer ditch was defended by a wooden tower on the counterscarp.[2] In the usual castle built according to this plan, the motte or mound varied from ten feet to one hundred feet in height and from one hundred to three hundred feet in diameter; often there was more than one bailey. The baileys were arranged in such order, dictated by the nature of the site, as would best defend the keep on the mound. If there were two or more baileys, often they were placed in line in front of the keep; again, they were placed in depth in front; often they flanked the keep or formed a semicircle around it. In some cases, as at Bramber and Skenfrith, the mound stood entirely within the bailey. The mounds were of three kinds: natural hillocks, partly natural and partly artificial, and wholly artificial. If the mound was artificial, the defenses on its summit must have been of timber. However, in France at least, reinforced clay was sometimes used.[3] Lambert d'Ardes, writing of an imposing timber keep of the eleventh century, described an elaborate structure of many stories and rooms; nevertheless, where conditions were favorable, the keeps were built of stone. William of Poitiers described the stone keep of Brionne, Normandy, which was built about 1045. The original early eleventh-century keep at Durham is reputed to have been of timber; the existing structure is of stone. In some cases, such as Corfe, the keep was built of stone, but the bailey was defended by stockades. Wherever the mounds were natural hillocks, and wherever stone was in abundance and timber scarce, there can be little doubt that their flat summits were defended by a stone building known as a shell keep. In these shell keeps the living rooms were built around and against the inside of the wall. These rooms enclosed a central courtyard or they occupied the whole walled space, in which case the roof timbers sprang from a central pillar. At Totnes the keep is a simple, irregularly shaped round shell, six and a half feet thick and fifteen feet high; the internal diameter is about seventy feet. Two stairways, built in the thickness of the wall, rise to the wall walk, which is carried

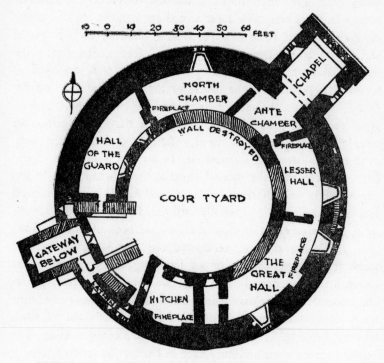

RESTORMEL CASTLE. PLAN OF KEEP, FIRST FLOOR.
(Reproduced by permission of Sidney Toy.)

all round the keep and is defended by an embattled parapet. Such internal buildings as may have existed have been destroyed, but at Restormel they have been preserved. Here within the shell keep there is another ring wall, concentric with and surrounding a large court. The space of eighteen and a half feet between the

shell and inner wall is divided by cross-walls into separate apartments, two stories in height. The ground floor contains the stores
and cellars, and the upper floor the halls and living roms. The
kitchen rises through both floors. A square tower, later converted
into a chapel, projects on one side of the keep.[4] The romancers, in
depicting castles, may or may not have had in mind this particular
plan; certainly the facts are not sufficiently detailed to offer proof.
Moreover, the facts as given are somewhat generalized; nevertheless, the wattle-clay described in the *Roman von Guillaume le
Clerc* bears strong likeness to the mote-bailey plan:

*En un castiel desus un val/ Manoit uns vilains de Pelande/ Ases pres
de la mer d'Irlande/ Desus une grante roche bise/ Ot sa maison most
bien asise/ Faite de cloies tote entor./ En son le pui ot une tor/
Q'N'ert, de piere ne de caus./ De terre estoit li murs fais haus/ Et
creneles et betilles.*[5]

Also, King Richard's men found themselves without any defense
establishment, so that they busied themselves to dig a wide and
deep ditch and to erect an exceedingly high castle of stone.[6] The
nature of the exigency here is comparable with that which called
forth the mote-bailey type: the necessity for protective quarters
which could be speedily and economically erected. In addition, the
nature of the construction of another castle gives a strong indication that it was of the mote-bailey type. One is led to believe that
a mound was raised as part of the structure:

Loke, þat tre & ston be riche,/ þe tour largge & depe þe diche! . . .
þis werkmen þider went þo,/ þre þousand þer were & mo,/ Hewen
schides & coruen ston/ & laiden foundement anon,/ Sum rammed &
doulen snel—/ & gun þat castel fair & wel.[7]

Meanwhile, the greater lords of England borrowed from France
the idea of massive square or rectangular keeps. These keeps, an
eleventh-century innovation, provided a powerful dwelling place
which was both convenient and secure. The usual plan was to
build on the firm ground of the bailey and entirely within the

bailey—as at London—or at a strategic point on the curtain wall, as at Kenilworth. The keeps, which were strongly built with walls of twelve-foot to twenty-foot thickness, re-enforced by flat buttresses, were from two to four stories in height. Often each story was divided into two or more apartments. Access to the keep was by means of a second-story doorway which was reached by a stairway built against the side of the keep; generally this stairway was contained in and protected by a forebuilding. At Dover a stairway reached to the entrance which was on the third story. Communication with the stories above and below the entrance floor was obtained by means of spiral stairways placed in the corners of the keep. The lower or basement floor had neither door nor loophole in its craggy walls, and was used as a storehouse. Dover was an exception because it had a postern in the basement as a means of escape if the entrance were taken by the enemy. The principal hall was usually on the entrance floor. Mural chambers, other apartments, and an oratory opened off the hall. Because of the combustible shingles which covered the keep, the outer walls were carried to such a height that the roof was effectively screened behind them. Within the keep was a deep well from which water could be drawn to any and all floors. The early eleventh-century stone donjon at Loches consists of a main building and a large forebuilding which is an integral part of the structure. The main building is sixty-five feet by twenty-five feet on the inside. The walls are nine feet two inches thick at the base, are strengthened by huge semi-circular buttresses, and rise in four lofty stories to a height of one hundred and twenty-two feet; there are no cross walls above the basement floor. Entrance to the keep is made on the second floor by means of a stairway which rises up on three sides of the forebuilding. The outside windows are relatively small; many of them have square lintels.[8] As in the case of the mote-bailey type, the romancers did not leave minute construction details of the square-keep type, but the broad outlines of the general plan may be identified with some assurance. The castle of Trebes bears strong resemblance:

So that to þe castel of Trebes they consentyd anon,/ that forto besegen with myht and strengthe/ On alle foure partyes in brede and lengthe./ For the castel stood wondirly hye,/ And strong mareys on boþe sides, trewelye,/ Also to that castel non entre there was/ but be a narwhe cause jn on plas,/ Which that was bothen streyt and long.[9]

Probably Balan was occupying such a keep when his enemies attacked him while he was at dinner, because he escaped by leaping out of a window which was "Syxty fote of heyzte, y wene, he lepe adown."[10]

Late in the twelfth century the cylindrical keep—at least a transitional form—came to England from France, where it had been introduced by Crusaders who saw the plan in the Levant. The cylindrical keep had three advantages over the rectangular form: it presented no angles to be shattered by oblique shots; its loopholes gave a wider field of fire for the defense, and in building, the scaffolding round the circular tower could be arranged into a circular ramp up which material could be wheeled at a considerable economy of labor. On the other hand, the rectangular plan was more convenient for the disposition of the rooms inside the building; consequently, many keeps combined the advantages of both. An example of such a transitional structure is the keep at Houdan which is square on the inside, with splayed corners, but which is circular on the outside, with four projecting turrets; each turret covers one of the internal corners. This two-story castle is of great height. The ground floor, which is the storechamber, contains a well. The upper story consists of the great hall, and chambers in three of the turrets. The fourth turret contains the spiral stairway which leads to the battlements. The roof is masked by the walls which rise sixteen feet above the gutters. The entrance doorway is in the north turret, twenty feet from the ground, and it is reached by a drawbridge from the curtain wall that passed near the keep at that point. From the doorway in the turret, a straight mural stairway on the left leads up to the hall on the first floor. During the late twelfth century, whenever keeps were built detached within the bailey, they were often surrounded by a narrow court and a high wall called a chemise. The approach to the keep was then by a gateway through the chemise into the court and then by a flight of steps within the court up to the wall walk of the chemise. At one point a causeway, with a drawbridge at the end, connected the wall walk of the chemise and the entrance of the keep. Etampes and Provins were approached thus.[11] Probably a romance castle seen by Godeffroy of Bologne was of this type. The donjon, which stood on the summit of a high mountain, was formed of very strong walls and thick towers. Because of its own strength and because of the precarious location of the keep on the precipitous peak, the romancer remarks that it could never be imagined how it could be mined. Moreover, the causeway between the keep and the town was so steep and so narrow that visitors had to proceed in single file, thus exposing any enemy to certain destruction.[12] Again, Melusine built a donjon which seems to have been of the transitional type:

Vppon the quicke Roche that it sett tho;/ The fyrste stones to put thay, and made/ In litell of tyme; Masons I—now had./ The walles hye deuised she echon, Wel founded was vppon the said wayley;/ Too strong toures made with a huge dongun, And Enuiron an hy with wardes strong that day./ Of it mervelyd strongly the contrary,/ hou ful sone men made this said strong repair,/ And when thys castell was bastiled fair.[13]

About 1190 the transitional keeps of the twelfth century gave way ultimately to the round keep which predominated until 1270. Crusaders returning from Palestine realized the necessity for more scientific planning in castles; consequently, many edifices were strengthened by the addition of another wall of towers. The keep itself, often no longer the ordinary residence of the lord but essentially his last line of defense, became round in shape as well as smaller and more powerful in design. Chateau Gaillard, located on a precipitous cliff above the Seine, consisted of three baileys. The triangular outer bailey was completely surrounded by a moat. The inner bailey with its surrounding moat was entirely encircled by the middle bailey. The curtain walls of the middle and outer baileys were re-enforced by a total of seven circular towers. Almost entirely within the inner bailey stood the keep, which was circular except that one side was thickened and shaped like the prow of a ship. Deep battered plinths and machicolations added to the defense of the castle. Entrance to this two-story keep was by means of a flight of steps from the courtyard to the second floor; the hall and domestic quarters were built in the courtyard near the donjon.[14] One weak point in the design of this keep and of earlier donjons was the one entrance or exit so that there was no way of escape in case the door were carried by assault. This defect was remedied in Pembroke and later castles by the addition of a postern.[15] Concerning the round keep, the romancers became more specific, and their descriptions are definitely realistic. In *Percival* a varlet saw a keep surmounting a pinnacle. On two sides he saw wall towers, and on the open side he saw four stone turrets. In the midst of the defenses he saw a huge, strong keep. The entrance to the castle was protected by a barbican and by a battlemented bridge.[16] Also, a similar castle was constructed by Melusine:

Soone was the Fortres made up not only with one warde [wall fortification] but two strong wardes, with double walles were there, on oon coude have comme to the stronge donjon of it. Round about the walles were gret tours machecoyled, & strong posternes and also barreres or wayes gooynd out fourth encysed and kerued within the hard roche.[17]

Moreover, Geffray passed through the first gate of a castle, entered into the inner court, and went toward the strong donjon which was further isolated by a drawbridge.[18]

In the early part of the thirteenth century, in many of the castles the keep was entirely omitted; the fortifications as a whole were considered as suffiicent. Moreover, castles were ceasing to be private strongholds and were becoming national institutions; therefore, they must be burgs rather than mottes, communal and not manorial fortresses. As a consequence, the general tendency was to concentrate the central defense on a four-square castle, surrounded by one or two lines of walls, and having a strong round tower at each corner of the inner wall. In addition, powerful gateways took the place of the keep, and there was a more liberal provision of gateways and posterns. Many were the variations of the plan, but Beaumaris Castle may be considered typical. The defenses consist of two lines of wall fortifications, forming the inner and outer baileys; the outer one is surrounded by a moat. The square inner bailey is enclosed in walls fifteen and a half feet thick and protected by six towers and two large gatehouses. Each of the gateways, which are in opposite walls, is defended by machicolations, three portcullises, and two doors. Both gatehouses are substantial structures, containing large halls and rooms. The wall of the outer bailey is built in the shape of a nonagon, is strengthened by twelve towers, and has two gateways. The hall and domestic quarters are built against the wall of the inner bailey.[19] Since the keepless castles were more numerous, and since this style persisted for a longer time, the romancers have treated it more often and with a greater degree of detail. One knight, after crossing a moat and passing through three portals, was kindly received within the hall. Soon accusations were hurled at him, so that he was escorted from the hall, the door of which was then locked by the master. Then he was ushered into a nearby strong tower in which were beds.[20] Also, Torrent of Portyngale entered a castle, passed the stable and other buildings, and sought his enemy, who was sleeping in a strong tower.[21] Another romancer described the actions of the people in the castle, immediately after dinner. Some went to various chambers, some to bowers, some to the high tower, and some stood in the hall.[22] Moreover, Floripas and some of the peers of France were besieged in a donjonless castle. A section of the wall having been destroyed and the domestic quarters captured, the defenders withdrew to a strong tower where they were safe.[23] A rather unusual castle described in *Sir Degrevant* seems to have some features in common with Caerphilly Castle. A girl, in order to have her lover visit her, instructed him to enter the castle by means of a waterfall:

Ther ys a place in the wall,/ Bytwyne the chambur and the hal,/ Thor lyzthe a muchel watur-wal/ Of fourty-feyt brede;/ There shalt thou come in a nyzthe/ Prevaly withouten syzth.[24]

Caerphilly stands within a lake formed by a stream, which is held in check by a great screen wall that forms the barbican. Through the screen wall run three sluices, by which the level of the lake is regulated. The main part of the rectangular castle is surrounded by two lines of walls, and a drawbridge connects the outer bailey with the barbican. This barbican, or great screen wall, is a formidable outwork three hundred yards in length. Certainly a secret entrance into such a castle would have to be made through some element other than the normal gateways.[25]

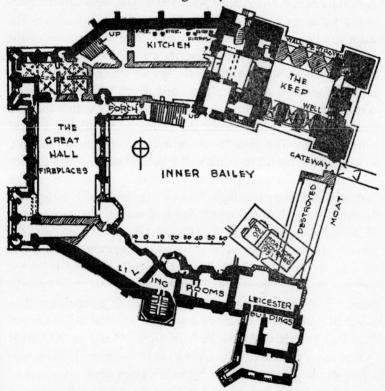

KENILWORTH CASTLE. PLAN OF THE INNER BAILEY.
(Reproduced by permission of Sidney Toy.)

By the early fifteenth century the center of gravity in castle construction had shifted away from the tower to the hall, a freestanding oblong building. Frequently a tower or towers were combined and this unified structure occupied the front of the construction as a whole. There was still the enclosure, but it trailed off behind. Such a castle was known as a palace. To the medieval writer "palace" was a variant for "hall"; it was a term descriptive of a particular type of building and had no reference to the rank of the occupant. In the palace plan it was not necessary that there be a complete quadrangle of buildings all in the same node. The palace building proper might occupy one or two sides and the remainder of the enclosure be walled as a close, or courtyard, with minor buildings against the wall. The term was applicable if the main building were of the hall character. The military side of the castle was yielding in prominence to its milder equipment; the castle enclosure was becoming the palace courtyard. Fifteenth-century Doune is a palace. The north front of the quadrangle consists of a two-story hall and a four-story tower with a rounded turret projection which flanks the entrance and affords a small suite of rooms. The great tower and hall are of normal character, as we shall see later. The south wall is pierced with windows which were intended for later erections that were never completed. The curtain wall is forty feet high. Ravenscraig, Morton, Huntley, and Linlithgow are all of this type.[26] Some, if not all, of the romancers identified the palace with a castle of this plan. However, the amount of external description is disappointing; more attention was paid to the interior. The hall was frequently referred to as the palace. One king opened his "chambre dore & so came into the palays."[27] Alexander, as well as Reinbrun,[28] entered a palace which he immediately described in terms of a typical hall.[29] Libeaus "rod into þe paleis/ And at þe halle alizte";[30] and so did Guy.[31]

One other general type of castle must be mentioned—the tower, a free-standing tower with its barmkin (a low wall from nine to eleven feet high) and minor buildings. In its simplest form, at least in Scotland, it was an oblong building containing a ground floor devoted to storage, a main floor or hall, a great chamber above, and usually an attic floor under the roof, which might be flat or gabled. The forty- to fifty-foot walls were crowned with a parapet which might rise flush with the walls or project on corbels. The most striking feature of these towers was their differences; however, some generalizations may be made. At least the ground floor was vaulted. The entrance was usually on the ground floor, and the stair, which was immediately adjoining, rose to the roof, served all floors, and terminated at the parapets in a small chamber that was available for an observation post. Usually the height exceeded any other dimension. At Threave (1400) the walls are eight feet thick, but at Comlongon they vary from ten feet to thirteen and a half feet in order to accommodate mural chambers. This latter tower measures forty-eight feet ten inches by forty-two feet seven inches and rises sixty-four feet ten inches to its flat roof, which is surmounted by the cap, or observation, house; a spiral stairway rises from the entrance on the ground to the roof. The vaulted basement is divided into two stories, over which there are the hall and two additional stories. Crenelated parapets project on triply-moulded corbels.[32] Certain romance towers are castles of this type. Valentine visited such a tower which had a great iron gate.[33] Gaffray saw before him in a field a square tower, a stronghold;[34] likewise, another knight, riding in the field, saw a great, square, battlemented tower with a barmkin around it.[35] Dunother was a marvelous great tower standing by the sea.[36] In a valley Percival spied a square, gray-stone tower with two turrets and a galley in front. Inside the tower he found a hall as wide as it was long.[37]

Now that we have considered the general plans used in the construction of castles, let us examine the various parts and discuss other pertinent facts. The selection of a city site had much in common with that of a castle; both were motivated primarily by the defense factor. Probably the castle site was conditioned secondarily by the terrain and the needs of the barony in which it was built; consequently, a large variety of sites was used. Pembroke castle was built on a promontory at the junction of two rivers, Bothwell on a promontory formed by a sharp loop-shaped turn in the Clyde, Flint and Warwick on the banks of rivers. Najac and Harlech stand on the summit of high hills, Gaillard on a three-hundred-foot, precipitous cliff, and Beeston on a high hill with sheer precipices on three sides. Caerlaverock crowns the summit of a high rock, and Conway a high rock on the shore of the estuary. Beaumaris stands on the seashore, Caerphilly on an island, Caernarvon on level ground, and Invernochty on the edge of a marsh.[38] Likewise, the romancers chose just such realistic sites. A king saw a castle built on a huge rock beside the Rhone;[39] Huon found one standing on a rock on the seaside;[40] Percival visited one built beside the sea, at the entrance of a bay.[41] Also, Huon, as well as Tydeus, visited castles built upon rocky peaks.[42] Other knights saw castles built upon the summit of mountains.[43] Others found castles built by the side of rivers.[44] In addition, Windsor was visited: "The army moved, and came to Windsor. . . . The castle stands above the Thames."[45] Alexander marvelled at one built in the midst of a river,[46] and Valentine visited one built on an island.[47] Trebes was surrounded by a marsh, but some others were constructed on a flat plain.[48]

The materials used in building a castle depended upon several factors: the material available, the resources of the builder, and the supply of skilled craftsmen. As I have already suggested, some of the early castles were built of timber, such as Durham was, and some of reinforced clay, such as the castle of Kinmont was, but most of them were built of more durable stuff. Some were built of stone and timber, as at Laval, and others were constructed of parallel stone facings filled with earth; Auchencass followed this usage.[49] But the more finished structures were built of rubble, which is rough or broken rocks or bricks, or they were built of ashlar; the core of the walls was of rubble of medium size, compacted with plenty of lime, and the faces of the walls were of dressed stone in nine- or ten-inch courses.[50] From the fourteenth century there are excellent examples of coursed ashlar building, such as

Tantallon; the stones are rather cubical in shape. During the fifteenth century the typical oblong stones tended to shorten on the bed and rise vertically, approximating a square face. Ravenscraig, Tulliallan, and Morton are of this type. Also in the fifteenth century random rubble walls were built. At Threaves the rubble is carefully brought to courses so that it gives a general feeling of horizontal construction; only the corners and stairwell are built of ashlar. The rubble of the fifteenth and sixteenth centuries shows itself in larger, roughly cubical blocks set in much mortar, as at Dirleton. Sixteenth-century Stonypath Tower is built of roughly cubical blocks with smaller packing; seventeenth century Saltcoats uses materials of all shapes and sizes.[51] Many of the rubble walls, like those of Amisfield, were plastered to cover up the rough stone surfaces. In general, the mortar used in medieval structures was good. If limestone was not available, shells were used to provide lime mortar. The core of the wall of Rothesay was set in plenty of lime filled with large gravel. The mortar used in the internal work of the piers of the sixteenth-century Bridge of Dee was of "strong red clay with a mixture of hot lime . . . carefully beaten together and mixed with rubble."[52] This was a very effective cement. On the subject of materials, the romancer did not overlook realistic material. Arthur considered building a castle "Of wode and lime, morter and stone."[53] Tristram built one of "ston and tree"; certainly a part of this was wood, for a servant spied on the queen by removing a board.[54] The Seven Sages of Rome ordered one built of "lym and of ston."[55] Godeffroy saw a strong wall built of "lyme and sonde."[56] The pillars and walls of Illium, the castle of the Earl of Pryncesamour, Castle Daroun, and a tower seen by Sir Eglamour were all built of stone.[57] No further description was given to indicate whether it was rubble or ashlar. However, Percival saw turrets built of hewn stone.[58] Windsor was built of hewn stone, and an Arthurian castle was of grey hewn stone.[59] Two fabulous castles were constructed of marble.[60]

Just as in the case of the city walls, the high walls framing the interior of a castle, as well as the wall circling the bailey, were known as the curtain. A noteworthy fact about these castle walls is the considerable variation that is found in their dimensions.[61] For example, Caerlaverock is twenty-five feet in height and Tantallon fifty. The thickness varied just as did the thickness of tower walls. Bothwell has walls fifteen feet thick, but the main tower of Dirleton is only ten. Totnes keep is six and a half feet thick and fifteen feet high; Launceston is twelve feet thick and thirty high. Bailey curtains were about eight or nine feet thick and were often in series of two or three. La Roche Guyon and Harlech have double walls, and Le Krak des Chevaliers has triple walls. Frequently the walls were strengthened by deep battered plinths. Sometimes the plinths were of great thickness, rose to half the height of the wall, and were continuous around the wall. Angers, built 1228-38, has widely battered plinths rising half of the great height of the walls, which are constructed of slate bonded at intervals by courses of dressed sandstone and granite.[62] The writers dealt fairly generally with the walls. The castle of Trebes and others were pictured as having very high walls, but a Saracen's castle did not have walls high enough to prevent their being scaled by means of a leather ladder and hooks.[63] Others were described as having steep walls [64] and thick walls.[65] A castle on the Rhone had particularly strong walls on the side where its natural defenses were weakest.[66] Moreover, a king ordered his builder to construct a great stone tower with good walls, fifteen feet thick or more:

Maistres, fait il, je vous requier/ Que de piere et de bon mortier/ Me faites ci une grant tour,/ Qui soit reonde tout entour;/ Les murs faites bons et espes/ De xv pies ou plus d'espes.[67]

Also, Melusine had a fortress built with two strong lines of defense, and a count had Windsor constructed with treble walls.[68]

The curtain walls surrounding baileys of the eleventh- and twelfth-century castles were sometimes plain, as at Yester, but in many cases they were strengthened at strategic points by square towers, projecting on the outside. At Ludlow the towers were spaced far apart, and at Richmond they were concentrated on the most vulnerable side. Later in the twelfth century, the towers were built closer together in order to command all panels of the walls. Mural towers were disposed, whenever it was possible, in a symmetrical fashion, though this amounted to little more than placing them at the angles of the enclosure. Skenfrith had a tower in each of its four corners. Some of the thirteenth-century rectangular castles had, in addition to a tower at each corner, a tower in the middle of each of three sides and a gateway near the middle of the fourth. One of the corner towers, built stronger than the others, became the keep. Najac had round towers built according to this plan. However, the number of towers varied with the castle and its needs. Le Krak des Chevaliers had eleven in the outer bailey and six in the inner bailey. Caernarvon had nine, and Beaumaris had fourteen in the outer bailey and seven in the inner.[69] The romances here carry realistic details. The poets went from general references concerning numerous towers or walls full of towers to specific data. Percival noted a keep surrounded by four towers; Huon saw one with thirteen great towers; a king saw a Rhone castle with thirty-three.[70] Valentine visited a castle possessed of "many greate thycke square toures," but Gawain stopped at one with fair, round towers: "Fayre fylyolez þat fyzed, & ferlyly long."[71] Godeffroy witnessed a tower of a castle being mined. When the defenders discovered this, they isolated the tower by building a wall inside the bailey, thus decreasing to a minor degree the extent of the bailey. Evidently this was one of the corner towers in a rectangular bailey.[72]

Also, the romancers have included the wall tower which was so strong that it served for a keep. When Huon and his men had to give up the town of Anfalerne, they withdrew to the castle, which was impregnable so long as the food lasted, because "at the corner of the castell there was a strong towre."[73] When castle Daroun was assaulted by Richard, the Saracens were forced to flee into the "heyeste toure."[74] When the French lords of Charles drove the Saracens out of the "strong tower," they were able to gain possession of the entire castle.[75]

During the fourteenth century some of the existing castles were strengthened by the addition of powerful towers, constructed either within the bailey, as at Foix, or in the curtain wall, as at Warwick. The nucleus of Foix is the eleventh-century rectangular tower standing at the north end of the bailey. Later, to this tower was added a long, one-story hall with a second rectangular tower at the other end of the hall. The second tower, being larger and stronger than the north tower, became the donjon. To reach the donjon entrance, which was on the second floor, one had to ascend the stairs in the north tower and walk across the flat roof of the hall. Still later a powerful tower was added at the south end of the bailey.[76] The author of *Partenay* must have had a similar structure in mind when he described a castle, built by Melusine, which had "Two strong toures made with a huge donjon, / And Enuiron an hy with wardes strong that day."[77]

Likewise, the castle of Douglas possessed a strong tower. When the castle was besieged, Douglas defended the hall and his warden defended the tower.[78]

Just as with the city walls, the castle walls possessed wall walks, or surmounting causeways which were protected by the outer parapet in front and by a low rear wall. The walk did not allow a very wide platform for operations or allow any massing of defenders at a threatened point, so that it was sometimes extended inward on corbels to give more room; this is the case at Caerlaverock and at Bothwell. At least half of the eight-foot thickness of the walls of Doune is taken up with the front parapet and rear wall.[79] Usually the walk was laid with overlapping flagstones, but if stone was scarce, lead was used. Lead flashings remain at Conway and at Beaumaris. At Conway the circulation of the wall walk is uninterrupted all around the curtain and on the cross walls, but at Caernarvon all the towers stood astride the walk, so that if any section of the curtain were carried, it could be isolated by closing

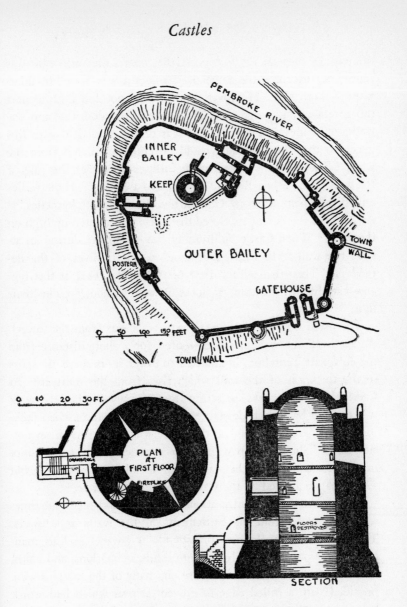

TOP: PLAN OF THE PEMBROKE CASTLE.
BOTTOM: PEMBROKE CASTLE. THE KEEP.
(Reproduced by permission of Sidney Toy.)

the passage through the towers. At Beaumaris the wall walk was continuous except at the gatehouses, where it was barred by doorways on both sides. Moreover the walk did not end flush against the gatehouse; a gorge was left between the doorway and the walk. A removable timber bridge was probably used to span this gorge so that the gatehouse could be entirely isolated from the walk.[80] The romance writers were fully cognizant of the role of the wall walk. When Richard approached a castle, "On the walles armyd they hem schewe;/ Out off tourelles, and off kyrnelles."[81] At Arundel the defenders closed the gate and mounted up high on the wall.[82] When Castle Kildrummy was set on fire during an attack, the wall walk with its defenses saved the lives of the defenders: "Than thai within drew till the wall,/ That at thet tym wes battalit all/ Within, richt as it was without,/ Saffit thair liffis."[83]

The usual way of reaching the wall walk was from the towers. At Bothwell the walk has been roofed for a short distance from the entry. At Tantallon, in addition to tower stairs there are stairs in the thickness of the wall which rises from the courtyard. At Caerlaverock there was no access from the towers, but the walk was reached by an outside stair.[84] Medea, of romance, when looking for her lover, climbed to the castle wall by means of an outside stair: "Sho went vp wightly by a walle syde/ To the toppt of a toure, & tot ouer the water/ ffor to loke on hir luffe"; but Charlemagne arrived on the wall by means of a tower.[85]

The defense of all fortifications in ancient and medieval times was principally from the battlements of the walls and towers. The crest of the wall was a breastwork of parapet at least man-height. The parapet was divided into solids, or merlons, and voids, or crenelles. From the third century on, many of the merlons were provided with a rolled edge to prevent arrows which had struck below from glancing over the parapet; that is the case at Caernarvon. Often the merlons, or embrasures, were fitted with removable wooden shutters, placed on the outside. The shutters were hung from the top, worked in sockets, and opened at the bottom so that an archer could shoot through the opening and be protected at the same time. At Alnwick the sockets are cut in the stone.[86] The walls of the romance castle built by Melusine were marvelously strong and surmounted with "wardes strong."[87] Charlemagne's men, besieged by the Saracens, were aided at the "kernels" by the women.[88] Also, a castle visited by Gawain was so well supplied with battlements that it seemed as though they were cut out of paper: "Among þe castel carnelez, clambred so þik./ þat pared out of papure purely hit semed."[89]

Another means of strengthening the battlements was the addition of hoards, and later, machicolations. Hoards were temporary wooden galleries constructed on the outside of the parapet in time of siege to protect the base of the wall and towers. The galleries were built upon rows of ten-inch square beams which were long enough to stretch across the wall walk, pierce the parapet, and project about four feet beyond the outer face. Boards were laid across these beams to form a foot-pace, and this gallery was protected on the outside by a screen and often covered by a pent roof. A wide aperture between the foot-pace and the stone wall was left for the purpose of dropping missiles on the enemy below; this feature was called machicolation. Because of the danger of fire, the wooden hoarding was replaced by stone machicolations, built on rows of stone corbels. Thirteenth-century Conway has stone machicolations on the gateways and wooden hoards on the lateral walls and towers.[90] The romance architect and builder, Melusine, was keenly aware of all defensive devices; her great donjon was protected by machicolations: "Round about the walles were gret tours machecoyled." A tower had a gallery, or wooden hoard, in front.[91]

Since the entrance to a castle was inevitably the weakest place, obstacles were multiplied about it. Probably the most universal of these was the moat, or ditch, which became a conventional boundary. Even the yard of the poor widow in Chaucer's *Nun's Priest's Tale* was surrounded by a fence of "sticks" and a dry ditch. On level sites the wall was surrounded by a moat, as at Sherborne, or defended partly by a moat and partly by a river, as at Skenfrith. But whenever a castle stood upon a promontory position and was flanked by precipitous rocks or deep declivities, only the neck had to be ditched across, as at Morton and Tantallon. Dunnottar, being entirely isolated, needed no artificial moat. Chateau de Bologne and Beaumaris were surrounded by moats. Beeston, which was almost inaccessible, needed no moat around the outer bailey, but the cautious builder had a ditch about thirty feet deep and thirty-five feet wide cut, in the inner bailey, through the natural rock from one precipitous side of the hill to the other. As we have already seen in the case of the motte-bailey type of castle, there was often a moat around the entire bailey and then another around just the tower, as at Bothwell.[92] The romancers described many realistic variations of the moat. One knight saw a castle and he found "by the castle moat the lord of that burg."[93] Daroun was provided with a spectacular moat.[94] Melusine's castle was provided with "ditches" which were presumably dry.[95] Another castle, built upon a peak, had a deep ditch; another, placed similarly, had "þe diches depe Inowh."[96] A Rhone castle had double moats, and Windsor had "treble . . . ditches."[97] A castle visited by Valentine, as well as one seen by Charles, was surrounded by deep ditches "full of rennyng water."[98]

The moat was crossed by means of a bridge, which in whole or in part could be raised, generally so as to lie against the inner entrance. Drawbridges were operated in several different ways. Some of them seem to have been simply drawn back upon a platform before the gate; this is the case at Burg Ez-Zefer, Cairo. Others were hinged on the inner side and, by means of chains attached to the outer side and by means of pulleys and windlasses, were raised up until they stood vertically against the face of the gate; thus the bridge became a kind of door blocking the passage. Conway is typical of this plan. At Caerlaverock a single chain was used to operate the bridge. Instead of windlasses, others used long beams, or gaffs, pivoted at the top of the passageway; at one end of the beam was fastened the chain which was secured to the drawbridge; the other end of the beam was weighted so that a minimum of additional weight would raise the bridge. These beams, when raised, lay back in long grooves in the wall of the gateway. Dalhouse still shows the grooves for the gaffs. St. Andrews had only one gaff, centrally placed, instead of the customary two. Other castles had an adaptation of the see-saw principle. The bridge, which moved on a pivot, was suspended over the moat on the outside of the castle and over a pit on the inside. Whenever the bridge was raised, the inner part descended into the pit and the outer part rose to block the gateway; the pit, such as at Caerphilly, formed an additional obstacle to anyone endeavoring to force an entry. Dunscaith has a different sort of drawbridge. The ravine between the castle and the mainland is spanned by a six-foot-wide bridge of a single arch. However, the footway of the bridge for a distance of eight feet is supplied only by a wooden floor swung upon a beam. The number of drawbridges depended upon the needs and strength of the castle. Conway had only one, Caernarvon two, and Caerphilly three. The main entrance of Harlech was defended by two drawbridges and that of Bodiam by three.[99] Such realistic bridges are found in the romances. The castle of Balam used a windlass to operate the bridge, for the defenders who kept the tower "woonde vp the brigges on hye."[100] The same bridge was described as being drawn up and tied fast. The bridge at Camelot was probably of this type; it was drawn up and all the pins put in place.[101] Another bridge was evidently of this type, for four porters were used in lowering it, but the bridge which was opened by Duke Neymoun was probably of the gaff type.[102] The bridge of Clereuauld's was of the gaff or pit type because a squire tricked him so that the counterbalance did not work:

He supposed to haue reculed & to haue lyft vp the bridge but the squyer & his peuple came so rudly that it was not in theire powere to haunce the bridge but bare it doune by force.[103]

Furthermore, Richard was warned to be careful in attempting to take a castle which had a pit-type bridge:

Under the brygge there is a swyke [trap]/ Corven clos, joynand quent-lyke;/ And undernethe is an hasp,/ Shet with a stapyl and a clasp,/ And in that hasp a pyn is pylt/ Thou myghte beware yiff thou wilt/ . . . .Though thou and thy folk wer in the mydde,/ And the pyns mete out were,/ Doun ye scholde fallen there,/ In a pyt syxty fadme deep.[104]

Of course, the depth of the pit was considerably exaggerated. Many castles had only one bridge, but Windsor had "draw-bridges."[105] However, a keep so defensible as the one seen by Percival needed only one bridge. The stream which surrounded the keep was crossed by a bridge built with stone arches. The bridge was battlemented, and in the middle stood a tower with a drawbridge.[106] Also, Valentine saw a castle which had a bridge that was made so cleverly that only one person could pass at a time without falling into the moat.[107]

Following out the principle of providing obstacles to access, the architect often built an outer gateway, or gate tower, con-nected with the main gateway by parallel walls; this entire struc-ture was known as the barbican. The term was also applied to any extension of the entrance passage by additional structures. The mote-bailey castle of Dinant had a barbican. The barbican at Launceston consisted of two parallel walls extending some forty feet from the castle wall, and crossing the moat on low arches; both walls were pierced with loopholes. A barbican often had its own gate or gates. The west barbican at Conway joins the protruding wall tower, runs parallel for the entire length of the west wall of the castle, and extends some fifteen feet beyond. This barbican has two gateways of its own in addition to a draw-bridge. One of the most imposing barbicans is at Caerphilly, where the structure extends nine hundred feet parallel to the castle. The north wing has two towers in addition to its huge-buttressed wall. One means of passage through the barbican was a series of three gates. Entrance from the barbican into the outer bailey was by means of a drawbridge.[108] The romance barbicans are not illuminating in details. Percival saw a castle with a "barbican washed by the flood," and a maiden saw a round tower with one.[109] The Macedonians, in fear of Alexander, shut their gates and barbicans.[110] Another castle was saved because there was a moat surrounding the barbican so that war engines could not be used effectively against the walls.[111] Beves went around a barbican in looking for a place to attack a castle.[112] Another castle withstood attack although the barbican was destroyed.[113] Richard found great solace in one which was "Heyghe wrought off harde stones."[114]

Regardless of the presence or absence of a barbican, the gateway to a castle was one of the most strongly fortified points. One of the protective devices was the portcullis, or heavy wooden grating, shod and plated with iron, which slid up and down in a groove, being worked from a room above. But this was only a device; the real strong point was a substantial building of two or three stories. The gateway of eleventh-century Exeter projected slightly on the outside of the curtain wall but extended forty feet within the bailey. It consisted of a three-story building and a lofty barbican. The outer end of the passage was probably closed by a two-leaved door, secured by a timber bolt. The three-story gateway of Newark-on-Trent was defended simply by a two-leaved door placed midway in the passage, and there was no portcullis. By the thirteenth century, considerable advancement in design had been made. The gateways were flanked by towers which formed part of the gatehouse, and the approaches were defended from the battlements of the gatehouse as well as from the meurtrieres in the towers. Also the gateway passages were defended by portcullises, machicolations, meurtrieres, and two-leaved doors. The machicolations opened out in the vault or roof of the gateway. Sometimes the machicolations were placed between the portcullis and the door, as at Pembroke, and sometimes before the portcullis, as at Parthenay, but the portcullis was always placed before the door which it defended. Often there were two or three systems of these defenses arranged at intervals through the gateway. The skillfully designed gatehouse of Denbigh consists of three towers arranged in triangular form round a central hall. Two of the towers, flanking the gateway, stand partially within the curtain wall, and the third tower is entirely within the bailey. The passageway, which is in two sections, has a right-angle turn. The outer section, leading from the drawbridge straight into the octagonal hall, is defended by two portcullises and two doors. Any enemy powerful enough to gain the hall found himself under fire from five meurtrieres in the surrounding walls, one of which in the south tower faced directly toward the entrance passage. The inner section of the passageway, which was at a right angle to the outer, led into the inner bailey; it was also defended by a portcullis and doors. The culmination of the development of the gateway is seen at Caernarvon, which is similar to Denbigh but stronger. There are also two passages at a right angle to each other and a large hall at the junction. The first passage, opening from a drawbridge, is defended by four portcullises and two doors and commanded from above by seven lines of machicolation. The outermost one covered the head of the first portcullis, so that, if need be, the portcullis could be drenched with water. The passage was under attack from numerous meurtrieres on either side; and its middle portion, from a level of twelve feet above ground, was commanded by six doorways—three on either side—through which heavy missiles could be dropped upon assailants. The second passage, which led from the hall into the bailey, was defended by two portcullises and two doors.[115] Although no romancer depicted a gateway like Caernarvon, the composite picture is realistic. When the Germans attacked a castle in which Huon was, he "mounted on the toure over ye gate," and he and his men successfully defended themselves. At another castle Huon had to pass through four gates in a series, each defended by a drawbridge, before he gained entrance to the hall.[116] A series of three gates protected the entrance of another.[117] The gateway of yet another castle was very similar to that of the historic Burg Ez-Zefer, Cairo. An exceedingly wide river flowed before the gateway. Doubtless, as at Ez-Zefer, a two-span bridge—the second a draw—was used to cross this barrier. The bridge opened on a small platform which was just in

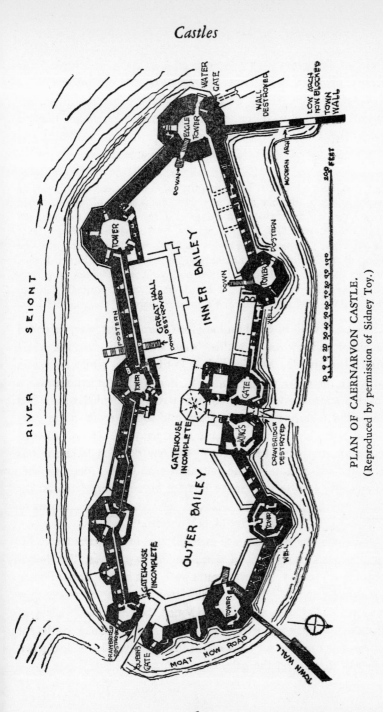

PLAN OF CAERNARVON CASTLE.
(Reproduced by permission of Sidney Toy.)

front of the gateway. The romancer says that the platform was wide enough for two chariots to meet there, and it was thirty paces in length.[118] Precarious, indeed, would be the position of any attacker who might be confined to so small a platform. But Sir Ewain actually found himself in great peril after becoming enmeshed in the devices of a gateway. The gateway was

fashioned like a trap that beheadeth the rat if he touch the key fastened to the knife; in like manner, a portcullis, sharp as sword, was sustained by a lever, which threw down the gate, if any man pass through, unless in the middle. The knight kept the centre, while Sir Ewain leant forward and grasped the knights saddle-bow; it was well that he stooped, for his horse trod on the pin, and the gate fell like a demon, cutting in twain the stead, and shearing his spurs, but doing no further harm. As he rode, the knight flung down a second portcullis, and in this manner Sir Ewain remained a prisoner between the gates.[119]

Likewise, Ywain rushed headlong into a similar gateway, defended at either end with a portcullis "shod wele with yren and stele/ And also grunden wonder-wele." Furthermore, while he was a prisoner there, he was surprised to hear a door open and see a maiden approach who led him into a room provided with a bed and other furniture.[120] This reference to such a room in the gatehouse is highly realistic, because quarters were always provided there for the porter or porters.[121] On one occasion Windsor was not attacked because of the portcullises and other defenses; but Clereuauld's castle was carried in spite of imposing defenses; the castle being surprised, the attackers set spears in the grooves of the portcullis so that it could not operate.[122]

Likewise, the structure and material of romance gates are realistic, the gates being built of wood and in two leaves. For the reception of Gawain, the broad gates were "Vn barred, & born open, vpon boþe halue."[123] Also, Bruce took a castle by stopping a wagon, loaded with straw-covered men, between the "chekys of the zet."[124] In another instance, Fortiger fled into a castle for safety, but the gate was of wood; consequently, all was lost when fire was thrown on the gate.[125]

Locks, or devices for securing the great gates, were of a simple character. Long wooden or iron bars, placed horizontally, fitted into sockets in the wall. Additional iron sockets attached to the leaves of the door gave added strength. Pins and padlocks were also used to prevent the removal of the bars.[126] One romancer depicted an enemy scaling a castle wall and breaking up the locks.[127] Another tells of a similar act in which the person was cautiously to "lift vp þe lach."[128] In a third parallel example the man on the inside was "The gate to unschette and unpynne,/ And stylly to unschette the lok."[129] Another writer pictures a knight approaching a gate that was "sperred ferli fast/ with lokkes, þat ful welle wald last."[130] Also, Rauf Coilyear, in order to admit his guest, seized hold of the bands—"Enbraissit the bandis beliue"— of the gate.[131] The band was the iron rod or bar by which one half of a gate was held fast and firmly closed.

As has already been indicated, castle gates were customarily made of wood; but in Scotland and the Border region, the gateways were often defended by iron gates, or yetts. These gates were strong forged grills formed of horizontal and vertical bars, hung on hinges, and secured either by long iron bars drawn out from a socket in the wall or by bolts attached to the yett. In Scotland the bars making up the gate were so forged that the vertical and horizontal pieces penetrated, or formed sockets for, the others in alternate series. In these the grill work was left open. In England all the vertical bars passed in front of the horizontal ones and the joints were riveted and clasped alternately. In these the spaces between the verticals were filled in with oak boards so that the gate was solid. Usually a yett was hung within a wooden door, the closing of which allowed time for the iron ones to be swung into place. At Doune the gateway was defended by a portcullis and a yett at the entrance and apparently another yett at the end toward the bailey. Each yett was of two leaves, hung on hinges two and three-fourths inches in diameter. It was made of one and three-fourths inches by one-inch bars, crossing each other in meshes seven and three-fourths inches square, and was secured, when closed, by a two and one-fourth inch square bolt. This bolt was drawn out from the socket in the wall by means of a handle and stretched across behind the yett in the same manner as the timber bars behind an ordinary door. There was a wicket gate in one of the leaves.[132] The realism concerning this feature in the romances is very striking. Torrent rode up to a gateway defended by "Two gattys of yron." Moreover, he went to another gateway defended by a gate made very craftily of "Irum and eke of tree."[133] A maiden approached a gate "That was of yren wrouzt with ful gret gynne,/ The barrys endentyd with stel with-oute and with-Inne,/ Sche brayde vp a vyket and hente vp a tre."[134]

A feature of the great gate of the larger castles was the wicket. This small door made in one leaf of the gate need not detain us since it is identical with that used in city gates and since it served the one purpose of providing a passageway to the outside without the necessity of opening the great gate.[135] Romance wickets served the same realistic purpose as that of Doune and other castles. Ywain, finding the great gates locked and barred, gained entrance through the "weket"; Sebylle admitted Huon to Dunoster through the wicket; and Floripas "brayde vp a vyket" for her friend to enter.[136]

Previously I have referred to the fact that, as the keep developed, defenders felt the need for a small side entrance, or postern. Usually it was placed in such a position that escape could be effected or a sally made unobserved by the enemy. At Dunnottar it opens on the steep hidden slope reaching down to the south bay. At Duntulm it is a sea gate. At Pembroke it is on the second floor and leads out on to the battlements of a building nearby. At Bothwell it is in the south curtain, overlooking the gorge; in addition, this one had a portcullis. At Dunbar and at Kildrummy the posterns had portcullises, but the one at Doune was warded by a machicolation.[137] The posterns in romance castles are very similar to these. The one in Susan's castle was in the garden wall, and another was in the rear of a castle.[138] Sir Degrevant entered a castle through the postern, and many escaped by the same means:

"At a posterne thai wente oute/ Pryvely aboute mydnyght,/ And passed through alle the route."[139] Another postern had a gate made of copper and quartered with iron, as much as a cart could haul; still another was defended by a portcullis.[140]

One of the most problematical features of a castle is the windows. These were fewest in the older buildings and varied according to their location in the castle. Generally the windows in the upper or living rooms of eleventh-century keeps were from one foot to one and a half feet wide and about four feet high. They had either round or flat heads that were flush with the outer face of the wall, and their internal jambs and arches were either splayed or opened out in orders. The windows were set in lofty internal recesses. At Canterbury, the upper windows, which have round heads, have a series of three internal recesses, that diminish in size towards the window opening. The first of these recesses is about ten feet wide, the second seven feet, the third five feet, and the window itself is about two feet wide. At Loches there are two internal recesses, and at Colchester one deep recess that is joined to the narrow window by splayed jambs. In most cases light was considered as secondary to safety—safety from missiles and from an enemy seeking an entrance. The size was also affected by the fact that glass was still a costly product, and the openings to the outside had to be fitted with shutters or wooden frames containing some suitable fabric or parchment, or both. At Edinburgh parchment and linen cloth were used. By the twelfth century there was a desire for more light in living quarters but a hesitancy to enlarge the external size of windows; consequently, two openings were built in one recess, as at Houdan. Here the lights are one foot wide by three and a fourth feet high and are placed two and three-fourths feet apart. The recess behind these twin lights is very wide and is provided with a seat on all three sides. At Coinsborough the twin lights of the window are larger than those at Houdan or Longtown, each being one foot ten inches wide and four feet eight inches high. The lights are recessed inside for wooden shutters, and the mullion—the stone division between the lights of the window—has a projection in the middle with a hole for the horizontal bar which secured the shutters when closed. Windows were sometimes equipped with a transom, which permitted the use of an upper and a lower pair of shutters. Sometimes the upper part was glazed and the lower was fitted with shutters. Later when windows became wider, they were blocked by grills of iron stanchions and saddle bars. On the ground floor of towers and castles, the windows were narrow, single lights, that gave air and some light to the storerooms. In the early buildings these same openings were flush with the outside face of the wall and the inner jambs and arches were widely splayed. Often the sill was rapidly deflected from outside to inside, as at Corfe, Chepstow, and Chateau de Foix. In eleventh- and twelfth-century keeps the windows of the ground floor, which were mere loopholes, were placed so high in the wall that they were often above the level of the first floor; the inner sills were deflected downward rapidy through the wall to the rooms. Canterbury and Skenfrith are examples. During the twelfth century the openings were sometimes splayed on both the inside and the outside, as at Kenilworth.[141] The romance windows are realistic. A knight, whose lover was imprisoned in a tower, approached to the "wyndowe, thynkynge to haue taken his louer by the hande, but he coude not, for the wall was to thycke."[142] By far the majority of the windows were of the shutter type. The windows in Sir Eger's chamber were of this type, for Winliane could not see when she went to inquire of her lover in his bedchamber, "the windows of which were partly closed, so that the features of the knight within the bed could not be discovered."[143] On another occasion Arthurian knights entered a room and opened all the windows to admit the light; one morning Merlin went into the king's bedchamber and opened two windows in order to see how to dress.[144] The maiden who visited Gawain's chamber locked the door and "Wayuez vp a wyndow."[145] Another woman was accused of having a lover and was almost caught: "Vp þou schotest a windowe & the persone þou out lete,/ & afterward þou schet it sket."[146] Usually there was a direct relationship between the location of the window and its size. A number of romances refer to windows large enough for a man to escape through. A Saracen, when attacked in a castle, leaped out of a window that was sixty feet above the ground. One writer described Saracens, caught in similar circumstances, who leaped out of windows to their death.[147] Another redactor pictured the windows as large enough for the escape of two or three men at a time:

þe Sarasynz, þat þo wer laft on lyur faste þay guune fle, & ful out at þe wyndowes blyve be twye & ek be three, & summe fulle out ouer þe wal in-to þe dupe dongoun, & breke hure nekkes to pieces smal so heze þay falle adoun.[148]

The traitor whom Huon chased from room to room effected his escape by leaping out of a chamber window which opened on a garden.[149]

Other romance windows were glazed. Huon entered a chamber, the windows of which were "rychely glasyd openynge vpon a gardeyne side."[150] The castle of Queen Candace had windows of "Riche glas."[151] In the buildings of the city of Damas the windows were "With laten sett and with glasse"; also, in Myldore's castle were "square wyndowus of glas" set in ornamented mullions.[152] In yet another castle "The wyndows of crystal were well fortyfyed."[153]

Three other features of windows received realistic consideration. One was the custom of affixing an iron grating on the outside of windows. Meleagans imprisoned a queen on the ground floor of a tower, and in order to insure her safety he ordered that there be placed over the windows "a sort of wicket composed of strong bars of iron, fixed on stout hinges, and locked every night."[154] A second feature was the wide seat formed in the window recess: "seþen zede to sitte same to solas & to pleie/ at a wid windowe þat was in þe chaumber."[155] A third feature was the custom of having mere slits for windows in strategic points such as the gatehouse. Ywain, held in the maiden's room in the gatehouse, was allowed to look out but "no windo was þare nane,/ Whare he myght oway gane."[156]

In a castle, the center of medieval domestic life was a large hall, which in its original state served all the necessities of shelter. The hall sometimes stood in the middle of the bailey, but more often it was built against the curtain wall which formed one wall of the hall. Sometimes the hall was the principal apartment among others in a single house, and sometimes it was an independent building. Generally the hall was a lofty one-story building with an open timberwork roof and with large windows opening on the court-yard. This apartment communicated with the private apartments at one end and the kitchen offices at the other. Sometimes, in a tower, the private apartments were above the hall and the kitchen below it, although a tower could have a kitchen on the same level as the hall. At one end of the hall was a raised platform, or dais, on which stood the high table. At the other end a passage, the "screens," was formed between the end wall and a wooden or stone partition which stretched across the hall from side to side and supported a minstrel gallery. Customarily the main entrance to the hall was at one end of the screens and a postern at the other. Often in the end wall were three doorways, as seen at Bodiam—one opening to the pantry, one to the buttery, and the middle one to a passage leading to the kitchen premises, whether these were on the same or a lower floor. In some of the early examples, the hall was virtually the keep. The great oblong hall of Chepstow, eighty-nine feet by thirty feet, was a powerful structure consisting of a basement and two upper stories. The hall and domestic buildings at Sherborne stand in the middle of the bailey and are built around the square courtyard. The hall is in the north range, the domestic offices in the east, and other buildings in the south and west. The twelfth-century hall of Leicester has a nave and two aisles, the pillars and struts of which are of oak. On the south of the hall are the kitchens, and beyond the destroyed kitchens is a vaulted undercroft fifty feet by eighteen feet. The living quarters were doubtless on the north side of the

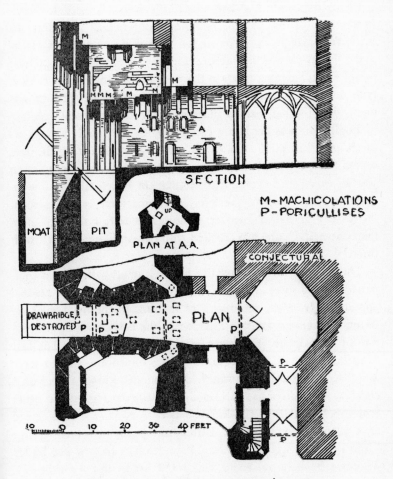

CAERNARVON CASTLE. THE KING'S GATE.
(Reproduced by permission of Sidney Toy.)

hall. The hall at Bothwell, built over a first floor devoted to
cellars, was reached by an outside stair and was lighted by a
range of windows high up in the wall facing the courtyard. A

handsome traceried window, a common feature in a complete hall, is in the dais end. The Earl of Huntly was instructed to build, upon vaults, a hall of lime and stone, one hundred by thirty by thirty feet, which was to be roofed with tiles. At one end of the hall at Bothwell was the kitchen, thirty-two feet high to its pointed barrel vault, having a hatch to the well and another to the bakery, both of which were in the basement. When greater privacy was demanded, the hall had to adapt itself. In the fourteenth century in England it was becoming customary for the family to take its meals in a less public apartment. At first a convenient chamber served this purpose; but by the sixteenth century the dining-room was an established room. Also, retirement to a parlor or "withdrawing room" became possible. At Doune there is such a room off the eastern hall. Moreover, some castles were built with more than one hall. Doune was credited with two and Caerlaverock with three.[157]

The romance writers have much to say about halls, but in comparison to the space allotted to the subject their depictions are disappointing from the standpoint of realism. In the main their accounts deal either with the function of the hall or with a description of its make-up. The latter we shall discuss later on. The first function of a hall, as recognized by the romancers, was to serve as a place of assembly. Gawain had a wounded knight placed on a couch at one side of the hall, in sight of the chief guests, in order that they might hear the knight's tale.[158] Next, the hall served as a place of refreshment. Partonope appreciated this service: "Into the halle wente he thoo,/ Fayre clothes he saw þer layde/ Thorowe þe halle on euery syde./ Off brede and wyne he saw grette plente."[159] Another writer presented realistically the social distinction of the hall: "sone þe semli segges were sette in halle/ þe real rinkes bi reson at þe heize dese/ & alle oþer afterward on þe side benches,/ eche dingneli at his degre."[160] Other writers recognized the dual function of the hall—assembly and refreshment:

than Guaryn toke Huon by the hand and lede hym in to his castell where as he was rychely reseyuyd/ Gauryns wyfe and iiii of hyr sonnes came to Huon, and he full courteously kyssed the lady and hyr iiii chyldrene, his cosyns. Greate ioy was made there in the hall, and the tabyles sette to supper.[161]

The hall as a distinct but integral part of a castle receives some realistic treatment; it is distinguished from the keep. Strangers entering Galafort saw the keep but could find no one; they proceeded until they came to the very center of the castle, heard voices, and continued until they entered a fair hall where were assembled all the men of the castle and the clerks of that country.[162] Also, Partonope visited a castle and its hall; he located the keep, but the hall was the center of the castle.[163] The hall of Lillias must have been built against the curtain wall, for Sir Graham, approaching the castle late in the evening, found the gate closed but was able to communicate with the desponding Lillias. A maiden told Graham that he could gain entrance only by going around through the castle.[164]

Two additional items regarding the hall were treated realistically. The number of halls in a castle was not always limited to one. A fictional countess received a prince into the "chef hal."[165] Also, the hall was the central apartment about which were grouped other apartments. Knights visiting a castle went through the great hall into a fair chamber, and when their coming was announced, "men made them to entre in to the chambre of parement, wher as" the beautiful lady was with her ladies.[166] When Gawain was received into a castle, he was brought into the hall, and the lord led him to a bedchamber.[167] Huon visited a spectacular hall with its adjoining rooms.

He enteryd into the hall, the whiche . . . was so fayre and ryche to beholde that there is no clarke . . . can dyscrye the beaute & rychesse therof; the ryche chambers that were on the syde of the hall were al composyd and made of whyght marbyll polysshed.[168]

In addition to the public apartment or hall, there were private apartments and domestic offices. These private apartments, known as "chalmers" or chambers, are very difficult to identify. In passages referring to the smaller edifices we may have no more definite reference than to the "great chamber" which was normally found in all cases and which was allotted to the head of the family. Otherwise chambers were distinguished by their occupants or by their position as "high" or "low." At St. Andrews, on the north side were the "gentilmenis chalmeris" for the use of single men. To refer to such rooms as bedrooms is essentially but not exclusively correct, for beds, as a rule, were numerous in any one room and might be distributed through all. At Caerlaverock there was a bed in the drawing room, an emergency bed in the dining room, and three beds in each of two wardrobes. Later on, other categories appeared, some of which I have just named. At Cardross there was a wardrobe, or personal storeroom in which were kept garments and personal possessions, such as money and important documents. Reference has already been made to the development of a parlor, or withdrawing room, and a dining room.[169]

Many aspects of the private chambers received realistic treatment. Primarily they were pictured as bedrooms and were presented, by inference, as being more than one to a castle. Ysolt went to her lover's chamber, fell upon his bed, and rehearsed her woes.[170] Another maiden in sorrow went to "hyr chambre" and fell upon her bed, in a swoon.[171] In "his chaumber" lay Ywain, his lion, and his maiden.[172] Melusine put a visiting knight in a "fayre chambre & riche" and put with him ladies and damsels, knights and squires in order to make him forget his loss.[173] Lot's quarters were probably restricted in bedrooms, for Antron, Sir Kay, and Arthur shared the master bedroom with Lot and his wife; again the king invited three kings, the bishop, and other dignitaries to share his own bedroom.[174] Other accounts referred to several bedchambers in a castle. A Saracen maiden, in an act of treachery, invited the enemy to "my chambre" to be armed in order to go to "my faders chambre" to kill him. Huon visited a giant's castle and found food in the first chamber, clothing in the next, a shrine in the third, and the giant's bed in the fourth.[175] Winliane, from her chamber, saw a light in the men's chamber and approached. Evidently, this latter apartment was on the ground floor and had a large window opening onto the courtyard, because Sir Eger and Sir Graham saw her when she rushed by the window.[176] Also, the king of Rome ordered the erection of a hall with seven chambers surrounding it.[177]

Previously I have referred to the fact that the location of the chambers was usually indefinite; however, a few romances are specific on that point. One bedchamber was on the floor above the hall, because from the hall the knight was escorted aloft: "To a chambre she ladde hym vp alofte,/ Ful wel beseyn, ther-in a bed right softe."[178] Winlaine's bower was in an upper story, for Sir Graham made his horse to curvet for some minutes under the window of the astonished girl before he dashed away.[179] In another castle "In a separate chamber, near the ground, were made two beds."[180] Medea received her guest in her bedchamber from which there opened a mural chamber.[181] The mural chamber would strongly suggest that Medea's apartments were in a keep, because mural chambers were rare in other types of castles. Other accounts showed that bedchambers might be entirely separate from the hall. On one occasion Medea's guest jumped from his bed and passed through a cloister until he came to the hall.[182] The cloister probably refers to the covered alleyway which connected the various independent buildings of a castle. Another maiden, who ate in the hall and then visited a knight in his chamber, referred to the fact that her father was in his chamber in "a holde of stane."[183] On one of his visits to Ysolde, Tristrem gained access to the queen's bower by tearing away one of its boards; and the bower was in a building separate from the hall: "Bitven þe bour and þe halle/ þe way was naru and lite."[184]

Living quarters were also located in wall towers, regardless of the type of castle. Sometimes these accommodations consisted of a projecting chamber, like a bretesche, which was wholly for residential use. Slezer's view of Linlithgow castle shows such a construction which is corbelled out on the north face of the tower. Likewise, mural towers in the curtain wall were used as lodgings subordinate to the great tower or principal residence. A survey of Alnwick castle showed that it had diverse fair towers and turrets which contained "diverse fair lodgings and other rooms or place of offices."[185] This utilization of space received realistic consideration. Florippe led her companions throughout hall and bour until they came to her chamber, which was in a tower.[186] Beves visited a chamber under a watchtower in which he found twelve knights asleep.[187] Torrent, riding into a castle, found no one until he looked high upon a tower, where he saw a lady sitting in bed.[188]

Just as in historical castles there were secret and private chambers, their counterparts appear in the romances. Valentine entered into his secret chamber in order to test the tables of Pacolet.[189] However, the private chamber for guests seems to have been a makeshift until the adoption of wardrobes and antechambers. Clarymonde had a wardrobe, "the most secretest" place, adjoining her chamber.[190] As a prisoner, Guinevere was assigned a ground-floor chamber, in the antechamber of which slept her fellow-prisoner, Sir Kay.[191] Also, Medea had an inner chamber housing her bed and an antechamber where she kept personal valuables.[192] The royal suite which Candace showed Alexander consisted of her bedchamber, a withdrawing chamber made of cypress, and "anoþer chambir."[193]

In consequence of the previously mentioned desire for more privacy in eating, private chambers were used for the serving of food if a dining-room was not available. For example, Guinevere sat "at meat in her chamber; . . . the others had eaten in the great hall."[194] And Floripas received Roland and Oliver in her chamber, where she fed them and gave them a bed.[195] However, Huon visited a castle which had a separate dining room.[196]

Other realistic apartments of a castle, which received mention, are the parlor, the "daunsyng" chamber, treasure chamber, washroom, disarming chamber, and nursery. No delineation was attempted by romance writers. A king was seated in his parlor, "with mirth and solas"; Aeneas was led into the "daunsyng" chamber, where he saw great riches: great pieces of plate, vessels of

78

gold and silver, jewelry, and "riche gownes hangynge on perches
of clothe of gold and syluer."[197] Lancelot was received at an
abbey and conducted to the disarming chamber, a chamber in
which a knight was divested of his armor and cloaked with a rich
robe belonging to the lord of the establishment; Geffrey went into
such a chamber where there were "cc harnes hangynge."[198] The
washroom, or lavatory, was an unusual feature in most castles. The
invariable ritual of washing before and after meals was usually
performed in a portable vessel for that purpose. At Borthwick, in
the screens through which the hall is entered, there is a beautiful
lavatory with elaborately carved canopy and wall shaft below the
basin. Coinsborough has a stone lavatory basin and a latrine on
each of its four floors.[199] In Arthur's castle, the people washed
in the order of their rank and then went into the hall to eat. Also,
Guy, who arrived late to a meal, went to a lavatory to wash before eating.[200] As to the nursery, a duke had one room so desig-
nated for his children.[201]

One means of providing more living space with some degree
of privacy was the addition of partitions. This was especially
true of the keep castle. Three of the four stories of the donjon at
Arques were divided by a partition into two large halls. The
keep at Corfe, which consisted of two tall stages and a basement,
was divided by partition walls into one large and two smaller
rooms at each stage.[202] Belisaunt, constrained by love to visit Amis
in his chamber, was spied upon by the false steward who occupied
the adjoining chamber and who looked through a small hole in the
partition.[203] When Havelock asked the lady of a castle for a
room, she gave him one in a tower; a partition made of fir separated his room from that of the lady:

It ne shal no þing ben bitwene/ þi bour and min, also y wene,/ But
a fayr firrene wowe;/ Speke y loude, or speke y lowe,/ þoy shalt ful
wel heren me.[204]

A private chapel held an important position in the life of the
castle. Sometimes it was a separate building of considerable size

and elegance, but that was the earlier and rarer plan; the chapel at Kildrummy stands by itself. Often it was situated in the keep. Colchester has an apsidal projection for a chapel at the southeast corner; on the first floor was a sub-chapel, but the principal one was on the third. Sometimes it stood in the bailey, as at Durham and Gisors. At Richmond and Beaumaris the chapel is in one of the wall towers. At Borthwick a chamber and window recess were adapted to a chapel containing a piscina, locker, and supports for an altar slab under the window as well as a *bénitier,* or stoup for holy water. The window recess served for a chancel and the chamber for a nave.[205] The chapels of fiction do not present the details of the exquisite beauty of many of the historical ones, but they are located in realistic places. A king commanded a priory and a chapel to be constructed within the enclosure of his castle.[206] When the chapel bell rang in the castle of the Green Knight, the lord and lady descended thereto and Gawain entered into a "comly closet."[207] Another romancer, describing the castle of a countess, says, "Of ther fair chapel doubt thereof had non,/ Wel apperailled was it, hie and bas,/ With riche iewelles stuffed manyon."[208]

A novel apartment which was rarely found in the traditional medieval castle was the gallery, a long corridor-like compartment which was not fully developed until the Elizabethan period. Viollet-le-Duc showed that by the fourteenth century the ordinary corridor providing access to several rooms had been widened until it was a veritable promenade, adorned with paintings and sculpture. At fifteenth-century Falkland there was a gallery which was partitioned off into two rooms.[209] Even this unusual feature did not escape the attention of the romancer. Erec went up into a gallery where he seated himself on a rug while his squire went to get his armor.[210]

An extra "room," associated with the larger castles, was the garden, or orchard, which was an adjunct of the ladies' apartments. Either a stairway or a postern opened from their quarters onto the garden in which flowers and trees grew. Frequently there was a fountain playing in it. Around all of this curled the castle wall. Henry III ordered a garden to be made between the queen's chamber and the encircling wall. A door opening on it was cut in the corridor connecting her chamber and the hall.[211] An illuminated manuscript shows a maiden and a youth, facing each other and leaning on a flower-covered trellis in a garden. Green grass, two sections of trimmed hedge, and two trees appear inside the crenelated wall, forming a background. [212] Another illumination shows the lovers' rendezvous in a garden. In the background appear the great hall and upper chambers of a castle as well as a formidable tower in the center of the picture. Domestic offices appear off to the left. The garden proper is separated from the courtyard by a low lattice fence. The lady is standing before her lover, who is seated on the edge of a three-level, flowing, stone fountain. Resting on a large square base is a much smaller but slightly raised square base. Upon this sits a six-sided tank filled with water, out of which rises an ornamental column topped with a small statue on a pedestal. Beneath the pedestal is a gilded spout from which water is flowing into the tank below. By means of a spout in the side of the tank, water is shot into a small square urn from which it empties into a pool by means of a third spout.[213]

Romance references to gardens are numerous and realistic. One visitor was led into a "foursquare herber wallyd round about."[214] Susan had the gates locked to her walled garden for "we wol wassche us Iwis bi þis welle strende."[215] Amidst another was a fair fountain, all of white jasper wrought richly with flowers of fine gold and azure.[216] Degrevant entered the postern of a garden and spent the night in a "rosere."[217] Melior's chamber was joined to a garden; Huon, looking out of a chamber window, saw the garden below so that he took the key, opened the door, and entered it.[218] In a place so convenient, the ladies entertained their lovers. Mildore and her maids went there to play and found Degrevant; Ywain and his maiden went into a garden and discovered two lovers under a tree.[219]

The domestic offices of a castle consisted of the kitchen, brew-house, etc. Alexander Necham, a twelfth-century writer, described these typically as being the kitchen, the larder, the sewery, and the cellar. When King David II occupied Cardross, it consisted of four bedchambers, a hall, a chapel, a kitchen, a larder, a brew-house, a bakehouse, and a winehouse.[220] Thus it is apparent that, early, these offices were housed in separate buildings.

Among the castle offices the kitchen played as prominent a part as the hall did in domestic life. Usually the kitchen in the thirteenth century was a separate building, open in the roof, the cooking being performed at an iron grate which stood in the center of it; however, in the Bayeux tapestry the cooking is going on in the open air. In 1382 a stone kitchen was built at Edinburgh, as well as other "necessary houses"—pantry, bakehouse, brewery, and kiln. The kitchen was to be near the great tower it served. Communication was by a connecting stair, or by hatches, as at Dirleton. At fifteenth-century Edinburgh there were the king's kitchen, the duke's, and the constable's. In towers, the kitchen was often built inside that structure. At Borthwick the kitchen was on the first floor of the wing, at the screen end of the hall. Two windows afforded light. At Dunnottat the kitchen was in the wing of the first floor but was moved to the basement. At Comlongon it is in one end of the hall, screened off by a wall with a service hatch. In all of these the kitchen is easily recognizable by its cavernous chimney and flue; the open hearth occupied only a part of the space. Frequently there was a stone sink, or drain, in the kitchen.[221]

The bakehouse, identified by its oven or ovens, was connected with the kitchen; sometimes it was merged in the kitchen, the oven being heated from the kitchen fire. If there were two ovens, the smaller one was for pastries. Of the exact position of the larder, the buttery, the pantry, and the sewery nothing definite can be said; they had no marked characteristics. The pantry or breadroom was the place in which grain and bread were stored. The sewery was the place for storing provisions for the household, such as linen and other table furniture. The buttery, or bottle-place, was the storeroom for wine and ale. The cellar, gener-ally vaulted, over which the hall or private chamber was built, was used as the storehouse where food supplies were kept in bulk. In some instances, in the twelfth century it was used not only as a storehouse but also as a brewery. The most important of these vaulted apartments on the ground floor was the larder, a place stocked with fresh or preserved meats—meats preserved by salting or larding with fat. In the case of a tower the basement floor was usually the cellar. Customarily there was a hatch for bringing up food to the hall; a stair was used in a tower, but at Coxton Tower there is only a hatch to the basement. Lochleven Tower has both hatch and stair, and Doune has two stairs from hall to cellars.[222]

Various features of the domestic offices received varying treat-ment by the romancers. Melior disguised herself as a boy when she wanted to run away and served in the kitchen where many men were busy skinning animals.[223] Once a knight was in a chamber of a castle and found himself hungry. He opened a door, descended a flight of steps, and was in a cellar which con-tained

a great ouen with ii mouthes, the whiche caste out a great clernes . . . ii delyueryd the louys to other ii, & they dyd set them downe on a ryche clothe of sylke/ then the other ii men toke the louys and deliuerid them to one man by ii louys atones/ and he dyd set them in the ouen to bake/ and at the other mouthe of the ouen ther was a man that drewe out the whyght louis and pastes, & before hym ther was a nother yonge man that reseyuyd them and put them into baskettis rychely payntyd.[224]

When the sight of Orson caused all the people to flee from a great hostelry, he and Valentine entered and went to the kitchen, where they found capons and various meats cooking on a great spit

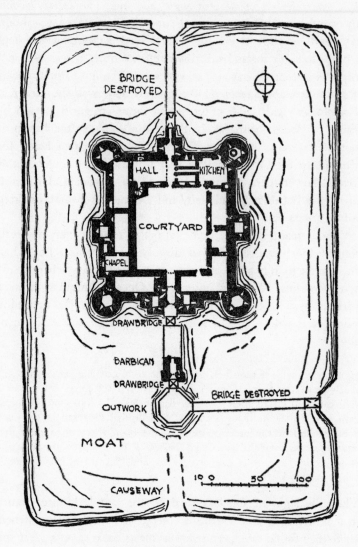

PLAN OF BODIAM CASTLE.
(Reproduced by permission of Sidney Toy.)

before the fire. Valentine then took a pot and led Orson into the cellar, which was open; there they drew off a pot of wine.[225] In the castle which Douglas took, at least part of the cellar was used for the buttery, and by inference, the other part was a storehouse; certainly the cellar served those functions. He went into the "vyne-sellar" and had his men to bring there all the "vittale," the salt, the wheat, the flour, the meal, and the malt; these he mixed together on the floor in order to deprive his enemy of the food.[226] Furthermore, a romancer illustrating the power of a carbuncle stone, said that there was no cellar so deep that this stone would not give enough light for the butler to pour both wine and ale.[227] Lancelot had the spacious cellar of Notingham cut out of rock so that its strength and its great store of food would protect the queen and him from the attacks of the king; "wiþ strengþe" he held the queen for three years and ten months.[228] Ipomydon, who was skilled in the ritual of table service and who hoped to win the princess, went to the buttery immediately after dinner;[229] spiced wine was customarily served after meals. Likewise Myldore was acquainted with the domestic offices. When Degrevant paid her a visit in her chamber, she provided him a repast which she had taken in the main from the pantry; the serving of "wylde swynne" she brought from the kitchen.[230] Although this reference is not exact, it would seem that there was only one kitchen in the castle.

The medieval predilection for building upon vaults would tend to place the hall on the first rather than on the ground floor. However strong this tendency was, there was no unanimity. At Tulliallan the hall was on the ground floor until it was moved to the one above. At Threave and at Halforest Tower the hall is on the second floor. At Rising and at Rochester the hall, which is on the second story, is reached by a covered stairway. At Newcastle and at Dover the entrance doorways are at the third story level and are approached by long covered stairways. Having the entrance well above the ground level was of military significance; an armed knight entering such a castle would have to do so on foot.

In other castles the inmates could enter with ease—on horseback— but the invader found formidable barriers which could be made insurmountable by a few defenders. The four-story keep at Colchester had the great hall on the ground floor, with the entrance opening directly into it. At Le Krak des Chevaliers a series of ramps made it possible for a mounted knight to approach the hall. At Conway, Caerphilly, and Harlech a horseman could approach the hall. Moreover, the doorway of the hall of Winchester was widened to admit the entrance of carts.[231] Both the castle which denied the horseman and the one which could admit him received the romancer's realistic attention. For example: In spite of a warning, a youth rode into Arthur's hall, which "was on the level of the ground," while the king was eating; haste caused a lady to ride into the same hall.[232] Octavian's son demeaned a hall to the extent of riding into it and then feeding his horse there.[233] Another knight shocked regal decorum by riding his steed so near to the king, sitting at dinner, that the mare kissed the forehead of the king.[234] However, other monarchs spared themselves this familiarity. Guy was not able to ride into a hall he visited; neither was Partonope:

Then sawe he where þe palys-yate/ Stode wyde open, and in þer-atte/ He rodde, and downe frome hys horse he lyghts,/ For ferther ryde he ne myghte./ And when he of hys hors lyghte,/ Hym thoghte he sawe mochte lyghte/ Off torches and off ffyre also./ Into the halle wente he thoo.[235]

Huon found his entrance into two castles very difficult because he had to go on foot; with much pain he mounted up the steps and came to the gate of the castle, where he sat down and rested.[236] Moreover, another knight had to enter a hall by means of an external stairway, similar to the one pictured in the Bayeux tapestry: "But discended don a-forn the gret hall,/ The grees ascended, many to counte.[237]

Although the external stair had some military significance, the internal stair was treated more as a means of passing from one level to another. Where the entrance was on the ground floor, customarily there was a straight stair in the thickness of the wall to the first floor, from which a winding stair, or turnpike, rose to the higher levels. At Dunnottar Tower the stair is in one straight flight from basement to garret. At Pembroke a spiral stairway leads from the basement to the battlements. In some towers one had to cross to the other end of the hall to reach the spiral continuation of the stair to the upper floors. The stair emerged at the level of the parapet under a low superstructure known as the caphouse. During the eleventh century, stairways in keeps and towers were built upon spiral vaults, winding around a central newel. From the twelfth century on, spiral stairways were composed of a series of steps, each being cut out of one stone and sufficiently long to form a section of the newel at one end and to tail into the wall at the other. By far the greater number of spiral stairs turned to the right, giving the defender the advantage in swordsplay. At Caerphilly seven turn right, two left; at Conway, seven right, one left; at Caernarvon, seven right, four left.[238] The romancers gave recognition, without detail, to this feature. For example, Gaffray, fearing for his life, fled up the steps to the battlements of his tower; Meliors went down the steps from her chamber to the graden below; and Dido "mounted the degres oll highe vpon her palayce, tyl" she came to an upper chamber.[239] In the palace of Arthur there were twin stairs leading into the great hall, for simultaneously the king descended the steps on one side and the queen on the other.[240]

Two other buildings always associated with a castle are the stables and the prison. About the stable, little that is definite can be said. It is to be assumed that it occupied one of the buildings surrounding the castle; however, it appears that not infrequently the cellar was used for this purpose when great security was needed. The stable at Aydon Castle is remarkable for the total absence of wood in its construction, even the mangers being of stone. Evidently it was contrived for the preservation of cattle during an assault. The windows are small oblong apertures, widely splayed internally and secured by iron bars.[241] The romancers were almost equally indefinite. Whenever a knight entered a castle, his horse was properly stabled by attendants.[242] When Merlin stopped at a hostel, the attendants took his horses to the stable and did there all that was necessary.[243] In escaping from a castle, Beues took a fine horse from the stable by surprising the pages "ase þai sete in here raging."[244] The stable was probably built against the curtain wall because Beues entered a watch tower in which he found twelve men asleep; as he came out of this tower he heard the pages playing.

An invariable feature of a castle was the prison, or prisons if it were a large castle. The prison at Skenfrith was the basement, entered through a trapdoor in the room above. The only other outlet was a ventilation shaft which passed steeply up through the wall to a small opening on its outside face. The basement of Caesar's Tower, Warwick, served as a prison, approached by a flight of steps from the courtyard. A small gallery was so placed that the warder could overlook the prisoners without entering the chamber. The prison was provided with paved floor, a latrine, and ventilation. At Peirrefonds there is a prison in four of the towers; in each case it occupies the two lower stages, which are all circular, stone-vaulted cells. The upper cell is reached by a spiral stairway leading from the chamber above and a passageway blocked by two doors. Two loopholes high in the wall and a latrine offer some comfort. A round hole with a stone cover is the only entrance to the lower cell which has a latrine but no light or ventilation. At Crichton the doorway to the prison is one foot eleven inches by two feet five inches; the lower sill of the doorway is six feet above the floor of the prison. It is ventilated but not lighted. The prison at Tantallon is twenty-two feet by thirteen feet; at Spedlins Tower it is seven feet four inches by two and a half feet and eleven and a half feet in height. At St. Andrews the prison is twenty-five feet from its floor to the entrance opening in its ceiling.[245] This subject which lends itself to realistic treatment has not been overlooked by the romancers.

Practically all are in agreement that the prison is of stone and that it is dark. For instance, Joseph was put into a "stronge prison of stone,/ In that darke house by hymselfe he lay./ Lyght he coude not se for wyndowe had it none."[246] Likewise, a maiden was confined in one in which "þer neuer day dewe," but four noblemen were in one that "ys dym."[247] Also, most of the writers pictured the prison as being in a tower. When a great host were captured, they were sent to Magence and put in prison in "towres and other places but ye duches was put all alone in a stronge towre, within the whiche there was a depe dongeon/ and therein she was set."[248] The depth of the prisons varied; two were forty fathoms, another twenty, and another fifteen feet.[249] Moreover, the depth or compactness of the structure determined the disposition of another prisoner. A maiden was ordered to be placed in a stone prison in order that her cries could not be heard.[250] One prison was like that of Pierrefords, one cell being placed over another:

In the dongeon was the mayden Galazye kepte. And vnder the sayde dongeon was a caue ryght profounde and depe, in the whiche the Emperour and the grene knyght was put.[251]

The entrances to the romance prisons were of the two historical types: a regular door and a hatch in the ceiling. Let me cite some examples. The imprisoned Huon could not see, because of the great darkness, what "prysoners they were that were let downe in to the pryson."[252] Brutamont put Olyuer and his companions down in a prison which was so deep in the ground that no light might be seen after he shut "the dore aboue them." However, Floripas came with a torch and did "open the pryson & put in the lyght tofore hyr for to see the prysonners. . . . She called hir chamberlayn and made hym to brynge a corde & a staffe bounden ouerthwart, & after lete it doun;" thus the prisoners were freed.[253] In other prisons the conventional barred door was used. Esclaramonde stole the jailor's keys and opened the door for a prisoner.[254]

Such prison latrines as were described were largely fortuitous. The jailor refused Floripas entrance because of the filth of the prison, "in whyche place al stenche was comprysed."[255] This prison, which was built by the sea side, was supposed to be flushed by the sea, for at high tide, water rose to a considerable height inside. Beues was more fortunate; a "water" ran through his prison that "bare the ffilth of that man."[256]

Associated with the prison was the practice of placing shackles on the hapless inmates. A romance said that Tirri had more iron about him, on his arms, legs, and body, than a pack horse could carry.[257] Furthermore, iron cages were sometimes used as adjuncts to prisons. Scott said that these were not like parrot's cages to be hung out over the wall but resembled those places in which wild beasts are confined.[258] Torrent entered a prison where there was an iron cage containing four men; and another knight saw a "grete yron trayll" containing many prisoners.[259]

A water supply and sewage disposal were necessary in the Middle Ages, but not to the extent that they are today. The main supply of water was from the wells; this was sometimes supplemented by drainage water from the roofs, caught in cisterns. Usually within a keep-castle there was a well which was carried up through two or three floors, with a drawing at each floor. The two hundred and fifty-foot well at Arques was carried up to the third story. In the basement of Orford there is a deep well, lined with dressed stonework and equipped with foot and hand-holds for descent to the bottom. On the ground story of Threave there is a large well and near it a stone sink with a drain to the outside. On the third floor of the keep at Dover there is a mural chamber containing a well. A recess beside the well contains a tank from which water was conveyed, through lead pipes buried in the thickness of the walls, to other parts of the keep. A similar system exists at Newcastle.[260]

The romancers were fully aware of the position of the well and of the water system. For instance, Douglas took salt and horse flesh to pollute the well in an enemy castle; probably this was in the basement, because he performed his other deviltry there.[261] Also, Susan wished to take a bath by the well which was in the garden.[262] Moreover, an ingenious individual had a well in a tower; the water from it he turned in "o pipe of bras,/ Whider so hit ned was./ Fram flore in to flore/ þe strimes of þis welle."[263]

Very likely the latrine was too realistic an object for the romancer to treat; nothing seems to have been said on the subject. The latrines, with one or more turnings in the entrance passage, were formed in the outer walls and opened from the principal rooms. An indication of their nature can be had from an account of the siege of Chateau Gaillard. The French having been balked in their effort to enter, two soldiers discovered a building which had latrines in it. They searched along the river bank for the outlet of the drain from the latrines, found it, crawled up through the drain, and gained entrance.[264]

Associated with the water-sewerage system is the bath, which early was of the bowl-and-pitcher circuit, but by the close of the thirteenth century formal baths were introduced in the king's houses. Edward I probably brought the idea of this luxury from the East. There were baths at Ledes castle and at the royal manor of Geddington.[265] Evidently there was some ritual associated with the bath, for usually the host was the attendant. For example, the queen led Tristrem to a bath; Princess Gonore took hot water to her father's guests to bathe "jn bacenis of gold"; after supper a royal party had "baynes chauffed"; in her chamber Floripas had a bath ready for Oliver and Roland; and a king prepared a bath for Eglamour, putting herbs in it, and the knight spent the night in it.[266] But Melusine enjoyed a real bath; she was "within a grete bathe of marbel stone, where were steppis to mounte in it, and was wel xv foot of length; and therein she bathed herself."[267]

A seeming essential in every castle would be a fireplace, but that was not always the case, as seen in the keeps at Chateau Gaillard and La Roche Guyon. The early fireplaces, which existed even in the thirteenth century, consisted of a hearth (formed of stone or tile) which appears to have been in the center of the room, and of louvres in the roof above. Fireplaces of the eleventh century were usually plain arched openings with semi-circular backs. The flues rose straight up for a short distance within the wall and then passed to the outside face, terminating in one or two loopholes which were generally concealed in the inner angles of buttresses. The flues to the twelfth-century keep of Conisborough passed up to the top of the wall where they terminated in a chimney. At Aydon castle the chimney was built entirely on the exterior of the wall. Typical of thirteenth-century fireplaces is one at Dirleton, in which the recess is somewhat shallow and a large stone-built hood projects to catch the smoke. The hood rests on corbels, elaborately molded and ornamented, and the corbels rest upon circular shafts with capitals and bases. At Borthwick the width between the jambs is eight and a half feet; on the wall side is a handsomely treated recess, a common feature in relation to fireplaces. Later on, the fireplace was carried deeper into the wall; consequently, the hood became unnecessary so that it diminished to a lintel, or mantel-shelf. The lintels at Dumfriesshire show traces of the common practice of ornamenting the fireplaces, and faint traces of the original coloring remain.[268] The fireplaces recorded by the romancers vary in form. These accounts trace part of the development of the fireplace from the simplest state. For example, Libeaus entered a hall and saw "Amidde þe halle flor/ A fier, stark and store,/ Was lizt and brende brizt." Furthermore, Gawain saw men playing in a hall about the fire upon the floor.[269] In other halls there were fireplaces of a later period. One visitor to a hall saw "charcole in any chymne," and another saw a chair before a "chemne þer charcole brenned."[270] Naymes approached a "chemneye," seized a brand with which he knocked out the eyes of a man, and then he threw the man into the fire, holding him down with a "fyre forke."[271] Another writer painted a realistic chimney and mantel, except for the material:

At the ende o the hall there was a chameney, wherof the two pillers that systeynyd the mantell tree were of fyne Iasper/ and the mantell

and herus,/ Gyf hyt be zoure wyll./ Austyn and Gregory,/ Jerome and Ambrose,/ Thus the foure doctorus/ Lystened than tylle:/ There was purtred in ston/ The fylesoferus everychon,/ The story of Absolon.[279]

Subjects of murals in the romances are Charlemagne, Godfrey of Bologne, and Arthur; the legend of Troy; great battles; King Elynas and Queen Pressyne; seasons, planets, and scenes from nature; Scripture; coats-of-arms, and knights in arms whose names and deed were also recorded.[280] The murals in one chamber extended from the base to the upper edge of the wall. Of interest is the decoration in another hall:

Painted full prudly with pure gold ouer,/ Drapred by þene with a dese riall./ There were bordis full bright about in þat sale,/ Set in sercle of Sedur tre fyn,/ Gret vp fro þe groung vppon gray marbill.[281]

The tapestries are described primarily as being without design; however, one of them portrayed the destruction of Troy. Other rooms were hung with cloths of gold and other rich cloths. The walls of still another room were entirely covered with bright tapestries embroidered all over. Above the tapestries, great escutcheons, enamelled and well set, were arranged properly along the length of the hall. Also, the royal chamber in one castle was so fully covered with the "hangyng" that a would-be assassin successfully concealed himself behind it."[282]

In addition to the ceilings already mentioned, one was painted red with designs of roses, columbines, and lilies. The walls to which this ceiling was affixed were decorated with gules shining on a green ground and flowers intermingling with fleur-de-lis.[283] However, the majority of the interior scenes under this category belong to open timber-roofed halls in which cypress or cedar beams and timbers are exposed to view.[284]

The floors of domestic and military buildings were usually of wood unless they were on the ground or on vaults. During the thirteenth century the flooring of rooms on the ground story was sometimes boarded, but more often it was the natural soil well rammed down, over which dry rushes were strewn in the winter and green fodder and flowers in the summer. Carpets, which were introduced into England by Eleanor of Castile, came into vogue in the thirteenth century, although some sort of carpet stuff or tapestry was made in England prior to the general use of carpets in royal houses. Also, about the middle of the reign of Henry II, plain tiles were applied to domestic buildings, and by the end of his reign ornamental ones were in use.[285]

In the romances three kinds of floors are referred to: carpeted, wood, and tile. Ewain was in a room which had rushes strewn over the floor, and another was strewn with sweet-smelling green herbs. The composition of these floors may have been dirt, but there is no proof.[286] Moreover, the timber floor in Myldore's chamber was painted and covered with a carpet. Other floors were covered with cloths of gold, several carpets—even Toulouse—or one large rug for the entire space. A figure of a lion was the design on the rug on which Erec sat.[287] Numerous floors were pictured as being paved, many without ornamentation; still others were of amber and "stanes of dyuerse colours."[288]

Roofs, especially in the thirteenth century, had a high pitch, and their ridges were often decorated with a running ornamentation. The plain open timberwork of the interior was covered with shingles of wood or stone, with tile, or occasionally with thatch. Lead gutters and gargoyles were ordinarily used. The crests of gables were customarily ornamented. Those at Oakham are ornamented with large figures; one is a figure in a long surcoat, mounted on the back of a lion; the other is a sagittary with bow and arrow.[289] On this subject the writers have little realistic comment. A royal palace was decorated with gargoyles of greyhounds, tigers, an elephant with a tower on his back, lions, a griffin, and a crouched moaning unicorn.[290]

The doors, which were of wood, were suspended from the jambs by means of hinges that projected almost entirely across the panel, and were more or less floriated; this was true, as seen in illuminations, from the tenth century on. The escutcheons of locks were often ornamented. A twelfth-century illumination (Cottonian MS, Nero C. IV) shows six bolts holding a rectangular escutcheon to the panel; each of the four corners terminates in a design similar to a fleur-de-lis. A large key is inserted in the sizeable keyhole. Two floriated hinges cross almost the entire panel. A metal ring, fastened to the panel with a large staple, serves as a doorknob. However, according to Necham, padlocks seem to have been the ordinary apparatus for securing doors. Ornamental nail-heads on doors seem not to have been used until the thirteenth century.[291] Certainly some doors were secured with padlocks; Joseph saw a romance door hanging from a wooden jamb and "haspet ful faste." Moreover, Lucafeer hit a door so hard that "þe henges boþe barste & þe stapel þar-with out sprong." Another romancer, depicting the same scene, said that the "barres & lockes" flew.[292]

CHAPTER THREE

aRchiτecτuRe ano fuRnishings

A. Domestic Architecture

IN THE MEDIEVAL period the place of habitation that attracted the most attention was the castle, the home of the feudal orders, of the personalities of glamor, of the well-to-do; however, there were other domestic habitations, which deserve some consideration.

Probably the earliest form of dwelling in Great Britain was round in shape. In Ireland such houses were made by constructing two basket-like cones, one within the other, and placed a foot apart. This intervening space was filled with interwoven wattles and with clay. A conical thatch cap was placed upon the top of this cylinder. To this day charcoal burners in England build huts of a similar nature. They are composed of a number of poles laid together in the form of a cone. These poles, placed in the ground about nine inches apart, are interlaced with brushwood upon which sod is placed, with grass towards the inside so that the dirt will not fall from the roots into the hut. The doorway, formed by laying a lintel from fork to fork, has sloping jambs. Such a hut has neither window nor chimney. A lair of grass is formed on one side and a fire is lighted upon the hearth in the threshold.[1] Doubtless such a hut was in the mind of one romancer who based his account on narratives connected with the history of Lincolnshire in the sixth century. When Havelock drifted to the shore of England, he constructed a little house of earth: "But grim it drou

98

up to þe lond;/ And þere he made a litel cote,/ To him and hise flote./ Bigan he þere for to erþe,/ A litel hus to maken of erþe."[2]

In Britain, as well as in Western Europe, a dwelling of similar antiquity was built underground and called a pit-dwelling. Near Salisbury the pits are carried down through the chalk to a depth of seven to ten feet. The roof is made of interlaced boughs coated with clay. Entrance is made by means of tunnels excavated through the chalk, and which slope downwards to the floor. Also in Cornwall there are subterranean dwellings. Near Bolleit is an underground gallery with two small chambers. The principal passage, thirty-six feet long and four feet seven inches wide, rises to a height of six feet two inches, but the entrance itself is much lower. The sides are crudely walled with unhewn stones; the roof is formed of granite slabs. At Chapel Uny, a narrow fifty-foot passage leads into a circular beehive chamber, fifteen feet in diameter.[3] Such a neolithic dwelling Tristram and Ysolt must have found:

They found a secret place beside a certain water and in a rock that heathen men let hew and adorn in olden time with mickle skill and fair craft, and this was all vaulted and the entrance digged deep into the earth, and there was a secret path far beneath. Over the house lay much earth and thereon stood a right fair tree.[4]

A much later development of the small or country house was the rectangular house. The hall, approximately sixteen feet square, was often in the center of the building, with the women's apartment—a chamber and the buttery—at one end and a barn or combined barn and cowhouse at the other. The main entrance to the building was a passage which divided the hall from the barn, and which was the threshing floor. If there was no barn in the house, the door opened straight into the hall but was screened by a "speer," a screen slightly wider than the door. Frequently lean-to shelters were constructed against the outside wall to house animals or goods. Near Pensitone is a house of wooden frame work built on "crucks," or curved oak timbers which when fastened together and put in position resemble the wishbone of a chicken, with the two prongs stuck in the ground. The original building consists of four rooms, two on the ground floor and two on the upper, and is equally divided by a massive oak partition wall. Entrance to the hall is by means of a doorway screened on the inside. Behind the screen and in the end wall is the fireplace. A round table is in the center of the room and another heavy carved oak table stands before a carved bench, affixed to the partition wall. Two other benches are moveable. In one corner of the buttery is a steep stair leading to the upper rooms. The walls of the house are two feet thick, are plastered, and apparently are built of stone. The floor is of stone.[5] In this instance the barn and other offices are in a separate building. Although the romancer affords little proof, it is probable that Rauf brought the unknown king to such a country house. Reference to the gate, to opening the door, to kindling the fire, to chickens in the shed, to homely fare, to servants stabling the horses, and to beginning the board would suggest a similar state in life:

To the Coilzearis hous baith, or thay wald blin,/ The Carll had Cunning weill quhair the gait lay;/ 'Vndo the due beliue! Dame, art thou in?' . . . 'Dame, kyith I am cummin hame, and kendill on ane fire,/ I trow our gaist be the gait hes farne als ill/ . . . Knap doun Capounis of the best, but in the byre,/ Heir is bot hamelie fair, do beliue, Gill.'/ Twa cant knaifis his awin haistelie he bad:/ 'The ane of zow my Capill ta,/ The vther his Coursour alswa,/ To the stabill swyith ze ga.'/ . . . Sone was the Supper dicht, and the fyre bet,/ And thay had weschin, Iwis, the worthiest was thair:/ 'Tak my wyfe be the hand, in feir, withoutin let,/ And gang begin the buird,' said the Coilzear.[6]

As I have already stated, in the rectangular house the barn was frequently part of the house, and sometimes the ox-house, or "shippon," was added to this. In that event, the barn part of the house was divided equally in half, one part for the storage of foodstuffs and the other divided into stalls for pairs of oxen. The oxen faced the foodstuffs, and behind them was an aisle leading to an outside door just for the use of the cattle. Frequently there was a loft in the barn. At Bolsterstone, six feet above the ground floor of the ox-house was a loft. A house of this plan at Rushy Lee is forty-four feet long and thirty-seven feet wide; two-thirds of the house is taken up by the barn and ox-house. The barns and independent buildings of more opulent establishments, such as a large manor house, were quite sizeable. The great barn at twelfth-century Walton was one hundred and sixty-eight feet long, fifty-three feet wide, and thirty-three and a half feet high—twenty-one and a half feet to the tie-beams and twelve feet from there to the ridgepole. The large barn at Gunthwaite was one hundred and sixty-five feet by forty-three feet by thirty feet; the tiebeams were fifteen feet from the floor and from the ridge-pole. The building was of timber framework filled up with stonework to a height of almost nine feet. The single span roof was supported by two rows of wooden pillars.[7]

On this subject, the romancers' contribution is negligible. Sir Randall Crawford was hanged in a "berne" in Ayr.[8] A more convenient place for such dastardly work could hardly have been found than a manorial barn with its accommodating tiebeams. Also, a woman went into a high loft ("hygh soler"), cast a rope about a beam, and hanged herself.[9]

The manor house, the chief of the country houses, consisted of a central "house" with a bower on one side and a hall on the other. Entrance to the building was by a central door opening into the "house-place." This is a description of a simple manor house; those even less pretentious contained only a bower and a hall. The manor house and its outbuildings were so arranged as to form a quadrangle. Twelfth-century Sandon consisted of a hall, a bower, and a latrine. To this were joined storehouses for grain, an ox-house, a washhouse, a brewery, a pig-cote, and a henhouse. Kensworth manor consisted of the "house" with a bower on one end and a hall on the other. The hall was thirty-five feet by thirty feet by twenty-two feet; the tiebeams were equidistant (eleven feet) between floor and ridgepole. The "house" measured twelve feet long, seventeen feet wide, and seventeen feet high; the bower, twenty-two feet long, sixteen feet wide, and eighteen feet high.

Also there was an ox-house thirty-three feet by twelve by thirteen, a sheep-cote thirty-nine by twelve by twenty-two, and a lamb-cote twenty-four by twelve by twelve. Little need be said about later changes in the manor house because it resembled closely the hall and adjoining chambers of Edwardian castles, devoid of the stronger defenses. The hall was still the chief feature, with one or more adjacent chambers; in fact, manor houses were often referred to as castles. At Charney a chapel adjoined the upper chamber in the south wing. The building at Woolmer consisted of an upper chamber (seventy-two feet by twenty-eight feet) with two chimneys, a small chapel, two stone wardrobes, and a hall of wood plastered over. The windows in the hall and chambers had wooden shutters, and the floors were boarded.[10]

In comparison to its importance in the medieval period, the romancers have almost neglected the manor house; however, there are a few realistic bits. Bruce and a few of his men came to a "vast husbandis hous" where they killed a wether and built a fire to roast it, but the king objected to any company at his fireplace so that he commanded his men to make another fire "in the End of the hous." This they did and "Thai drew thame in the hous and,/ And half the veddir till hym send;/ And thai rostit in hy thair met."[11] A knight, seeing a "gret hous" in a valley, approached, entered the open gate, and saw a great fire burning within the hall.[12] The general opulence of another manor amazed the spectators:

From the ton Ende to the tothir with-owten dowte,/ And so many Riche things seyn they there/ that Evere to-forn seyen they In ony Manere;/ For Moner was þer Neuere so Ryaly dyht/ that Cowde Comprehende to Mannes Myht.[13]

Another was built of marble, and all "of divers Colowres it was."[14]

Little can be said about domestic furniture in the early part of the Middle Ages except that it was scanty and that it was made on the spot. In the hall, tables and benches constituted the customary furniture, and in the sleeping room a bed and a chest were the chief appendages.

Prior to the twelfth century beds were seldom represented with canopies, but during the thirteenth century the tester was certainly in use; the bed was provided with a canopy for the protection of the head. The substructure of the bed was probably little more than a bench. On this was placed a mattress, often of a very elaborate character, covered with rich stuffs and quilted. An upholsterer was ordered to cover the king's mattresses with silk, velvet, and other costly and fitting materials.[15] A fifteenth-century York house had a bed with a tester ornamented with a figure of the Blessed Mary. In the great chamber were two feather beds. A bed inherited by King Richard was of red velvet, embroidered with ostrich feathers in silver, and heads of leopards in gold, with foliated ornaments and devices issuing from their mouths.[16] Illuminations from the Caedmon manuscript of tenth- or eleventh-century furniture show two beds and a cradle, all of the same general design. The bed itself is V-shaped with a diamond-shaped headboard and footboard. None of the substructure shows. In two of them, ovoid, figured pillows and coverings of an indefinite nature are seen. In the Benedictional of St. Ethewold are illuminations of two oblong wooden beds which have square posts that extend above the head- and foot-boards. The base and crown of the posts are highly ornamented. Ovoid pillows, richly designed, support the heads of the reclining figures.[17] A similar bed is seen in an illumination of the Nativity, except that the ends of the bed are draped in a blue material. The pillow is green-checkered; the sheet, white; and the coverlet, red.[18] In a farmhouse there were four alcove beds, one over the other.[19] A woodcut from *Quatre Fils d'Aymon* shows beds in an inn arranged in separate berths, like those of a ship's cabin.[20] Later on, draw-curtains, often very rich, were placed around the bed; they were hung on a frame. Because of the lack of privacy and of chairs, the bedroom became a kind of reception room, and the bed was used as a seat. This was the origin of the day-bed, or couch. The couch was a compromise between the bed and the bench. An illumination (manuscript Life of St. Cuthbert) shows a person reclining on a couch. The couch stands on cylindrical legs with square bases. There is a back to the couch, which seems to be filled with wicker work. The arms, which are draped with some kind of cloth and which are crowned at either end with a post, are of the same height as the back.[21]

Accessories to the bed were the pillows and bolsters, many of which were equally as rich in character as the king's mattress, just described. Counterpanes and linen sheets were in common use. In 1293 the inventory of a small farmer showed that he had a bolster worth 2d. and a rug and two sheets worth 10d.[22] An inventory in 1464 of a manor house near Durham described an outer chamber containing two sheets, two "dormonds," and three bolsters filled with feathers.[23]

Romance beds are exceedingly realistic and of all types. There are the bed of "tre," wonderfully devised,[24] the richly wrought bed,[25] the richly ornamented bed,[26] beds of silk white as milk,[27] "bedstedes" all of white ivory,[28] beds of gold,[29] the "lityl bedde,"[30] the bed improvised of cushions and spread with grass and reeds,[31] the hermit's grass couches,[32] the bed with the "fowre postes that vp bare,"[33] the tester bed, the couch, and the soft bed—probably a feather bed.[34] Degrevant admired a tester bed which had enwrought on its border the story of Amadas and Ydoyne, escutcheons of knights, true loves, and the king's own banner:

Hur bede was off aszure,/ With testur and celure,/ With a bryzt bordure/ Compasyd ful clene;/ And all a storye as hit was/ Of Ydoyne and Amadas,/ Perreye in ylke a plas,/ And papageyes of grene./ The scochenus of many knyzt/ Of gold and cyprus was i-dyzt,/ Brode besauntus and bryzt,/ And trewelovus bytwene;/ Ther was at hur testere/ The kyngus owne banere.[35]

Other beds were equally as elaborately covered and curtained. When Gawayne visited the Green Knight, he lay in a bed "Vnder covertour ful clere, cortyned aboute."[36] The curtains of fair silk had bright gold hems. The interesting canopy was made of a kind of fine, bright linen; on the sides it was embroidered. The curtains, attached to gold rings, ran on a rope.[37] In another instance the cord on which the gold rings ran looked as though it had been woven from the yellow tresses of mermaids.[38] The curtain of Beues' bed was fastened on a "rail tre." The romancer remarked that it was the custom to have a curtain around the bed.[39] Another "hanged Bedde" had curtains of gold silk.[40] Rauf Coilyear had a curtained bed, and Huon admired a bed adorned with rich curtains, covering, and pillows.[41]

One romance bed had sheets of lawn and another of silk, but the color was always white.[42] Some beds were covered with quilts of silk or gold; but others used counterpanes.[43] These coverings were of cloth of gold, of purple and gold, of silk, of rich cloth, and of fleur-de-lis.[44] One bed was covered with "sente," a kind of rich, thin, silken stuff, highly esteemed.[45]

The romancers were well aware of the custom of using the bed for a bench, or couch, in the daytime. Rimnild led a knight into her chamber and seated him on the bed with her.[46] Iosyn so treated her guest, and Eglantine made Blanchardyn sit beside her on a couch.[47] The romancers seemed to make a distinction between a bed and a couch, although it was not always clear. At one time it seemed to be the same as a bed, for the king led Galahad to his chamber and placed him in the "couch where he himself was accustomed to lie."[48] But in another case the king was brought unto "bedde as the custome was" and Orson lay down on a "couche bedde."[49]

The cradles were referred to without explanation except when one was overturned by a faithful animal trying to kill a snake. The child was not hurt, because the cradle was held off of it by the "stapeles."[50]

Tables of this period were of two fundamental designs, the trestle table and the fixed table. The trestle table was a removable table which was set up in the hall for meals and removed immediately thereafter. It was made up of two or more trestles across which boards were laid. About the fourteenth century there came into use the fixed tables which were similar to our solid tables today; frequently these were carved with rich designs. An illuminated manuscript (MS Arch. A. 154 Bodl.) shows a table on two trestles which have flat heads. The oblong table top sems to be made into a solid piece with a bevelled moulding all around the top edge.[51] A thirteenth-century fixed table in the charterhouse, Salisbury, has a round top of two leaves. The base of the table is a wooden ring of almost the same circumference as the top. Connecting the two are eight legs, carved on the outside to give the appearance of a cylindrical pillar. Between each pair of legs is a carved ornamentation in the shape of a trefoil arch. In the Strangers' Hall, Winchester, is a fixed table attached to the wall. The oblong top has been cut on the far side to accommodate a semi-circular pilaster of the wall. The two solid wooden legs, each almost as wide as the table, are elaborately carved on the front edge in a leaf-and-vine design. In a Midhope cottage there is a small round table at which it was the custom for the master to eat, and an oblong table for the servants. The oblong oak table has four round, carved legs resting in the corners of a rectangular wooden base. The sides of the top are carved in a scroll design. Also, in a manor house near Durham, one chamber had a long dining table with two trestles. In the hall were five dining table leaves and four pairs of trestles.[52] The romancers well recorded the ritual of beginning the board— the board lying on trestles; consequently, great emphasis was given to the trestellated table. Gawain was warming himself in a great hall when "sone watz telded vp a tabil, on trestez ful fayre."[53] Likewise, Gawain entertained in a pavilion where they "prayd vp with a burd."[54] Again, afterwards, the guests were served with hypocras and spices.[55] In another case, for the king they "sette tresteles, and layde a borde."[56] In addition, many references are found of guests entering a hall where they found the "tables set and couered."[57] The order of procedure here—the table being "set" and then the tablecloth placed—would indicate that these were trestellated tables. But in the hall of Amiloun there was a fixed table. When he developed leprosy, he was no longer allowed to eat at the "heize bord" but had to eat at the end of the common table, the place of the lowest menial.[58] This was a fixed table fastened to the floor. This last reference suggests the distinction, based on social standing, between the tables. The sultan sat at dinner at his dais, but Richard put the Saracens at a side table; moreover, Torrent began a "syd bord" for knights and squires.[59] The romancers were not very revealing about the ornamentation of tables. One table had an ivory top and the trestles were of ebony; that of Darius was of gold.[60] One passage refers to the "tablet flure." This has been interestingly interpreted as possibly referring to the upper part of the table where Arthur sat as being decorated with flowers.[61]

Early medieval chairs were, for the most part, benches or forms. In a royal establishment the king's seat was often of stone, elaborately decorated with gilding and painting; it was in the center of a stone bench which extended from one side of the dais to the other. Sometimes the king had an additional seat at the high table. The seats used for dining in the hall were long benches, usually without backs. In private apartments chairs seem generally to have been fixtures. In small country houses a bench was always built against the screen in the hall. Edward ordered a moveable chair to be built for his bedchamber. The coronation chair in Westminster is a thirteenth-century moveable chair, elaborately carved with an architectural design. The panels of the chair were once lined with gypsum, diapered and gilded.[62] In the Bayeux tapestry there are representations of seats. Two are low seats on legs but without backs. The legs terminate in carved head and feet of animals. Two seats have a horizontal bar across the back; ornamented cushions are in the seats. Illuminations (manuscript Life of St. Cuthbert) of the twelfth century show a bench without any back; the rear edge is rolled. Another is of the same design except that the top of the seat is absolutely flat. Another has a back made of two widely spaced horizontal pieces. The ornamented legs extend a bit higher than the back; all three of these were designed to accommodate two persons. Another seat, shown in an illumination (MS Canonici Bibl. Lat. 62), is in the form of an X with a cushion across the upper angle; there is no back. A fixed seat, illuminated (MS Douce, 180), resembles very much a straight chair of today except that the forelegs extend above the seat, and except the elaborate ornamentation in painting. The seats were often covered with mats made of osiers. About the fourteenth century, the mats gave way to real cushions; many were beautified with needlework. Mats were also used in royal establishments to put under the feet to protect them from the cold; from this practice developed the hassock.[63]

Chairs depicted by the romance writers were often very vague in outline. Such descriptions as seats of gold and soft seats are not very revealing; fortunately others depicted the general nature.[64] Some of them were pictured as being of ivory or set with gems.[65] Doubtless the "gud vif on the bynk sytand" whom Bruce visited in her small country house was sitting on a bench fixed to the screen.[66] In the dining room the bench came into its own. In one hall the heroes sat at the dais and others sat on the "side benches" which were fixed.[67] Other romancers referred to these long benches: "to benche went the bold/ When thai were semly set on rowe."[68] The chairs were generally described as being made of carbuncle stone,[69] as being rich and garnished with gold and gems,[70] as being a rich chair with a cushion. [71] In one rich chair there was a cushion of cloth of gold, embroidered with pearls and precious stones.[72] Another chair was definitely moveable because it was brought to Gawain and placed before the fire in order that he might be warm; it possessed both cushion and hassock.[73] The bench was also affixed to the chamber. One maiden seated her guest on a bench; another, on a bench large enough that "seiven mizt sit þer on."[74] Also, a count placed himself beside the maiden, "on a low stool";[75] probably this was one of the benches without a back. Evidently benches or chairs were not always available, for Huon and the king sat together on the rich carpets; Eric sat on the leopard design on a rug, and a maiden sat in her chamber on a cloth of Thessaly.[76] Two other realistic facts were given. The king's throne, of gold and ivory, was fancifully carved. Two of the legs were leopards and two "cockatrice."[77] Lydgate described the visit of a person to the "banket" in the palace of Apollo. A banket was a fourteenth-century cloth or covering for a bank or bench on which dessert was served.[78]

Reference has just been made to a rich cushion in a chair. A number of instances are found in which a servant was ordered to bring a chair and a cushion.[79] Other references were made to a bench covered in a silken cloth, or in tapestry, or spread with a coverlet.[80] In one instance a woman went "to tapestry" a bench, and in another, birds were embroidered on the bright coverings of a bench.[81]

In the dining halls of the larger establishments, an additional article of furniture was the cupboard, or buffet, on which the plate was displayed. Doubtless it was the most attractive feature in the hall. In the thirteenth century it consisted of merely three open shelves, but in the fourteenth century it was often adorned with the choicest carving and with the most ingenious efforts of the metalworker. A canopy of carved wood was frequently suspended over the buffet, hung with cloth of tissue, deeply fringed with passement of gold and silver weaving. The top shelf was covered with a cupboard-cloth of needlework or white diaper, and the bottom one was spread with a carpet. The plate on the top was seldom touched, being designed primarily for show; the plate in use was placed on the lower shelf. The center division was often enclosed with doors, carved with open foliated tracery so that the treasures within might still be visible.[82] With realistic fidelity the romancer has presented this article. Partonope saw on the "cuppe-borde" cups and spoons of gold and silver.[83] The king's son, sitting at the dais, was royally served. He saw many trusty men at the "sidbordez" as was the custom. Arthur's cupboard was covered with silver; there were on it sixty silver cups over which the chief butler had supervision.[84]

Another piece of furniture, so necessary to the people, was the chest or coffer, made of oak or cypress and richly carved. It seems to have had three essential uses. It was used as a press or storage place for clothes and other personal effects. It was a strongbox in which was kept treasure of money, gems, and silverware. Also it served as a trunk when the owner went traveling. The manor of Beaurepaire, in 1464, had three chests in the bedchamber.[85] Huon of romance discovered rich presses in which there was regal apparel:

. . . presses made of fyne Iuory rychely wrought & entayled, so that there was no beast no byrd but there it was wrought; in the presses were gownes and robes of fyne golde, and ryche mantelles furryd with sabyls.[86]

The coffers held great wealth. Richard pillaged a ship and took coffers containing jewelry and silverware.[87] In a treasure room Huon saw coffers with similar wealth.[88] Ysolde kept Tristram's sword, which she valued highly, in a "coffer newe."[89] Also, a wagon train was pillaged, and in the luggage were "cofers fulle riche."[90] Amadace found chests and coffers filled with treasure.[91] Lancelot had mules bearing chests in which he had his arms,[92] but Guinevere opened a coffer and took out two pasties.[93]

Linen was used extensively for table covers; it was manufactured chiefly in the southwestern counties. Enormous quantities were used in royal naperies. The tables were probably covered with clean cloths even when beggars were fed. Henry III had his bailiffs of Wilton to buy five hundred ells of fine linen for tablecloths and the same amount of a coarser linen for the same purpose. At a later time the cloths used by the wealthy were of diaper or damask. Like the table, the cloth was usually long and narrow; it was sometimes fringed with a deep border which hung down over the ends but left the front of the table exposed.[94] An illustration from an early manuscript (Royal MS., 2 B vii, folio 71 b) shows four persons seated at a dinner table covered with a cloth that reaches to the floor. Another illustration shows a king, a queen, and a guest seated at a table covered with a cloth that hangs a few inches over the sides.[95] The romancers were solicitous to have the tables covered. Probably this was due in a measure to the ritual of setting the table; the cloth was spread with great ceremony by two ushers. "A bord was sett, a cloth was spred,"[96] and "A ryche clothe on borde was spredde"[97] are characteristic of the depictions of this ceremony. One tablecloth was described as being as white as any ever used by a cardinal or a pope.[98] Similarly, one table was "clad wyth a clene cloþe," but another was made of silk, richly wrought.[99] Napkins are also mentioned: "Siþene þei braide vp a borde, and cloþes þei calle,/ Sanape and scaler, semly to sighte."[100]

Associated with the topic of table linen is the towel, which was used to dry the hands in the ceremony of washing just before and after meals. One writer said that one damsel entered carrying a gold basin and another followed with two "towayle whyt and fyn." Another mentioned towels of "Eylyssham," white as sea foam; napkins were made of the same material.[101] Others merely referred to the bringing of water and a towel for use at the table.[102]

Silverware and china for the medieval table were often scanty. Even in the twelfth century the huge salt shaker was the chief ornament. On the royal table the goblets and plates were of silver, often gilt and enamelled, but in ordinary houses wooden bowls and trenchers were used. In these lesser houses, counterfeit vessels of pewter were for the feast whereas those of wood were for everyday service; the latter were sometimes square and made of white maple. Until the end of the reign of Edward I, earthenware had not been applied to the making of plates and dishes; previously it had been used to make pitchers and jugs. Cups were often made out of exotic material, such as cocoanut, teeth of walrus, and horns of buffalo. Henry III had three cups made of cocoanut, one of which he valued at £2. 9s. Also he had a gourd mounted in silver and set with precious stones; this was valued at £10. 17s. In addition, he had a glass cup set in silver, one of crystal, and one of alabaster. Agate was sometimes used. Often cups were tall, highly ornamented vessels, usually without a lid. They stood on a foot or stem. The ornamentation often consisted of repoussé work depicting scenes from romances or history or conventional designs. Although forks were a rarity in the thirteenth century, spoons were quite common, and the middle class owned numbers of silver ones. A Bristol Jew possessed 141, valued at £70. 7s. The knife suffered somewhat the neglect of the fork; fingers were used instead of the knife. However, the knives used by the wealthier class of the thirteenth century frequently had handles of agate, crystal, or silver enameled. But it was the custom during the Middle Ages for the gentlemen to bring their own knives. Lydgate warned those who wished to gain the reputation of a man of courtesy to "Bryng no knyvys unscouryd to ye table." Gaston, Count of Foix, carried in his pocket the knife with which he cut his meat at the table.[103] The fashion of serving is shown in the Bayeux tapestry: a servant passed around the meat on a spit and each person cut a portion with his own knife. The spits used by the nobility were usually of silver and sometimes gold.[104]

Kitchen utensils centered primarily around the large metal cauldrons. An illustration from a manuscript (Arch. A. 154, Bodl.) shows a large metal cauldron over a fire. It is of a kettle-drum shape, and has a curved handle caught in a hook which suspends the cauldron.[105]

The romancers have given full recognition to the variety as well as to the splendor of the cups. Some writers referred to them simply as drinking cups. Ywain saw on a table a pot of wine and a cup to put it in. One mentioned four hundred cups of brass.[106] Others talked about cups of gold. For instance, Richard acquired great and small cups of gold by pillaging a boat.[107] Utherpendragon had a cup of gold worth a "shire of lond," and Amis had two identical cups made which cost him £300.[108] Likewise, a queen had cups made out of a large gold chain:

She badde þe wesselle were made vpon alle wyse:/ The goldesmyth goothe & beetheth hym a fyre & brekethe a cheyne,/ . . . He toke þat oþur fyue & fro þe flyer hem leyde,/ And made hollye þe cuppe.[109]

MAY SCENE OF BOATING PARTY

(*Horae*, Brit. Mus. Add. 24098)

ROYAL BURIAL

(*Mandeville's Travels*, Brit. Mus. Add. 24189)

Another depicted a richly wrought cup which had a gold pin in it.[110] This reference is in keeping with the practice of putting gold or silver pins into goblets to regulate the draught of each guest. Still other writers described cups of gold, enriched with jewels. For example, when the king wanted to make a sacrifice to Apollo, he took a cup "Ful of gold and precious stones." A similar cup contained relics as well as jewels.[111] Another writer envisaged a gold cup enamelled with azure; the design was "so corouse and so nobill" that he could not describe it.[112] Still other cups were engraved. Let me illustrate. The richest cup in a king's treasury weighed fifteen marks of gold, but the "work" on it was more costly than the metal, yet the most valuable part was the gems which covered it.[113] Also, one other cup was enriched with repoussé work that delineated "How Paryse ledde awey þe Queene," and the story of their love was on the lid, and on the knob of the handle was a brilliant stone.[114]

Unfortunatey the romancers did not treat spoons and salt cellars with the comprehensiveness of cups. In one hall Partonope saw gold and silver spoons on the cupboard, and Gawayne at one time saw the salt cellar and silver spoons before him.[115] Myldore had a gilt salt cellar in her hall.[116]

In the romances, forks were seemingly scarcer than they were in medieval life, and the knives—with emphasis on table use—were none too common. This latter combination instrument received realistic treatment. For instance, in the romance of Beues, one person became angry while he was eating so that "he cast his knyfe ouer the borde,/ To haue hit the messangere."[117] Again, while a king was eating, he threw his knife at the steward, who moved in time to escape with only an arm wound.[118] A would-be murderer drew out his knife, which had a blade "a foote long."[119] A traveler to Carthage had a rich knife, hafted with jasper, enriched and garnished with fine gold, and hanging at a silken lace by his side.[120]

The treatment of dishes is realistic, describing the commonplace as well as the unusual. One writer referred to platters, dishes, and cups of brass, and another discussed dishes and cups of gold.[121] Other writers referred to all the plate's being of gold and silver, cupbearers carrying cups in a golden tray set with gems, a king and a duke both eating out of the same dish and platter, gold vessels bordered with gems, meat chopped in a charger of chalk-white silver, plain pots containing wine, and golden jewelled pots.[122] The use of rich vessels can best be summed up by a direct quotation:

there, come in at the fyrste course, be-for the kyng selvne,/ Bare-heuedys [boars head] that ware bryghte, burnyste [served] with syluer/ . . . Pacokes and plouers n platers of golde/ . . . Grett swannes fulle swythe in silueryne chargeours/ ffesauntez enflures chit in flammande siluer/ Than Claret and Crette, clergyally rennene,/ With condethes fulle curious alle of clene siluyre/ . . . Vernage of Venyce vertuouse and Crete;/ In faucetez of fyne golde.[123]

The basins, used in the ceremonial ablutions connected with the meals, were in general depicted as being very rich. Reference was made to a plain basin and ewer,[124] but more general was the reference to gold ones; for illustration, in one hall a maiden carried a gold basin to all the guests; in another there was brought before Partonope " A payre of bassennys fayre Icuryd,/ Off ffyne golde ryghte welle pured."[125] Some few were further enhanced by gems.[126]

To the romancers, the kitchen utensils seem to have been almost a forgotten item. A cauldron of brass has the earmark of reality.[127]

The chief method of lighting was by candles, and the holders for these were generally inexpensive in the thirteenth century. Even in the churches the candles were often stuck in a row on a wooden beam which was fitted with wooden pickets. When branched so as to hold more than one light, the holder was called a beam or tree. In old inventories, records are given of beams and trees with four or six candlesticks. There were several orders by Henry III to have iron branches or candlelabra attached to piers in a number of royal halls. Silver candlesticks were used in churches, but rarely for secular purposes. A candlestick in the king's own chamber was worth only 8d., but a thirteenth-century one, preserved in the British Museum, displays much beauty and is enriched with Champleve enamel. An illumination of a royal dais shows two lighted candles held in brightly polished brass or gold candlesticks. The torches commonly used were made of rope steeped in pitch, tallow, oil, and rosin.[128] The lighting fixtures of the romancers were both moveable and stationary, but simple; richness seems to be almost absent from this feature in their picture of domestic establishments, although some is recorded in ecclesiastical use. Candles, lamps, and torches were the devices presented. Esclaramonde used a "torche of wax" when she walked through her castle, and Valentine carried a large taper in his hand.[129] Huon saw two torches burning in a hall; Medea had "grete torches and cyrges" attached to the pillars in her castle.[130] Chandeliers were referred to, but candlesticks were the usual device.[131] For example, Gawain and his guests called for "torches and brochetes."[132] These latter were candlesticks fitted with small broaches or spikes on which the candles were placed. No description was given of the composition of these items. Lamps also came in for consideration. Lamps were burning in Crystabelle's chamber and in Floripas'.[133] These last two references represent an interesting custom of having a light burn all night in the bedroom.[134] Floripas awoke and saw, by the lamp light, the intruder in her room. Also, after supper Eglamour went with Crystabelle to her chamber; "There lampus were brennyng bryght;/ That lady was not for to hyde,/ Sche sett hym on hur beddys syde." If a lady did not want to be recognized entering a gentleman's room, she would want the torches extinguished:

I have a lady of hegh bloode./ Bot sche wyl have mykyl good,/ And dyrke scho wolde that hit bee,/ Scho nylle that no man hyre see,/ Parfay, quod the kyng anoon./ Lette quenche the torches ilkon![135]

B. Ecclesiastical Architecture

Since all art had its origin in religion, it is not surprising that in this period of great religious enthusiasm, churches were so magnificent. The basis of the plan of the early church was the Roman basilica. Later the pointed style of architecture pushed aside the round style, so that by the time of the emergence of the medieval church the essential features were fixed: arched windows and portals, towers and spires and radiating chapels, compounded columns or piers and multiple arcades, pillared nave and flanking aisles, triforium and clerestory, transepts and encircled sanctuary.[136] The nave or place of worship of the laity was a high vaulted enclosure in the west portion of the church—the altar always faced east. Ornamented walls on either side rose to support the great weight of the stone roof. The walls were pierced by the bays of the triforium, which was a gallery built over the arcade and opening onto the nave by means of three-light windows. The range above the triforium was the clerestory, which contained a series of stained glass windows, with gorgeously resplendent stained glass windows in the end walls. These large, round windows, filled with traceried designs, were known as rose windows. Often over the very center of the transept rose a tower of great height. The semicircular projection east of the transepts, generally referred to as the apse, contained the choir, the altar, the ambulatory, and chapels. On the western side of the high altar was the choir, separated for the women on the north and the men on the south. The walls which shut it in were about seven feet high. Circling part of the choir and of the altar was an ambulatory from which opened small chapels. The high altar in the early church, placed in the apse, was far away from any wall and was overshadowed by a small dome which rested on four columns and about which hung precious ornaments. Between the columns ran rods holding rings to which were fastened rich curtains, often of cloth of gold flowered with garlands of pearls running round imagery illustrative of sacred subjects. Whether of stone or wood, the altar received its decoration from magnificent palls and moveable adornments or frontals made of thick plates of gold or silver, exhibiting the figures of Christ and the saints standing out in bold relief from a ground sparkling with gems. The palls of the richest purple dye were woven of fine silk and edged with golden borders. Upon the altar at all times stood the cross, usually sheathed between plates of gold or silver. Often beautiful carpets embroidered in fanciful designs of flowers and wild beasts, and rugs made from expensive furs were spread on the steps and floor before the altar. The holy of holies, the chalice, and often the cruet for holding the wine were made of gold and set with gems. Later on, the dome ceased to overshadow the altar and only the two eastern columns remained; across them ran a thick beam for relics and saints' images to stand on. Immediately from the altar rose the crucifix.

The walls on the inside were frequently decorated with paintings of the Virgin, the apostles, the saints, and illuminations of different passages of Holy Writ. In addition to this, painted vaults, pavements of mosaic, tinted carvings, and resplendent windows showed the most glorious embellishments that the Byzantine tradition could afford. On the outside, carved portals, edifying friezes, flying buttresses, and lofty spires and towers completed the picture of grandeur. Such was the cathedral; such was the independent chapel—only in miniature. In the less wealthy churches and chapels the grandeur gave way in part to simplicity, but the general plan of construction was retained.[137]

It is disappointing but understandable that, in a period when the church loomed so magnificent and so splendid on the horizon, it should find such a paucity of realistic note in the romances. Certain parts of or facts about the church were mentioned, but the detailed grandeur of them was lost. For example, the church was located in the midst of the market, which was quite common.[138] A queen went to the "mynstre," and a knight took his sister there to be wedded; whereas an emperor gave a maiden in marriage at the church door.[139] Regrettable in this instance is the romancer's failure to depict the beauty of the door. Again, Partonope visited St. Peter's in Rome, and Huon went to Notre Dame of Paris.[140] Inside the church, the decoration of the walls was hinted at. In several churches there were representations of a star, and in the star was the sign of the cross with the Christ-child above.[141] The church in which Arthur was buried was painted in four colors.[142] Philip had his church hung with broad and long "bawdekyn":[143] would that we could see the colors and design! In another the vault above was checkered in amber and crystal, and the floor was paved in stone tiles that were powdered with gold fleur-de-lis intermingled with red roses.[144] The pillars of St. Sophie were of marble.[145] The choir and the high altar were shown in the proper relationship. At midnight some monks went into a church, entered the choir, and kneeled down before the high altar.[146] Also, Athelston, probably praying at the altar before the rood screen, looked up into the choir and there saw the archbishop;[147] the choir, divided from the transept by an ornamented partition known as the rood screen, was reserved for the monks, etc. Also there was a commemorative oratory in the apse, near the high altar.[148]

The vessels and furnishings of the church were also sketchily recorded. Charlemagne provided the church of St. James with bells, vessels of gold and silver, adornments of precious stones, cloths, books, vestments, and chalices.[149] Another church was provided with a basin of silver, a cruet, a little pitcher for holy water, and a censer.[150] In another the ornamental coverings were of cloth of gold trimmed and set with pearls and other gems. A crucifix, the figure of Our Lady, and other figures were well carved in another.[151] The order of the mass explains further the nature and use of the objects. When mass is said, a gold crown is hung over the altar; and when the communicants sing it, the clergy cut bread four-square and place it in a "disshe of gold or of syluer." Above that they lay a star, and cover it with a white cloth. After the offertory the elevated host is carried through the church, with burning candles and swinging censers.[152] Likewise, the chapel was presented in no greater degree of detail. The chapel was recorded as being built of "stone and tre," or of "lim & ston."[153] To one was attached a steeple: "a pilere of stone made aboue þis chapel, of a wonder heithe."[154] Inside one, Sir Amadace found pillars as well as a glass window.[155] Another was skillfully carved and had all kinds of rich ornaments.[156] Yet another had a fireplace inside[157]—that was a common practice; a knight suffering from the cold "into the chappel zede . . . and by the fyre he hym sete."

Of great importance in the extensive holdings and numerous establishments of the church was the monastery, which consisted primarily of the great church, the abbot's lodge, the cloister close, and numerous buildings, all enclosed in a stone wall with an imposing gate-tower. The heart of the monastery was the quadrangular sodded cloister around which were arranged the church, the chapterhouse, the refectory, the dormitory, and other buildings. Usually around the four sides of the cloister close was an ambulatory, having an open arcade on the side facing the court, which supported the groined roof. Sometimes the open arcade gave way to glazed windows, even painted ones. Usually there was a fountain in one corner of the cloister where the monks washed before meals.

The principal building of a monastery was the church, with its shrines, tombs, altars, costly furniture, and great splendor. Many of the existing cathedrals today were abbey churches. Peterborough, Christ Church at Oxford, Gloucester, and Westminster were originally Benedictine abbey churches. The monks entered the church on the south side, and in some churches there was a newel stair in the south transept so that the monks could enter from their dormitory without going out into the open. Usually the laity entered on the north side. The great western door was reserved chiefly for processions, accompanied by the tolling of the bell, chanting of hymns, and displaying of cross and banners. The internal arrangement was similar to that of cathedrals of today. In the ornate choir stalls sat the members of the convent. In the choir aisles or in the apse behind the high altar were placed the shrines of noted saints or benefactors. Stained glass windows, the choir hung with hangings, banners and tapestries hanging from the arches of the triforium, the altar bedecked with jewelled plate, and monuments lighted with tapers completed the internal picture. Almost as a rule the cloister was placed on the south side of the church, in the angle between nave and transept. The chapterhouse was always on the east side of the cloister, unless it was part of an establishment of secular canons; in that event it was multi-sided with a central pillar to support the groined, conical, lead-covered roof. The chapterhouse was a room, of much architectural ornamentation, with the western end frequently divided off as an anteroom. Pillars often divided the room into two or three aisles. Seats for the monks were arranged around the wall, with a higher seat at the east end for the abbot; a desk stood in the middle. In Cistercian houses there was a long building south of the chapterhouse. The lower story of it was the fraterhouse, or place of retirement after meals to talk and take the alloted indulgence of wine and food. The upper story was the dormitory, a long, vaulted, or open timberwork room in which pallets were arranged in rows against the walls. On the south side of the close was the refectory, which commonly had a row of pillars down the center to support the groined roof. At one end was the dais and at the other the screen; a pulpit took the place of the oriel window of medieval halls. The scriptorium, or room used by the scribes, was usually over the chapter house. The abbot's house sometimes formed the western side of the cloister close, but more often it was a detached building placed conveniently within the abbey close. Since abbots were powerful noblemen who entertained honored guests, the abbot's house consisted of the hall, great chamber, kitchen, buttery, chamber, chapel, cellars, etc. The hall of the abbot of Fountains was divided by two rows of pillars and it was one hundred and seventy feet long by seventy feet wide. Other buildings were usually detached. One of them was the infirmary, which had its own kitchen, refectory, chapel, and chambers. The guest house was sometimes detached, being a part of an outer court, westward of the cloister court. At Canterbury this house was one hundred and fifty feet long and fifty feet wide; it was raised on an undercroft. The guest house usually consisted of the hall, a drawing-room, sleeping chambers, and a chapel. The gatehouse was a large, handsome tower with the porter's lodgings on one side of the arched entrance and a prison on the other. Often there was a handsome room over the entrance, in which the manorial court was held. A variation of this plan, notable in the Carthusian monasteries, is seen in Chartreuse of Clermont, in which the cloister court consists of about twenty enclosures. Each enclosure, or cell, is a little three-apartment house and a garden. These and the oratory form the cloister court; in the small outer court are the prior's cell and the guest house.[158]

The romancers have treated monastic buildings with fidelity but not with meticulousness. When Huon visited a monastery, he found the porter a venerable man of authority who allowed him to enter. He told Huon that he would find the abbot in the abbot's own hall.[159] After going to mass in the church, Huon and the abbot went into the hall to eat; the knight, being a noble guest, sat by the abbot.[160] Sir Guroun was greeted in the guest hall by an abbess, and a knight-errant was received at a monastic gate with joy by the friars who took his steed and led him to the hall, which was on the ground floor.[161] The size of another monastery can be determined from the fact that it housed one hundred canons and a prior.[162] Also, Athelston, who found the archbishop praying in the choir of Westminster, accompanied the prelate into the "wyde halle."[163] Although these references are not specific, they clearly indicate certain known features of monasteries. However, one other reference, depicting the Carthusian plan, is so highly realistic that I shall quote at some length. Geffray visited the monastery at Mountferrat where he saw the

chirche & the place there. . . . And thenne came to hym they that were ordeyned for to lodge & herberowe the pelgrymes. . . . Thenne were his horses stabled and they gaf hym a fayre Chambre for hym & for his men. And in the meane while Raymondyn yede & vystyed the hermytages but he went no ferther than to the Vth celle for that place was of so grete heygth that he myght not goodly goo thither/ and fonde the IIIde celle exempt. For the hermyte there was deed. . . . And there was stablysshed of old a custome that yf within a terme prefix none came there to be hermyte, he of the nerest Celle gooyng vpward muste entre into that other Celle so exempted/ and so al the hermytes benethe hym to chaunge theire places vpward.

The next day Raymondyn entered his cell as a monk, and the monks

went & hanged the chirche, and made al the place fayre & clene to theire power as god hymself had descende there. And thenne mounted Deffray toward the first hermitage that was wel LXXX stepes highe vpon the mountayne. . . Geffray beheld vpward the great mountaynes whiche were high & ryght vp and sawe the Capell of Saynt Mychel which was the Vth hermytage, and after locked dounward . . . and to hym appered the chirche and housyng of thabbey but as lytel Chappelles.[164]

Monserrat, which rises abruptly from the plain of Catalonia, contains a number of natural caves. A monastery was founded there in the tenth century, and later passed into the hands of the Benedictines. The cells, now in ruins, were all built alike. Each had an antechamber, a cell with a recess, a kitchen, a study, and a plot of garden with a chapel.[165]

A hermitage was really a miniature monastery in which one person, accompanied sometimes by a chaplain, performed all of the duties. It consisted of a chapel, accommodations for the hermit, travellers, servants, and a chaplain—when one lived in the hermitage. It was not unusual for hermitages to be built for more than one person; in such a case the hermit had his cell outside the chapel. Frequently the chapel was used as a bedroom for guests. Generally hermitages had a courtyard and a garden. The material used in the construction of such a retreat varied from wattle to stone. An illustration from a Book of Hours (Brit. Mus., Domitian A. xcii, folio 4 v.) shows one hermitage which is partly of wattled work, and another of stone. On the gable of the little chapel is a bell in a bell cot. Near Rowsley there is a cave that was a hermitage. St. Roberts Chapel, Yorkshire, is a hermitage hewn out of the rock. On the outside there appears a simply arched doorway, an arched window on the left, and a small square opening between. Inside, the cell is fashioned like a little chapel with groined ceiling. At the east end is an apsidal recess in which the altar stands. A piscina, a credence, and a stone seat are in the north wall. There are a row of sculptured heads in the south wall, and a gravestone in the middle of the floor. The chapel also seems to have been the hermit's dwelling.[166]

Hermitages were a great comfort to romance characters. Lancelot and other Arthurian figures took full advantage of their hospitality.[167] Ywain found a little hermitage in a wood, opened the gate, and approached the hermit who sat at "his window."[168] Also, Sir Agloval found a hermitage, went to the gate, and looked through the wicket.[169] Lancelot found a hermitage which was well built; he stopped at the little window and asked for tidings. The hermit, who had a servant, invited the knight to stable his steeds and spend the night "within my chapel."[170] While the servant fetched water from the spring, the hermit prepared a couch in the chapel.

The habitation of a female hermit was a reclusorium, a house of timber or stone built in the churchyard and usually against the church. Such a cell had a little altar at the east end. A little, square, unglazed window, with a shutter, had a black curtain hung across it so that the recluse could converse without being seen. Another small window gave a direct view of the altar in the church. Through this window she could participate in worship and receive the sacraments. A third window gave access to the outer apartment in which her maid lived and in which guests were sometimes entertained.[171] Early romancers seem not to have delineated this structure. On one occasion Lancelot passed a chapel where there was a reclusorium which had a window for the hermit to see the altar. After talking to Lancelot, she invited him to dinner.[172] When Percival was looking for Lancelot, he returned to a reclusorium. After he had knelt at the lady's window, she opened it and recognized him and ordered that he be entertained, but she seems not to have participated.[173]

C. Statues and Tombs

The dead in the medieval period were buried in the graveyard, in the crypt, or in the ambulatory of the apse. The graveyard grew around the church, but the church was always built on the north of the cemetery in order that its shadow might fall clear of the graves. There the bodies of most of the common people returned to dust, but the more notable figures were buried in the crypt beneath the chancel. By the end of the Norman period it was the fashion to translate saints and similar dignitaries to some part of the chancel. In the arcade around the choir and presbytery there were tombs also. Frequently members of royalty, archbishops, or the founders of chantry chapels were buried in the chapels encircling the arcade of the apse. If a person were buried in the crypt, a plain marble slab covered his grave in the floor, but if he rested in the nave, a tomb of great wealth and splendor perpetuated his memory. By the thirteenth century, sepulchral sculpture in the form of effigies became important. The figures were generally of knights in their close-fitting mail, and of ecclesiastics in draped robes. The figures were usually recumbent, but the knight was often represented in action, such as drawing or sheathing his sword, and the bishop in action, such as giving a blessing. However, by the end of the century, figures were usually represented in repose. In York Minster is a fine effigy of Archbishop Walter de Gray (d. 1255), combined with the graceful architecture and decorative sculpture of the period. The earlier effigies were made of hard Purbeck marble, but softer stones as well as alabaster and oak were used later. Generally the figures were painted and gilded with ornamental decoration, sometimes molded or stamped on a coating of plaster. By the fourteenth century, an important feature in churches was the canopied tombs, the upper portion of which was either an arch under a gable, or an erection of open tabernacle-work in several tiers. An example of the former is the rich Percy tomb, elaborately decorated with the beautiful foliage of the period. The tomb consists of a freestone canopy over a gray marble tomb, inlaid with a metal effigy of Lady Percy. In the spandrels of the arch are family shields held by knights. On a pedestal below the finial, Christ is seated and is holding the lady's soul in a cloth. The tomb of Edward II is built in five tiers of tabernacle work. On one side is a projecting pedestal which probably supported a light.[174]

The romancers have buried their heroes with realistic fervor and splendor. One deceased knight is recorded as being buried under stone;[175] this could have been in the crypt of some manor church. Gawain was buried amid the choir of a chapel.[176] The making of a tomb was depicted by Sir Archibald, who ordered that alabaster be taken to fashion a tomb worthy of his father.[177] Charlemagne was buried in a rich tomb, having a canopy of the arch-under-gable type. Over his tomb was an arch made of gold, silver, and gems. The effigy was of the king richly clad, crowned, and sitting on a chair of gold. Upon his knees was the open text of the Four Gospels, and with the right hand he held a letter and in his left the royal scepter. The crown on his head reached to the arch.[178] Another tomb was adorned with gold and gems. The tomb sat upon six pillars, and above it was the prone figure of a knightly-armed crowned king; this was made of chalcedony. Near the king was the figure of a woman looking at him with "alabaster" eyes and holding on her knees a table of gold which identified the deceased.[179] The tomb of Hector was set on four pillars of gilt, and on each pillar stood an image with a lovely face like an angel. The roof over the tomb was of gold set with green, red, blue, and black stones. Over the tomb was a gilt effigy of Hector with drawn sword. "Many a proude pynacle/ Stode aboute that tabernacle."[180] Around the tomb were carved and painted leaves of oak, of hawthorn, of the vine, and grapes, flowers, and fruits.

Tombs, especially of the great, were often lighted at all times, and additional tapers were added for special occasions. Henry VII made an agreement with the monastery of Westminster that there should be four tapers burning continually on his tomb. These tapers, placed one on each side of the tomb, were to be eleven feet long and weigh twelve pounds each. For his weekly obit there were to be one hundred tapers nine feet long and twenty-four torches of twice the weight.[181] A romance account of the tomb of King Elynas says that there were great candlesticks of gold in which great white tapers were burning. Another reference to this same tomb adds to the candlesticks "lampes & torches which brennen both day & nyght continuelly."[182] At Arthur's gray marble tomb, one hundred tapers were burning on the "herse," which was a frame designed to carry the candles lighted in honor of the dead.[183]

D. Ships and Wagons

English ships received their primary design from the galley, a swift ship of from fifty to one hundred and fifty feet in length, and fifteen feet or more in width. The galley had a great sheer, or rise at stem and stern, and had one mast and sail, although it was propelled principally by twelve to thirty-five oarsmen. Some of the larger ones were decked, with cabins below and a raised platform aft. An illumination in Froissart's *Chronicle* (Harl. 4, 379) shows a galley which is a long, low boat with outrigger galleries for the rowers. The hold is full of soldiers. It has a forecastle like ordinary ships; the soldiers who occupy it have their shields hung over the bulwarks. The commander stands in the stern under a penthouse covered with tapestry.[184] Returning Crusaders brought back ideas about rigging and sailing, so that the galley was forced into a secondary role. Its limited storage space, inability to carry cannon, lack of maneuverability, the impossibility of laying alongside and boarding hostile vessels because of its oars—all these relegated it to coastwise work. However, in 1544 a glorified example of the galley was built. It was a two-hundred-ton ship manned by a crew of two hundred and fifty mariners, with three brass guns in the bows. Her hull was painted horizontally in three colors: yellow at the gunwales, timber-color below, and dark brown beneath; the beak was yellow, then timber-color, and scarlet below that. The awning at the bows was yellow and the canopy at the stern was scarlet inside but yellow on the outside, decorated with the royal insignia. The projecting dragon's head was green and its tongue scarlet. Ornamental shields painted along the gunwale showed various heraldic devices. The mast was scarlet; the yard, timber-color; the top, white and yellow; and the sweeps, white and scarlet. Nine large, brilliantly colored flags were placed on the hull. The streamers from the top of the mast and from the yardarm bore St. George's cross with a yellow border and Tudor fly.

By the time of King John, barges and merchant ships were in common use. The barge was an adaptation of the Viking longship. It used oar and sail, and sometimes had two decks. The merchant ship was a tub-shaped, round-bowed, and flat-bottomed boat. A wreck of a thirteenth-century boat proved to be of this type. It was built of oak, was single-masted, flat-floored, with no keel, and had one cabin fore and two aft. The caulking was of moss. The yard was fitted with braces, and the decorated sail had brails, reefs, and bonnets. Such things as sheets, cranelines, bowlines, collars, trusses, davits, halliards, bolt-ropes, hawsers, shivers, pulleys, handpikes, hatches, buoys, windlasses, etc. were used then as now. Also, the rudder had supplanted the oar for guiding ships. The forecastle and the poop gradually developed from "castles" or temporary wooden structures in the bow and stern. These could be used for warfare as well as could the fighting-top, or crow's nest, which was placed at some point along the mast. By the fifteenth century, large ships, developed along modern lines, had more than one mast. In addition to the decorated hull and brilliantly colored sails, banners and streamers were used. In 1514, one of the streamers on the *Great Harry* displayed a dragon forty-five yards long. Also, figureheads of animals were in use. Carved, gilded figures decorated both the inside and outside of cabins; cabins were painted and upholstered in green and white. Moreover, topmasts were then raised and lowered instead of being fixed. The warship as such was practically non-existent; merchant ships served the purpose until the late advent of the armed vessel. Boats, similar to rowboats today, were used as ferries from shore to ship.[185]

With striking fidelity, the writers have depicted ships of all kinds. The entire category of ships is referred to: galleys,[186] cargo or merchant ships,[187] boats,[188] great ships,[189] barges,[190] and warships.[191] One ship was a galley, probably without a rudder, for no one aboard could stop "fra steryng, and fra rowyng."[192] Another was a merchant ship with sails, because the sailors were helpless after the tempest destroyed their tackle, anchor, sail, rudder, ropes, and cords.[193] The boat served its usual function of ferrying; a provost had a boat manned with eight oarsmen to take him out to a galley.[194] Furthermore, certain parts of ships received notice: cables,[195] anchor,[196] oars,[197] sail,[198] mast,[199] ropes, cords, rudder,[200] caulking of tallow and pitch,[201] and gangplank.[202] Partonope laid a strong broad "brygge" from ship to shore in order "nozte to wete hys fotte a delle." Also, top-castles were quite common; one served to defend the ship because men climbed there with spears, darts, and stones.[203] In addition, a forecastle was depicted; within it was a chamber which was richly curtained.[204] The after section of another vessel had a pavilion over it, and another had over it a canopy shining like gold.[205] Moreover, practically all the sailing vessels had moveable topmasts. To illustrate: "þen þai turnyt hor tackle tomly to ground,/ Leton sailes doun slide, slippit into botes,/ Launchet vpon land."[206] In addition, the ornamentation was well presented. The mast of one and the top-castle of another were painted gold.[207] Another ship had white sails and the sign of Troy painted on the mast.[208] The decoration of yet another consisted of red sails embroidered with animals and birds; also, on the sails were displayed the arms of Laban—"Of Asure and foure lions of goolde."[209] The four sails on one ship were yellow, green, red, and blue.[210] White and red,[211] yellow and blue, red and green[212] were other

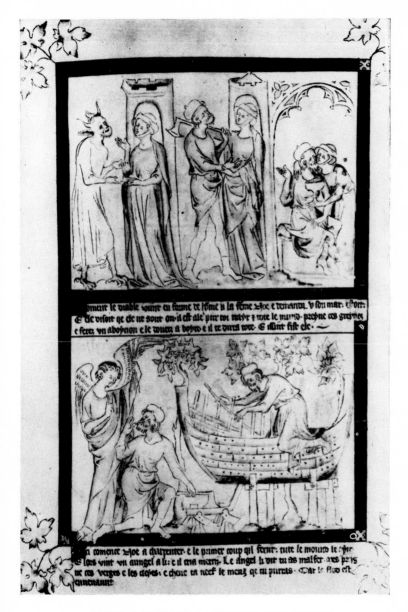

DEVIL INSTILLING JEALOUS SUSPICIONS
IN NOAH'S WIFE

(*English Psalter*, Brit. Mus. Roy. 2 B vii)

THE CONE MARRIAGE FEAST WITH SERVANT OFFERING
NEW WINE TO THE RULER OF THE FEAST

(*English Psalter*, Brit. Mus. Roy. 2 B vii)

color combinations for sails. One romancer knew so intimately the ordering of a ship and the function of a navy that I shall paraphrase him at length as a kind of summation. When the barges were ready, men rowed to the shore and loaded the vessels with horses, armor, clothes, chests, and food. When this was completed, the tide was ebbing so that the ships crossed their yardarms. Vigorously the men on the gunwale weighed anchor, quickly hoisted sails and turned the tiller, while some sailors on the prow of the ship coiled the ropes. Then they took soundings, went with full sail, hauled in the little boats entirely without damage, smartly closed the ports, heaved the lead to take another sounding, looked at the lode star when it was dark, and skillfully shaped their course.[213]

One other interesting practice in connection with ships was the putting of heavy chains across a harbor to prevent the entry of enemy ships. The romance city of Aeres,[214] as well as historical Upnor and Rochester,[215] were thus protected.

Travel on land was very slow and difficult because of the poor condition of the roads; consequently, much of it was done by means of packhorses. However, the transportation of heavy objects, such as chests, necessitated stronger modes of conveyance. Chief among these were the wagon and the cart. The wagon was a four-wheeled vehicle drawn by horses; the present-day wagon seems to have made little improvements in design. Scenes of country life from a fourteenth-century manuscript (Bodl. MS. 264) show a heavily loaded wagon drawn by a team. The front wheels are somewhat smaller in diameter than the rear ones; there are eight spokes to a wheel and the tread or tire is studded with great nails. The wagon has a low open-frame, or hay-frame, body. Clearly seen are wagon tongue and crosstree, as well as the harness on the team.[216] The carts were smaller vehicles, having two wheels and shafts. An illustration from the fourteenth-century Luttrell Psalter shows a cart drawn by three horses; only the third one in line is between the shafts. The seven-spoke wheels are nail-studded, and the frame is of wickerwork on timber. A small timber gate is seen at the rear of the wagon.[217] Street scenes from the *Alchemy Book* (Plut. 3469) picture a wagon drawn by four horses and two carts drawn by one horse each.[218] A funeral procession from Froissart's *Chronicles* depicts a four-wheel wagon drawn by one horse in shafts. The low wooden body of the wagon is covered by a black canopy in the shape of a covered wagon.[219] More luxurious transportation for the delicate maidens was provided by the litter, a rectangular box carried on shafts by one horse in front and one horse in the rear. A miniature from a fifteenth-century manuscript depicts a gilded litter in which a maiden is sitting on the floor, probably on cushions, and propped up by an ornamented red and blue spangled pillow. The interior of the litter is upholstered in a green diamond-shaped design.[220] The cabriolet served the same purpose as the litter. It was an ornate vehicle of the same design as the cart—a two-wheel vehicle with shafts for the horse. The body of the cabriolet was in the form of a rectangular pan in the midst of which was fixed a bench with low back and sides. Ornamentation was often added to the sides of the body and to the ends of the seat.[221] Ladies of rank travelled in a car or chariot which was a covered vehicle drawn by two or more horses. Artistic decoration was lavished on these chariots, which were provided with a weather-proof roof from which there were hung curtains of leather or of heavy silk. The woodwork was painted and the nails and wheels were gilded. The interior was appropriately fitted with ample cushions and other appliances. The external ornaments of the chariot of the daughter of Edward I were enamelled.[222] More spectacular than these was the state carriage of royalty. One of the fourteenth century is a four-wheeled wagon. The low wooden body has an ornamented wheel in either end; this serves as the framework of the canopy above. A regal chair is fixed within. Elaborate designs appear on the body.[223]

Literary accounts of these vehicles are, for the most part, vague. Oliver, besieged in Spain, saw twenty-four packhorses approach.[224] Upon another occasion wagons were loaded with tents and other supplies.[225] An attacking force had wagons "with yrne qwhelis and barris long and sqwar."[226] To other forces came wagons loaded with food.[227] Another wagon was turned into a hearse in order to carry the slain Sir James back to Germany.[228] One group of soldiers barricaded themselves with their carts and wagons.[229] Iosyan and other maidens rode in chariots.[230] King Philon's chariot was

clene and al yvore/ Bothe behynde and eke be-fore,/ Siluer and gold on ayther whele/ Was layd aboute fair and wele;/ Al was begon, syde and hemmes,/ Ful of riche precious gemmes.[231]

Another account of the same chariot says it was covered with a cloth of gold.[232] Also, when Eric was wounded, his men "cut poles, and crossed staves . . . and harnessed two horses" to the improvised litter on which they placed him.[233] Likewise, when Uther was sick, he ordered a litter in order that he might accompany his men in battle.[234] An associated reference is one given to a "crude-wain" or pushcart, probably a wheelbarrow such as is seen in a fourteenth- century manuscript (Bodl. MS. 264).[235]

E. Musical Instruments

Musical instruments were the livelihood of the medieval minstrel, and every gentleman of estate had one or more minstrels as a regular part of his household. The minstrels played for religious services and dances, provided entertainment in the hall, sounded the trumpet announcing dinner, and participated in the ritual of serving, wherein they preceded the servants at the bringing in of each course. An illustration from a fourteenth-century manuscript (Brit. Mus. Royal 2 B vii., f. 184) shows the royal minstrel playing a viol, who is followed by two servants bearing a dish each. Also, a harper frequently recited during meals. Another illustration (Royal MS., 2 B vii., folio 71b) presents a harper seated on the floor and playing for four persons at dinner. Moreover, minstrels sometimes played just before a tourney took place. An illustration (Royal MS. 14 E iii) shows the herald arranging the preliminaries between two knights while a band of four minstrels inspires them.[236] The instruments commonly played were varied. The pipe was an instrument of cylindrical bore— twenty-four to thirty inches long, which possessed two fingerholes in front and one behind for the thumb. The pipe was usually associated with the tabor. With the pipe held in and played by the left hand, the right hand was free to beat the tabor, or small drum, which was generally hung on the left arm or fastened to the left shoulder. The cymbals, as seen in a thirteenth-century illumination, were a pair, either flat or hemispherical, of thin plates which produced a din by being vigorously clashed together. The trumpet was formed of a cylindrical metal tube; it had no fingerholes. The cylindrical bore opened out towards the end into a broader bell. The horn, as distinguished from the trumpet, was of the type that included those instruments in which the tube tapered gradually from the mouthpiece to the bell, and was represented by the bugle and hunting horns. The clarionet was a trumpet of very high pitch. The bugle, which received its name from the bugle or wild ox, was made of a fine, twisted horn thirty-six inches in length, and was terminated at the larger end by a copper bell. The kettledrum was a hemispherical body, usually metal, which was covered with skin over its open top. The harp was a triangular instrument with seven, twelve, or more strings of hair, gut, or wire; these strings were plucked with the fingers. The characteristic feature of the Western type was the stay or pillar. The citole was an instrument of four strings plucked with a plectrum. The string holder was attached to the front table and acted also as a bridge. The neck, which was free, often terminated in a figurehead. The viol, played with a bow, was an instrument very similar to the fiddle. A twelfth-century manuscript shows a viol with incurved sides and a well-formed head with eight pegs inserted in the side. The hurdy gurdy, associated with the symphony, was an instrument producing all the intervals of the musical scales by a series of moveable bridges. Devices were adopted for shifting the bridges more readily, and the bow was superseded by a well-rosined wheel, revolving beneath the strings. A handle at one end of the box-like instrument turned the wheel.[237]

The romancers were aware of the functions of the minstrels as well as of their instruments, but apparently they failed to depict them. The catalogue of instruments mentioned by them includes trumpets, clarionets,[238] pipes, kettledrums,[239] bugles, tabors,[240] brass horns,[241] citole with cymbals,[242] harp and viol.[243] At a tourney the minstrels played on trumpets and clarionets;[244] Tristram, disguised as a minstrel from Ireland, was received by Mark, before whom he played on his hurdy-gurdy, which he carreid around his neck; this hurdy-gurdy of ivory "Richelich it was wrouzt."[245] Just as a bell summoned the monks to prayers, it was used to summon men to the defense of the city or castle; but a horn was sometimes used.[246] The trumpet not only announced that meals were ready to be served but also the serving of them: "þen þe first cors come with crakkyng of trumpes."[247]

F. Pavilions

One of the most spectacular features of the medieval period was the tent or pavilion, which was used as a place of shelter whenever no lodge was available. Also, in the summertime, occupants of a castle often set up tents in the courtyard or garden and resided there instead of indoors. These tents, square or round, were often castellated above, with rich ornamentation at the top of the pole from which banners and pennons were flying. Made of rich cloth, the curtains were striped of alternate breadths of gay colors, such as gold, red, green, and blue. Armorial bearings and other devices were often enwrought. Internally the pavilion was provided with such furnishings as were essential. An illumination of a bell-shaped pavilion shows a knight seated at a table covered with a white cloth. Two lighted candles in massive candlesticks, a wine flagon, a cup, and a knife are visible. The curtains of the tent are alternately striped in gold, red, green, and blue. Another illumination shows the exterior of a bell-shaped pavilion which has two rows of dormer windows in the dome. The ornamented tent pole is surmounted by a decorated ball. An elaborate scroll border encircles the upper portion of the curtains, which are further decorated with shield designs.[248] The fictional pavilions were highly colorful and varied. As to shape, they were both "quarre and rounde" as well as in the "schape of castelles."[249] The materials recorded were all very fine: silk, cendale, and syclatoun.[250] Some of the colors used were gold, "yellow and green, blue and red richly adorned, gilt and embroidered with gold," vermilion and green, and "one side vermillion and the other green, striped with gold; at the top was a gilded eagle."[251] Some of the ornamented designs on the curtains were birds,[252] a gold lion,[253] eagles,[254] herons,[255] borders of bright blue beaten with gold,[256] an eagle on a gilded apple with two lions lying beneath, armorial bearings, crowds of people, and representations of historical stories.[257] The banners flying above were of gold and silver on the standards of the chief.[258] The interior furnishing in most cases was specifically a bed; others had seats, coffers, and tables.[259] Some pavilions were of more than one room,[260] and one tented army was pictured as having a large tent reserved as a dining hall.[261] A good general view of a large pavilion used as a balmy weather retreat may be seen in the pavilion to which Gawain led the people from the hall of the castle. It was made of rich cloth, highly adorned with purple and "palle"; birds were embroidered in bright gold. Inside was a chapel, a chamber, a hall, and a chimney with charcoal. On the table which Gawain called for were placed a tablecloth, napkins, salt cellars, candlesticks, and silver.[262] Possibly another romancer had in mind a large pavilion when he called a gilded building with similar accommodations a summer hall.[263]

G. Implements of War

Medieval military engines, confusing because of nomenclature, long retained the designs inherited from classical times. The chief difference between the two is that the classical machines were constructed on the principle of the bow, and the medieval ones on the principle of the sling. Three of the most important engines, generally referred to as guns or engines of war, were the mangonel, the balista, and the trebuchet, which worked respectively by torsion, by tension, and by counterpoise. The mangonel, or catapult, a machine for throwing heavy stones, was composed of two fixed uprights and a moveable beam worked by twisting ropes which, when drawn back and then suddenly released, threw a missile through the air in a high curve. The balista, a device essentially for shooting great bolts and javelins, was made like a huge cross-bow that threw its missiles pointblank, in a low trajectory. The trebuchet, a thirteenth-century slinging device, consisted of a balance beam, one end of which was loaded with a heavy weight. The other end, which was dragged down by force and which held the missile, threw the missile violently into the air when the beam was released. Among the other engines and equipment were the ladder, the springal, the ram, the sow, the moveable tower, the mantelet, the stink pot, Greek fire, the crossbow and quarrels, and the cannon. The ladder, made of wood or of rope with iron hooks at the end, was used for scaling walls. The springal or arbalast was a huge crossbow mounted on wheels; it threw pointed bolts. The ram, designed to beat down walls but rarely used in the Middle Ages, consisted of a heavy square timber which was suspended by a rope from a frame, and worked by hand. The sow or hog or mine was a temporary penthouse designed to protect workers undermining a wall. Built on wheels, the sow had a roof covered with boards and wicker-work, and the sides were protected with hides. The moveable tower was a wooden structure of several stories, protected from fire by hides or metal plates.

When the tower, on wheels, neared a wall, a drawbridge was dropped from one side of it onto the wall so that the besiegers could rush out to overcome the garrison. The pavis was a tall shield, broad at the top and tapering to the foot, behind which a bowman stood. The mantelet was a shield more ample, capable of being fixed upright by a prop so that it formed a kind of moveable fort. The name of the stink pot indicates the nature of this device for repelling the enemy. Greek fire, used to destroy objects by fire, was ejected through pipes, affixed to javelins, hurled by engines, or thrown in shells by hand. Hot oil, lead, or pitch were also used by defenders of buildings. The crossbow was a device for shooting an arrow which was called a bolt or quarrel. The quarrel was shorter and stouter than the ordinary arrow. The bow of the crossbow was made of steel, and the instrument was sometimes strung by putting the foot into a loop at the end of the stock and pulling the cord up to its notch by main force. A cord and pulley and a winch were other means of stringing it. Cannons, introduced in the fourteenth century, were small, clumsily built guns. They were made by casting or by welding together iron bars around which iron hoops were placed for strength. Smaller firearms at first were hardly superior to bows.[264]

Many siege instruments were mentioned by the romancers, but few were described. The terms *gun* and *engine* were frequently used very loosely. *Engine* referred to any of the rock-hurling devices, and *gun* was used to refer to those as well as to cannons: for example, "The gynour than gert bend in hy/ The gyne, ans swappit out the stane,"[265] and "Waspasian . . . benden engynes,/ Kesten at þe kernels & clustered toures."[266] "Bombardis and gonnes" were cannon because their noise was "hydouser than thonder."[267] The ladders were both of wood and of rope. The Greeks gained entrance into a castle by means of a rope, and Bruce entered Edinburgh by means of hempen ladders which had square iron hooks to catch on the kernels.[268] Arbalast and springal were both referred to. The "quarels floze out pike of arbelastes," and men's brains were split with "sprygaldis."[269] The trebuchet was referred to without comment, but of the mangonel it was said "þat þurch quentise of mannes strengþe/ It mizt cast þre mile o lengþe."[270] Mentioned without comment were bows,[271] crossbows that hurled out quarrels,[272] pavis behind which bowmen had protection,[273] great round balls for the engines,[274] hot lead, pitch, and brimstone to drop on attackers,[275] Greek fire shot on quarrels "þat setlede so on the walle zerne hit gen to brenne,"[276] and such minor ordnance as the one and a half inch bore serpentine and the culverine.[277] The sow was often mentioned; Godeffroy attested to its value in bringing down a tower.[278] Once, when a sow was attached to a wall, the defending gunner dropped a missile on its chief beam so that the sow was torn asunder.[279] The moveable tower, "castle," or "fortress," received the most detailed consideration. One constructed on twelve posts was very wide and high;[280] a second was built with six floors;[281] a third was square, and the side towards the city was doubled in such a way that one of the "panes that was without mught be aualed vpon the walles" like a bridge;[282] and a fourth was made of wood in three stories:

þan þe hexest stage of al fulde he wiþ men of armes. . ./ And on þat oþer stage amidde ordeynt he gunnes grete,/ And oþer engyns y-hidde wilde fyr to caste & schete/ . . . In þe nyþermest stage þanne schup he him selue to hove,/ To ordeyne hure fyr þar-inne & send hit to hem above.[283]

An interesting protective device against the tower was pictured by one romancer. The citizens built a tall crane mounted on wheels so that they could move it as needed. Whenever a tower approached the wall, giant bundles of faggots were fired, then suspended by iron chains from a crane, and held against the side of the tower until it caught fire.[284]

CHAPTER FOUR

the supernatural

THE ROMANCES, SO indebted to realistic art and so realistic in essence, would not have fallen into the romantic classification if they had relied entirely on fact. There had to be elements of the unreal, the mystical, the supernatural, in order to raise them to the level of romance literature. Consequently the writers included elements designed to excite the admiration, to enchant the imagination of the reader. Under the guise of verisimilitude, the romancer introduced into his descriptions fabulous things, such as the most sumptuous castles and palaces, the most magnificent gardens, the rarest curiosities, and the most exotic prodigies. Because of this desire to astonish and to find more than their predecessors, the French romancers went progressively from the curious to the extraordinary to the fabulous. However, since the English romancers in large measure gave a fairly close translation of the French accounts and often rationalized some of the originals, we are interested in tracing the origin or origins of these fabulous elements as well as in noting the rationalizing.

In general it may be stated that the marvelous came from popular tradition, from legends, from the Orient—introduced by the Crusaders—from literary sources, from the Bible, from the lives of the saints, from certain classical works, and perhaps from the influence of certain romances.

Let us begin with fabulous architecture. Frequently the romancers depicted the interior as well as the exterior of castles as being characterized by a richness and sumptuousness that defies imagination. To illustrate, the palace of Illium was of surpassing grandeur:

In al þis world was þer noon so riche,/ Of hize devis, nor of bildynge liche,/ þe whiche stood, þe more to delyte,/ . . . Of alabastre, shortly to conculde; And twenty pas was þe latitude,/ þe ground y-pauyd þoruz-out with cristal,/ And vp-on heizt parformyd euery wal/ Of alle stonys þat any man can fynde,/ Of diamauntis and saphiris ynde,/ þe royal ruby, so roient and lizt,/ þat þe dirknes of þe dymme nyzt/ Enchacid was with his bemys shene;/ And euere amonge wern areraudis grene, With stonys alle, þat any mane man/ In þis world deuyse or rekne can,/ þat wern of pris, valu or richesse./ And þer were wrought, of large and gret roundne/ (As seith Dares) of yvory pylers,/ And þer-vp-on set at þe corners,/ Of purid gold, al aboue on heizt,/ Þer were ymages wonder huge of weizt,/ With many perle and many riche stoon;/ And euery piler in þe halle had oon, Of massif gold, burned clere and brizt,/ And wonderful to any mannys sozt;/ For of þis werks þe merveillous facioun/ Was more lik, by esty-macioun,/ A þhinge y-made & founded by fairye.[1]

And another romancer added to this marvel the fact that the huge hall was made of twelve great stones:

On stones twelue was hit al set/ Off Alabaster that wele were wrouzt,/ It was gret meruayle how thei were bouzt/ Vnto that werk to rayse that ground,/ It was meruayle where men thei found. He was worthi be called a clerk,/ That of twelue stones made suche. The halle flore was paued al/ Throwout with clene cristal/ . . . The walles of that halle streyzt/ Were two thousand fet of heyzt,/ And zit ther-to ffyue hundrid als.[2]

Moreover, the Palace of Canace had a gold roof with precious stones. Her chambers were of the same material; the stones used were onyx. The floor and the benches were of ivory, "smaragdez," and amethyst.[3] Also, Darius' palace was wreathed in gold. The walls were of pure polished gold set with stars and various gems "with brizt blasynand bees [jewels] as bemes of þe son." The building itself of his summer hall, the bath, the table, the seats, and the vessels were all of bright gold "set full of stanes."[4] Furthermore, Tristram had made "with great cunning a house of pure gold."[5] The walls of another castle were also cunningly made "clear and transparent as glass; naught that passed therein might be held secret."[6] These glass walls remind one of Merlin's glass house on the sacred isle of Bardsey, as well as of the Glass Fortress mentioned in the Celtic *Harryings of Annwn*.[7] Still another rich palace sparkled with brilliant jewels and unusual kinds of wood:

On þat place was a paleis on:/ Swich ne sez neuer non,/ Ne of so meche mizte./ Þe walles were of cristal,/ Þe celing was of fin ruwal/ Þet schon swiþe brizte. Þe reftes al cipres be,/ Þat swote smal casten he/ Ouer al aboute./ Þe resins wer of fin coral/ To-gedre iuned wiþ metal/ Wiþ-inne and ek wiþ-oute./ On þe front stod a charbokel ston:/ Ouer al þe contre it schon,/ Wiþ-outen eni doute./ Postes and laces þat þer were/ Of iaspe gentil þat was dere/ Al of one soute./ Þe paleis was beloken al/ Aboute wiþ a marbel wal/ Of noble entaile./ Vpon eueriche kernal/ Was ful of speres and of springal.[8]

All of these descriptions seem to have been imitated from the famous chambers, ornaments, etc. of Byzantine palaces. Accounts in Julius Valerius of the palace of Porus and of the palace of Candace probably influenced the romancers.[9]

The tower of Babylon, although greatly simplified in comparison to the French account, is quite extraordinary with its two hundred foot height surmounted with a light-giving carbuncle.[10] Such a structure seems to have been based on some designs which derived from Bagdad. The secret door, round tower, etc. correspond to the characteristics of oriental architecture.[11] As Paris says, the occidental imagination was stirred by the recital, by pilgrims who had visited Constantinople on the way to the Holy Land, of the magnificence of the imperial palace of Constantinople.[12]

Another palace, the habitation of the sun god, was indeed fabulous enough for a deity of such brilliance:

Þay come till a Mountayne of adamande; and at þe fute þare offe þare hange chains of golde. Þis Mountayne hadd made of saphyres twa

thowsande greez & a halfe, by þe whilke men ascendid to þe summit of
þe Mountayne . . . þare he fande a palace wonder faire and curiously
wroughte; and it hade twelve zates and thre score & ten wyndows.
And þe lyntalles bathe of þe durs and of þe windows ware of fyn
golde, wele burnescht, and þat Palace was called þe howse of þe son.
Þare was also a temple all of golde & of precious stanes, And bi-fore
þe dores þare-off þare was a vyne of golde, berande grapes of char-
buncles, of Rubyes, Dyamandez, and many oþer maneres of precyous
stanes. . .[13]

Doubtless the mythological trait in this passage would lead one
to find the source in a palace like the Prytaneum, the representative of Zeus on earth, and in the palace of Minos, the abode of
the sun king.[14]

The house of Dedalus was unusual because it was built in the
form of a maze "where were as many walles as were there cham-
bres, that were in grete nombre; & euery chambre was walled and
closed rounde aboute, and yet myghte one goo from one to nother.
And yf some body had be shette therein he coulde never fynde
the firste entree thereof, for to com oute ayen; For an hundred
dores were there."[15] Doubtless the classical source here is to be
found in the legend of Theseus and the Minotaur, in which
Ariadne aided Theseus to escape from the labyrinth by means of
a piece of string.[16]

In addition to the thickness of the walls of another palace,
the fabulous element consists of the garden and of two stones
lying in the hall; one is hot and one is cold:

an hall, þe feyrest vndir sky:/ The wallis been of marbill, I-wyned &
I-closid/ And the pilours cristall, grete & wele purposid;/ The keueryng
of-bove, is of selondyn;/ And the pavemt be-neth, of gold & asure fyne.
But who-so passith þurh þis hall, hath nede to renne blyve,/ Or els
he myzte be disware of his owne lyve; ffor þerewithen lijth a stoon,
þat is so hote of kynde,/ That what thing com forby, a-noon it woll
atend,/ As bryzt as any candel leem, & consume a-noon;/ And so
wold the hall also, ner coldness of a stoon/ That is I-clepid 'dyonyse,'
þat set is hym ageyn/ So, & þow lepe liztly, þow shalt have no peyn;/
ffor ethir stone, in kynde proporcioned they be;/ Of hete, & eke of
coldness, of oon equalite/ . . . Ther be been to libardis, loos and eke

untyed;/ If that thy blowing of þat othir in eny thing be spyed,/ ffor nys thing in erth þat he so much doith hate,/ As breth of mannys mowith: wherfor refreyne the.[17]

This description of Duke Isope's castle and garden reads, says Furnivall, "like—what it is—a leaf out of an Oriental romance." A similar palace is depicted in the Arabian romance of Antar. The whole edifice, with its gems, its fabulous devices, and its perfumes, was "one of the wonders of the period, and the miracle of the age."[18]

A royal castle had walls built of adamant, which had the power of drawing to it all things of metal. This magnetized castle was "walled with admantes whiche draweth by violence/ Accordynge to they power and thy stones fortitude."[19] This idea was perhaps inspired by certain tales related to the legend of Alexander. It is found in the *Commonitorium Palladii.*[20]

Associated with this subject of magnetism is a rock of adamant such as that which drew Huon's boat to it:

for the Adamant drewe the shypp so sore that, yf they had not quickly stricken theyr sayle, the shypp had broken all to peses . . . because the Adamant drew so sore the Iron to hym by nature.[21]

This rock appears in the Bavarian folktale of Herzog Ernst von Baiern and in the tale of Sinbad in the *Arabian Nights.* John Mandeville describes it in almost identical terms. He localized it in a China sea;[22] other writers, such as the author of the *Arabian Nights,* place it between Tonkin and Cochin China. The myth doubtless had been orally current in Europe long before the date of *Huon* or of *Duke Ernest.*[23]

The fabulousness of the palace of Porus consisted primarily in the great variety and in the lavish use of precious stones:

Porus Palace, whare-In he fande mare reches þan any man will trowe. For he fande þare-in xl peleres of Massu golde, ilkan of a grete thiknes & a grete lenthe, with þaire chapytralles and bitwene þe pelers of golde ware hyngande venettez of golde & syluere, wit leues of golde. And þe brawnchez of this venett ware sum of cristalle, sum of Margaritez, sum of Smaragdes, & sum of Onyches, and þay semed as þay hade bene verray vynes. Þe walles also of þe palace ware couerde all ouer wit plates of golde, þe whilke when þe Macedoynes cutte in soundre & brakke, þay fande þat þay ware a gret ynche thikke. And þir walles ware sett full of diuerse precious stanes, þat es at sat, of charebuncles, Smaragdes, Margarites & Amatistes. And þe zates of þe Palace ware of Euour. Þe chambris, also, of þis Palace were of Cipresse, and þe beddez in þam ware sett full of Margaritez, Smaragdez, & charebuncles.[24]

Another version of the same palace is equally rich:

He past in-to his palais & in þe place findis þat semed no synfull seule is selcuthe to trowe./ First fand he þare of fyne gold a foure hundreth postis,/ With crafti coronals & clene coruen of þe same./ Betwene þe peleres was pizt with precious levys,/ Gilden wynes with grapis of gracious stanes./ Sum were of cristall clere clustrid to-gedire,/ Sum made ware of Margartis þe mast of þe werd;/ Sum was smeth smarag-dyns & oþire smal gemmes./ And new nychometis nemellus endentid/ Þat ware as semely quen þai ware samen,/ And all pargestis of plate as pure as þe noble./ Þe Messedons in þam merkid with þaire mekill brandis,/ And þe thinnest was a nynche thicke quen þai ware þurze persed;/ And þo ware strenkild with stanes as sterne o þe heuyn,/ With charbokles on þe champ & with chefe perles,/ Smeten was smaragdans in-to þe smeth werkis,/ And athill amytists als in aungels licknes;/ Of Euor & of olifants was ordand þe zatis,/ With barrers of ane Ebyn-tree bonden with cheynes./ Þe Ebyn, as þe buke sias brin neuir. . . .[25]

The tradition of employing a superabundance of gems comes from the popularity of the lapidaries as well as from the Bible. In the Apocalypse and in Exodus, so often drawn upon in the Middle Ages, there is given a list of essentially the same precious stones.[26]

Certain stones possessed the extraordinary power of giving light so that no lamp was needed at night; the stone most commonly associated with this trait was the carbuncle. The altar in Priam's palace had a statue wearing a crown studded with all kinds of gems, and "for most chefe al dirkenes to confounde,/ Was a charbocle, kyng of stonys alle."[27] In Illium's palace "Ther stode many a charbocle-ston,/ That as bryzt aboute mydnyght,/ As doth the somerday lyght."[28] Upon the top of an Emir's tower stood a "charbugleston" which gave light both day and night so that it was never dark inside the tower.[29] On the front of another palace stood a "charbokel ston:/ Ouer al þe contre it schon."[30] In a fabulous room visited by Huon there was an image of a two-year-old child with eyes of carbuncle stone which lighted the palace.[31] The source of light in Illium's hall, as pictured by one romancer, was the "royal ruby, so roient and lizt,/ þat þe dirkness of þe dymme nyzt/ Enchacid was with his bemys shene."[32] In the summit of the throne fashioned by Alexander was set a ruby "þat schane on þe nughte as it hade bene þe mone."[33] Certain rich rooms visited by Huon were made light by "reason of shynynge of the precyous stones."[34] Another romancer described a chair made of carbuncle stone, "Swylke on ne sawgh they never non," but he failed entirely to mention any light-giving property of the gem.[35] Rich pavilions were sometimes crowned with an eagle having carbuncle stones for eyes.[36] This superstition of light-giving stones, which is very ancient, was even attributed to St. Augustine. It is described also in the *Pèlerinage de Charlemagne* (v. 423). By the Middle Ages it had become a kind of commonplace for which it is almost useless to seek an exact source. Benjamin Tudela, who visited Constantinople in 1161 A.D., told of the jewel-studded gold throne of Emperor Manuel. The crown was reported to be so bright and sparkling from the numerous jewels that their glitter rendered needless any other illumination at night. Also, Marbode in *Liber de Gemmis* said that of all the burning gems, the carbuncle is chief, shedding its rays on all sides like a burning coal and giving forth a light that darkest night cannot extinguish. Isidore of Seville, long before him, made the same assertion. The *Lapidaire en Vers* ascribed the same property to the ruby, which was made to stand for Christ. Doubtless the high degree of phosphorescence of some stones had something to do with this legend. Also, the analogy between the flame of a lamp or the glow of a burning coal and the radiance of a ruby resulted in the fancy that such stones were luminous in the dark.[37]

The withdrawing room of Candace was a marvel of mobility:

scheo ledd hym in-till a withdrawyng chambir made of cypresse. Þis chambir was sett apon foure wheles by crafte of clergy; and twenty xxti Olyphauntes drewe it wheþir as scho wolde hafe it.[38]

Moreover, on the hill of Vaws, which was higher than all the "hills of þe eest," there was a tower surmounted with a star that turned with the wind and threw sunlight by day and moonlight by night far into the country.[39] Similarly the turning castle is found in the *Prose Perceval*[40] as well as in Chaucer's *House of Fame.* The question of the exact source of these turning structures is unanswerable, but the influence may have come by way of some literary treatment of the motif, or the notion may have come from some folktale. The motif of the revolving house or tower, preserved in folktale and artistic literature, is very old, having its origin seemingly in myth-making days. In *Karls des Grossen Reise Jerusalem und Constantinople*[41] is found the turning castle. In the Irish *Fled Bricrend,* in *Prester John,* and in Russian folktales as well the same feature appears. Rhys thinks the turning castle is a form of the abode of the king of the dead.[42]

So often associated with cities or castles were automata. Over the gates of Rome Vergil erected two brass statues of a man:

Vpon þe est zate of þe toun/ He made a man of fin latoun/ And in his hond of gold a bal./ Vpon þe zate on þe west wal/ Virgil kest an ymage oþer,/ Rizt als hit were his owen broþer,/ þat al þe folk of Rome said/ Wiz þat bal to gider þai plaid./ Þat on hit hente þat oþer hit þrew,/ Mani a man þe soþe iknew./ Amideward þe cite on a stage/ Virgil made anoþer ymage,/ þat held a mirour in his hond,/ And ouer segz al þat lond./ Who wolds pes, who wolds bataille./ Quik he warned þe toun, saunz faile./ Aboute Rome seuen Jurneys þous he warned nizt and dais,/ And þo þat were rebel ifounde,/ þe Romains gadered hem in a stounde,/ þai wente þider quik a non/ And destrued here fon.[43]

The magic mirror which warned of enemies is found in *Prester John.* Also, in the lighthouse of Alexander, as one of the Seven Wonders of the World, was placed a mirror which enabled the defenders to see the fleet of an enemy at a great distance. Benjamin de Tudele spoke of this mirror when referring to a voyage which he had made in the Orient, between 1160 and 1170. Perhaps the fable had its origin from the installation of an observatory in the isle by the Arabs and from the employment of optical instruments. Visitors to the tomb of St. Mark in Constantinople carried back an account of it when they returned home.[44]

Other automata are found at the gate of the castle of Dunoster: "than he sawe ii men of brasse that without seasynge bet with there flaylles. . .At last he saw nere to a pyller of marbell a basyn of gold fast tyed with a chayne." Huon finally gained entrance when Sebylle opened a small wicket from which issued such a wind that the two men were forced to stop beating with their flails.[45] The automata here were probably derived from the Dolorouse Garde episode in the prose *Lancelot*[46] which may have been influenced by the Vergil legend. These automata, which had only a limited intelligence, were created for a single purpose. The invention seems to be in keeping with the usage of placing guards before the gate of buildings, and with the late usage of putting on doors the figures of guardians, such as the representation of dogs on ancient Roman thresholds or door sills. Moreover, in the widely known *Roman d'Alexandre* two figures were used to defend a bridge.[47]

Two unusual machines or objects, usually associated, were a garden, indoors or out of doors, which had in it a tree of precious metal and singing birds of various merit that were frequently placed on its branches. In the center of Illium's hall was a tree so cleverly made that one could not determine whether it was natural or artificial:

In-to þe paleis as þei to-gidre goon,/ þat pauyd was al of Iasper stoon—/ Of a tree þat amyddes stood,/ Of whiche to loke hem dozt it dide hem good,/ Musing wher it were artificial/ Erect or set by magick natural,/ Or by engyne of werkmen corious,/ þoruz sotil craftis superticious,/ . . . þe stok. . . In sothfastnes was of purid gold,/ Whiche schon as brizt as þe somer sonne/ To enlumyne þinges þat wer donne;/ And þe body as a mast was rizt, Proporcioned most goodly to þe sizt,/ Substancial, & of huge strengþe;/ And xii cubites þe body was of lengþe;/

And þe crop, rounde & large of brede;/ And in compas gan so florische
& sprede,/ þat al þe pleyn aboute enviroun,/ With þe bowis was
schawded vp & doun./ Þe riche braunchis and þe levis faire,/ Tweyne
& tweyne Ioyned as a psyre—/ Oon of gold, anoþer of siluer schene,/
And meynt among with stonys whit & grene,/ Some rede and some
saphirhered./ And euery day þe blomys wer renewed;/ And þe blosmys,
with many sondri swt;/ For stonys ynde it bare in stede frut,/ As
seith Guydo—I can no ferder telle.[48]

Another romancer describing the same hall said that the fruit was
of many kinds:

The brede of his bowes borly to se,/ Large and longe, [light as the
sun]/ ffro the dese to the dorse doblit on brede/ And the sydys, by a
sercle of þe same hall./ The braunches were borly, sum of bright gold,/
Sum syluer for sothe, semlist of hew;/ With leuys full luffly, light of
þe same;/ With burions aboue bright to be holde;/ And frut on yt
fourmyt fairest of shap,/ Of mony kynd þat was kuyt, knagged aboue,/
þat shemert as shire as any shene stonys.[49]

In the *Tale of Beryn* the tree stood in the middle of the evergreen garden:

In mydward of this garden stant a feire tre,/ Of alle maner levis þat
vnder sky there be,/ I-forgit & I-fourmyd, eche in his degre,/ Of sylvir,
& of golde fyne, þat lusty been to see./ This garden is evir green, &
ful of maye flouris,/ Of rede, white, & blewe, & othir fresshe colouris,/
. . . ffor ther beth viij tregetours þat þis gardyn kepith;/ ffour of hem
doith waak, whils the foure sclepeth;/ . . . They make semen (as to
mannys sight)/ Abominabill wormys, þat sore ouzt be a-frizte/ The
hertiest man on erth, but he warnyd were/ Of the grisly siztis þat he
shuld see there./ Among al other, ther is a lyon white,/ . . . And hath
to-fore this tyme, v c men & mo/ Devouris & I-ete, þat therforth have
I-goo./ Zit shalt þowe þas suyrly, so þow do as I tell./ The tre I told
to-fore, þat round as any bell/ Berith bowe & braunces, traylyng to þe
ground,/ And þow touch oon of hem, þow art saff & sound;/ . . . Then
shalt þowe se an entre, by the ferther syde;/[50]

Within a chamber in another castle there were mechanical birds

that sang "so marvaylous swetely that ioye it was to here them."[51]
Outside another castle stood a tree with many kinds of birds, singing continuously.[52] A similar tree with perpetually singing birds
was located outside another castle.[53] The sweet music emanating
from another garden made the visitor think he was in paradise:

When thou art passid this hall, anoon þen shalt þowe com/ In-to the
fayerest gardyn þat is in cristendom:/ The wich, þurh his clergy, is
made of such devise/ That a man shall ween he is in paradise,/ At
his first coming in, for melody & song,/ And othir glorious thingis, &
delectabill a-mong/ The wich Tholomaeus. . ./ Did it so devise, þurgh
his hize connyng,/ That there nys best in erth, ne bird þat doith syng,/
That he nys ther in figur, in gold and sylvir fyne.[54]

In the palace of Porus there were images set on thrones, over
which were built gilded tabernacles that were ornamented with
filagree work and with whitened birds of all kinds. These were
painted, both feathers and wings, just as they are in life; their
bills were of gold. Furthermore, they were so constructed that
their actions appeared realistic. Naturally, these birds sang.[55]
Another romancer, describing this garden and its birds, said that
the birds had gold bills and claws, and "ay when Porus liste,
thir fewles thurgh crafte of music walde synge."[56] This singing-
bird device originated in a very widespread ancient myth. In the
Katha Sarit Sagara we read of trees with golden trunks, branches
of jewels, and clear white blossoms which were clusters of pearls,
etc. Also, Aladdin found in the cave where was deposited the
magic lamp, trees bearing fruit of emeralds and other rich gems.[57]
But evidently the source of these devices was in Constantinople,
where there was, in the palace of the emperor, a machine in the
form of a tree filled with singing birds. Gibbon, quoting Abu-'l-
Feda, stated that in the palace of the Khalif Moktador, among
other spectacles of stupendous luxury, was a tree of gold and silver
spreading into eighteen branches, on the lesser boughs of which
sat all kinds of birds. The tree and the birds were made of the
same precious metal. The machinery affected spontaneous motions,

and several birds warbled their natural harmony. Again, it may be that the origin of this machine is to be found in the sacred tree and the oracular dove of Dodonaean Zeus.[58]

Fountains were likewise fabulous at times. Huon approached a fountain with the desire to drink and found the gravel in the bottom all of precious stones:

he sawe the masonrye therof ryche, all of whight Iasper wroughte rychely with flowers of fyne golde and Asure . . . & sawe the gravell in the bottome all of presyous stones . . . All the grauell in the water were medelyd with presyous stones/ when Huon sawe that he toke a scope and cast into the shyppe so moche of those presyous stonys that it gaue as great a light as thoughe x torchys hade bene breynnynge/ so moch of this grauell Huon dyd cast into the shyppe that he was wery of laboure.[59]

The water in a similar fountain came from paradise:

þe strimes comed fram paradis./ For in þe strimes þe smale stones,/ Hi beoþ þer funden eurech one,/ Boþe saphirs and sardoines,/ And suþþe riche cassidoines,/ and Iacinctes and topaces,/ And onicle of muchel grace,/ And mani on oþer þerewerde ston/ þat ich nu nempne ne can.[60]

The origin of this wonder is clearly Eastern. This river of paradise is the Euphrates, which flows around the tower of the Emir of Babylon. This same wonder of gems in the bed of the river was related by Mandeville.[61]

Certain fabulous objects served either as tests, as talismans, or as oracles. Oberon gave to Huon a cup of plenty which filled immediately with wine after the sign of the cross was made. One other condition was imposed: "If the cuppe were in the hands of any man beynge out of dedly synne, he myght drinke thereof his fyll."[62] The same cup proved Charlemagne sinful, but Huon and Gerames were shown to be innocent. These magical testings of chastity occur in many Asiatic as well as medieval European romances and tales. In an eleventh-century Sanskrit collection,

Katha Sarit Sagara, a merchant named Guhasena was about to depart on a long trading journey, and he and his wife had misgivings about each other's fidelity during their separation. The deity Siva appeared before them and put in the hands of each a red lotus which would fade if either were unfaithful. In the Persian *Tuti Nama* a soldier's wife gave her husband a nosegay which would betoken her chastity as long as it bloomed. In the Arabian tale of Prince Zaynal-Asnam the king gave his son a mirror in which, if he saw the reflection of any maiden undimmed, he could be sure she was chaste. Accounts of tests were doubtless brought back by Crusaders who probably had pondered such questions about their own lovers while fighting in the Levant. In *Amadis de. Gaul* the test was a garland; in *Perce Forest*, a rose; in *Tristram,* in *Percival,* and in *Morte d'Arthur* a cup of wine which, if spilled while in the hand of either male or female, indicated the unfaithful lover.[63] Hypocras had a cup which prevented the imbiber from being poisoned. If poison were placed in the cup, immediately its strength was dissipated.[64] This protective power was also associated with precious stones and became a medieval commonplace. Doubtless the practice of placing a large gem in the handle of a cup arose from this belief. In an age when poison was a widely used means of murder, probably everyone was eager to protect his life by such an effective device.[65] Magic gems and cups appeared in innumerable tales. Frequently the gems were obtained from grateful serpents, as in an Albanian tale (No. 9 of M. Dozon's French collection) in which a grateful serpent gave a youth a wishing-stone.[66]

Melusine possessed a number of rings imbued with magical power. One made the holder proof against death, another gave the wearer victory in war and in law, a third gave victory and protected against enchantment and poison, a fourth gave victory so long as the wearer fought in a good cause.[67] Magic rings appear to have come from the East; in many Arabian tales reference is made to them. This is also true to some extent in classical literature. The legend may have had a Semitic source. Also, Plato's story of the ring of Gyges, that made the bearer invisible, was well known. Moreover, Solomon had a ring that gave him command over the genii. This ring was made of copper and iron and was engraved with the name of the deity. Solomon sealed orders to refractory genii with the iron part and to the good genii with the copper. Once, when he was bathing, he took off the ring, which was then stolen by an evil genius. Afterwards it was recovered from the stomach of a fish that was served at the king's table. Petrarch related that Charlemagne became infatuated with a woman of low degree and neglected the cares of state. The woman became ill and died, but the charm was not broken, and the king would not let her body be buried. Archbishop Turpin found a ring in her mouth; this he removed and kept until the king worried him with his presence. In desperation, the archbishop threw the ring into a lake at Aix-la-Chapelle, and thereafter Charlemagne refused to leave the place.[68]

Huon possessed a most extraordinary horn. When Oberon gave it to Huon, he related its "grete vertu. . .that yf thou be neuer so farre fro me, as soone as thou blowest the horne/ I shall here the/ & shall be incontenent with the with a c thousaunde men of armes for to socoure and ayed the."[69] This horn was made by four fairies in the isle of Cephallonia, and one endowed it with the power of curing by its blast all manner of sickness; a second endowed it with the power of satisfying hunger and thirst; a third with the power that whoever heard it, "though he were never so poor & feeble by sickness, he should have such joy in his heart that he should dance & sing"; a fourth, with the power of forcing whoever heard it to come at the pleasure of him who blew it. Musical instruments that make one dance are common in the folk-tales of all Europe, as seen in the magic pipe in the Old English tale of the *Friar and the Boy,* in the violin in the German *Das Jude im Dorn,* and in the harp in the Icelandic *Herauds ok Bosi Saga.* The virtue of calling up a hundred thousand men to aid the blower has its counterpart in the horn that drew crowds which were presented by the little man in red to one of the three soldiers journeying together, according to Grimm's story of "The Nose."[70]

A progenitor of the airplane was the fabulous flying chair drawn by griffins:

Comandid þam þat þay sulde make hym a chayer and trelesse it wit barrez of Iren ilk a syde so þat he myзte sauely sitt þare-in. And þan he gart brynge foure gripes and tye þam faste wit Iren cheynes vn-to þe chayere, and in þe ouermare party of þe chayere he gart putt mete for þe grippes.[71]

According to the story of Duke Ernest of Bavaria, the duke was whisked alive through the air by a bird to a rock, whence like Huon he traveled down a river in the heart of a mountain.[72]

Other fabulous accounts are found in the descriptions of cities, some of which were comparable to those of oriental splendor. Beues visited the city of Damas, in which the windows and walls were of crystal, the pillars and doors of brass; there was a bridge of brass over the moat. Protecting this bridge was a tower on which stood a golden eagle that had eyes set with precious stones.[73] Moreover, Alexander visited a country in which there was a "noble citee all of precyous stones made withowtten lyme or sande, sett apon an hill."[74] Both of these citations imply a more or less definite following of the legend of Alexander, which was so popular during the Middle Ages.[75] A temple in Jerusalem glowed with oriental splendor:

Þe roof with rubies grete,/ With perles & peritotes alle þe place ferde/ As glowande gledfur þat on gold strikeþ./ Þe dores ful of dyemauntes dryuen wer þicke/ & made merueylous-lye with margeri-perles;/ Derst no candel be kynde whan clerkes scholde rise,/ So wer þey lemaunde lyzt & as a lampe schonen/ . . . þer was plente in þe place of precious stonys,/ Grete gaddes of gold . . ./ Platis, pecis of peys, pulsched vessel,/ Bassynes of brend gold & oþer bryzt ger,/ Pelours, masly made of metals fele,/ In copre craftly cast & in clene seluere/ Peynted with pur gold alle þe place was ouer.[76]

This sumptuousness is reminiscent of the splendor of the temple of the gods in the city of the Islands of the Blessed, described by

Lucian in his *Vera Historia,* but more likely the source is to be found in the legendary temple of Ephesus and in Solomon's temple; the latter building was considered at one time as one of the Seven Wonders of the World.[77]

Within another city there was a castle which possessed a great marvel which we have already discussed: "For nyghte hyte was vppon þe see,/ And in þe Cuntre hyt was bryghte/ As thowe hyt had be day lyghte."[78] This and similar passages were probably an interpretation of the Seven Wonders of the World, among which the lighthouse of Alexandria was one. Also, the citadel of Carthage in *Eneas* may have afforded another source.[79]

Statues and images were made fabulous either as the work of the devil or as the habitation of fiends. One such statue possessed the power of an oracle:

And in his temple large, longe, and olde,/ Þer was a statue al of purid golde,/ Ful gret and hize, & of huge weizte,/ And þer-in was, þourz þe deuels sleizte,/ A spirit vnclene, be false illusion,/ Þat zaf answere to euery question.[80]

The same power was ascribed to a "heade of brasse that of old antiquite had bene composed muche subtyllye by Nygromancye of a Fee, the whyche head was of suche nature that it gaue answer of al thynges that was asked it."[81] In Apollo's temple in Thebes there was a statue of the goddess placed in a chair of gold "On wheles four boornyd bright and shene;/ And with-In a spirit ful vnclene,/ Be fraude only and fals collusion,/ Answere gaf to euery question."[82] Also, Medea gave Jason a white silver image, charmed with enchantment: "Hit was wroght all by wit and wiles to helpe,/ And mighty suche mawmwntry made to destroy."[83] To Mohammed was ascribed the construction of two other similar images:

That ydolle was made of the honde of Machommete in the tyme that he lyved, & was named Mahommet in thonour of hym; and by arte magyke and dyabolyke he closed therin a legyon of deuylles. . . The stone vpon whyche thydolle was sette was meruayllously made. It was a stone of the see, wrought of sarasyns, and grauen subtylly of grete ans ryche facyon, the whyche was enhaunced vpryght, not without grete crafte & connyng. Toward the erth it was meruayllously grete, & alway vpward it was lasse; and that stone was so hye as a crowe myght flee: vpon whyche stone was thydolle sette, whyche was of fyn yuorye, after thas-semblaunce of a man stondyng vpryght on his feet, & had hys face torned to the south, & helde in his ryght honde a grete keye.[84]

And:

an image of gret pouste,/ Stode on a roche bi þe se,/ In þe gilden lond;/ His name was salanicodus/ As a man y-schapen he was,/ & held a glaive an hond/ Mahoun maked him wiþ gin,/ & dede mani fendes þer in,/ As ich vnderstond./ For to susten þe ymage,/ & sett him on heize stage.[85]

A common notion in the Middle Ages, ultimately derived from patristic writers, was that oracles were really the voice of evil spirits concealed in images of pagan deities, and that the gods of Greece and Rome were merely devils. Even for Milton (*Paradise Regained*, I, 430 ff.) oracles were the utterance of devils. This conception of oracles was also familiar to Mohammedans.[86]

Devils were called forth to perform a sort of work which Milton has since treated and made famous:

Conioured þre hundred fendes of helle/ þat þai schuld make a brigge/ Ouer þe se for to ligge/ Aday þai schuld to helle gon. & fram þennes bring þe ston/ þat schuld to þe brigge go/ & þe siment onizt in derke/ Opon þe brigge þai schuld werke/ On þis maner it to dizt/ þe brigge to make & wirke onizt/ So al in a litel while/ þe brigge was maked xx mile/ & þo anon þe conqueror/ þer lete make a strong tour/ Wele yhoused & wele ybeld/ T chambers & halles wiþ mani teld/ Zef he oþer his went ouer þe see/ þat he mizt þer herberwed be.[87]

This obviously had its source in Church magic, which was a commonplace in the medieval period.[88]

The marvelous tomb of Hector is striking because of the gems, the four statues on which the sarcophagus rests, and the embalming fluid:

Ther werk was al of pure gold,/ Ther thei made his sepulture./ But
he was mad, he schold not greue a grot,/ He was mad so he myzt
not rot,/ Thei held him hole & alle entere/ In his colour fair &
clere,/ . . These Maystres and these riche clerkes/ That witti were
of craffty werkes,/ That this thyng schold vnditake/ And that crafft-
werk to make,/ Off brede & lengthe toke thei met,/ Or it were raysed
or vpset./ Thei set it alle In foure pilers/ Off pure gold at foure
corneres,/ The pilers alle of red gold/ From a-boue to the mold;/ On
eche a pilere stod an ymage/ With louely chere & fair visage . . . Ther
were stones of alle kynde,/ Grene, rede, blewe, and Inde;/ Ther
stood many riche ston/ That as bryzt a-boute hem schon,/ As doth In
somer the sonne bem;/ A man may se to sowe a sem/ In the furthest
of the chirche/ A-boute mydnyght that thanne wold wirche./ Al was
wrought of balewerie/ Opon the erthe al vpon hye,/ And men clombe
op on greces smale/ That were wrought of clene cristale./ The maystres
that were wise & slye/ Thei sette an y-mage al vp on hye/ Off gold
fair, of his gretnesse,/ . . . To hem of Grece he turned his vyce"[89]

"And amyddes al þis grete richesse,/ þei han y-set, by good avise-
nesse,/ þe dede cors of þis wordi knyzt,/ To sizt of man . . . as he
were lyvynge,/ . . . For in his hede, like as it tolde,/ þoruz smale
pipes wrouzt & made of gold,/ . . . To eche party and extremyte/
Of his body lyneally correct./ Whereby þe licour myzte doun discende/
To kepe hym hool fro corruptioun.[90]

The passage in Guido, which these romancers said they were
translating is quoted here:

*Statuerunt enim predicti magistri iuxta magnum altare templi predicti
quoddam thabernaculum constitui spacii condecentis, quod super illior
columpnas ex auro purissimo fusiles regeretur. In quarum qualibet
representans, ab ymo usque ad summum ex ipsarum substancia colump-
narum, sic quod in columpnis ipsis erant ymagines et columpne habentes
bases et capitella in mirabilibus celaturis. Testudo uero ipsius tabernaculi
licet tota fuisset ex auro, incrustaciones eius tamen omnes erant ex
lapidibus preciosis cuiuslibet generis et in mirabilis copie quantitate,
quorum splendor claritatis et lucis de nocte diem et de die solis radios
effundere uidebatur. Tabernaculum autem ipsum ab infima soli super-
ficie extitit eleuatum, et suppositis quibusdam gradibus crisallinis, per
ipsos gradus ad ipsum tabernaculum erat ascensus. In excelso uero
testudinis ipsius tabernaculi supra culmen predicti magistri constituerunt
quandam auream statuam, similitudinem Hectoris describentem, haben-
tem ensem nudum in manu, cuius aspectus et facies erat ex ea parte*

in qua Grecorum exercitus in eroum tentoriis morabatur, qui cum eius ense Grecis minas inprimere uidebatur. Corpus uero ipsius Hectoris in mirabilis magisterii eorum artificio statuerunt in medio, ipsius solii subnixa firmtate, sedere, sic artificiose locatum ut quasi uiuum se in sua regeret sessione, propriis indutum uestibus preter pedum extrema . . . Cuius balsami et rerum liquor primo deriuabatur ad frontis ambitum per partes intrinsecas, deinde ad oculos et nares, necnon recto decurso descendendo per easdem partes intrinsecas perueniebat ad genas, per quas ginguias et dentes conseruabat ipsius, sic quod tota eius facies cum suorum multitudine capillorum in sua conseruacione uigebat. . . . Sic et liquor ipse descendens per utrunque latus, copiose diffusus, latera ipsa sic conseruabat in statu ut quasi uiui latera uiderentur. . . . Constituerunt predicti sapientes artifices illior lampades, ex auro compositas, ignem inextinguibilem continentes.[91]

Certainly these authors had their minds filled with Oriental things. Very similar to this tomb was the tomb of Camille (*Eneas* v, 7646 ff.) and of Pallas (*Eneas* v, 6467 ff.). The statue of Hector on the summit probably had its origin in the famous equestrian statue of Justinian in Constantinople. This elaborate bronze statue was reached by seven white marble steps. The emperor was facing the Orient as if to march against the Persians. One hand held a globe and the other was extended toward Asia.[92]

Of interest is the grave of Ninus, which the Macedonians found when digging in the field. It was hollowed out of a single amethyst and engraved on the outside with palm leaves and sundry kinds of birds. And so bright was the amethyst that even from the outside the man's body appeared whole:

Was of ane athill amatist & all within grauen,/ Plantid full of palmetres & many proud fowles,/ And slike a cleret it kest þurze kynd of it-selfe/ þai mizt haue kend without þe kist þe corps all-to-gedire.[93]

This passage is almost a literal translation from *Historia de Preliis*. Also it is based on the Latin text of the *Letters of Alexander to Aristotle*.[94]

Marvelous indeed was the throne of Cyrus, of which Alexander came into possession. It was seven cubits high from the ground

and was approached by means of seven rich steps, each made of a
different kind of stone which had a symbolical meaning for the
king:

þe first was of an Amatist þat all chaye demes/ Riche, said þe romance
& ronkenes of wynes,/ Lattis na dronkynnes þam þere þat douth at it
beris/ . . . þe secunde was of Samaragdone þat ay þe sizt kepis;/
Quat berne as beris it him on it briztens his ezen/ . . . þe thirs was a
Topaz, I trow at to þe trone lengis;/ þat is so clere of his kind þe
clause me recordis,/ þat qua-sum-euire in þat ilk his ymage behaldis,/
þe face is to þe fold-ward þe fete to þe firment/ . . . þe ferd was a
garnate, I gesse goules althire fynest;/ Is nane so redy, as I rede of
all þe riche stanes/ . . . þe fift was all of adomant as þe buke tellis;/
þat is he þat is so hard þat hurt may nane tole;/ Is nothire stele ne na
stane so stife it may perce/ And growis out of the grete see in graynes
& in cragis./ If any Naue to it neze þat naylid is with iryn,/ þen
cleuys it ay to þe clife carryg & othyre;/ þe sext was of gold graciously
hewen,/ Of all metals o mold þe maister & þe syre;/ . . . þe seuynt
vp to þe sege was of þe selfe erth/ Bot blode of body, sais þe buke
bees it neuire percid.[95]

Again, this passage is almost a literal translation from the Latin
text of the *Letters of Alexander to Aristotle*. The reference to the
adamant stone is not found in the Latin text but is found in *Mandeville's Travels*. The generally accepted idea, referred to here,
that adamant could be broken by the blood of goats is found in
the *Bestiary* of Philip de Thaun (p. 25). The combination of seven
steps of different kinds of stones or material may have some connection with the Assyrian amulet of seven stones worn by kings.
Among the Babylonians the number seven was looked upon as
especially sacred.[96]

Another fabulous object was the ship in which Partonope found
himself. In spite of the absence of sailors to steer and row, the
boat proceeded at a rapid rate in a direct course to a wonderful
city: "thys shyppe was mervelus made./ In alle hys lyffe he ne
hadde/ Sey so cvryous a wroughte thynge./ He then trowed þer
was no man leuynge/ By crafte of honde cowde suche on make."[97]
The same vessel returned him to France. A probable source for

this marvel is found in continental as well as Oriental literature. A similar journey was made by Sinbad and also by Herzog Ernst.[98] Another strange ship is depicted in the *History of the Holy Grail*:

> The schipe, Al of Silver it was,/ The naylles Of gold In that plas;/ . . . So Riche thilke litel vessel was,/ That Sire Nasciens thowhte In non plas/ . . . So Riche a vessel that Myhte han be;/ For withowten it was Set so ful of precious stones,/ Every bord ful thikke for the Nonis/ . . . And zit was that Schipe In Other degre/ Anoured with diuers Iowellis Certeinle.[99]

Ships of an unreal nature were quite common in the oldest Irish fairy stories, as in the *Voyage of Bran*. In the *Adventures of Connla* a supernatural damsel came in a wonderful ship of glass and carried the hero away to a superbly beautiful land. A more likely source for this passage as well as for the description of France. The romance ships, just as Manannan's coracle and Solo-Perceval's magic, self-propelling ship, with the rich bed of cypress and ivory, is the account of the coracle of Manannan in the *Fate of the Children of Turenn* and the legend of Solomon's ship, which was probably introduced into the romance by Marie de mon's ship, moved by magic to predestined places. Doubtless the fame of Solomon's skilled craftsmen led the romancer to make Solomon, the builder of the temple, become the builder of a fantastic barge which, in the Grail legend, symbolized the Church, both of the Old Law and the New.[100]

Of considerable interest is the marvelous storm-raising spring:

> By þat well hinges a bacyne, þat es of gold gude and fyne,/ With a cheyne, trewly to tell,/ þat will reche into þe well,/ þare es a chapel nere þarby [and before the well the stepping-stone was a single emerald, hollow, and mounted on four rubies, more radiant than the sun when it rises in the orient].[101]

The spring of Barenton in the forest of Broceliande was regarded in the Middle Ages as a storm-raising spring. Popular tradition held the belief that, if water was taken from the spring and poured on a slab of stone lying by the side of the fountain, a fierce thunderstorm would burst immediately afterwards and rain would fall in great quantities. Lewis contends that the legend of the spring is based on the sacred spring of Zeus at Dodona, which bubbled up from the roots of a giant evergreen that never shed its leaves. Also, not far from the sacred spring of Dodona stood the temple of the storm-god Zeus; similarly the romance fountain was near a chapel. The emerald slab was a "streaming stone," and its function was to produce rain whenever water was poured on it. The basin is a much impaired version of the cauldron of bronze, or gong, at Dodona which had the function of producing thunder-storms by the process of sympathetic magic; that is, by imitating the phenomena of nature which constitute the thunderstorm, namely thunder and lightning.[102]

In the Grail romances the cup plays a dominant role. In Love-lich's account of the Holy Grail, the cup or dish was kept in the ark: *"Et en mi lieu del autel si auoit i moult riche vaissiel d'or en samblanche d'un hanap."*[103] This rendition of Robert de Boron's poem is clearly dependent on purely Christian sources. The source is found in the part played by Joseph of Arimathea in the Bible story of the Passion and Resurrection, and in the apocryphal tales like the *Gesta Pilati* and *Vindicta Salvatoris.* In the original account the Grail was the cup in which Joseph of Arimathea caught up the blood of Jesus when he took the body from the Cross. This chalice shed a bright light, but no mention was made of a lance. But other elements were later added to this basic legend, as seen in the story of Perceval and the Fisher King. Lewis thinks the Grail, christianized by Boron, was originally an heirloom of the house of Atreus. It was the golden Lamb of Atreus which some writers of antiquity described as a silver bowl or cup enriched with a gold lamb in the center of it.[104] The lance, associated with the Grail, he identifies as the royal sceptre of Agamemnon, which, says Homer, was given to Pelops by Zeus as a symbol of dominion. Later this spear was identified with the lance of Longius when the classical legend came under Christian influence. The broken sword he identifies with the sword of Menelaus, which smashed in pieces at the critical moment in the single combat with Paris before the walls of Troy.[105] Loomis finds that all manner of sacred vessels of the Irish and Welsh have contributed to the conception of the Grail, particularly the pearl-rimmed caldron of the Head of Annwn, the Caldron of Britain of which Manawyd was perpetual guardian; the caldron of Bran, Manannan's cup of truth, the cup of sovereignty in the palace of Lug, the caldron of Blathnat. The Grail's curative virtues probably came from the caldron of Blathnat, its power as an inexhaustible provider of food and drink from the caldron of the Head of Annwn, and its property of denial of food to the unworthy to Manannan's cup of Truth. The spear or lance he identifies with the Fiery Spear of Lug, or with the lightning spears of Irish legend of which Lug's spear is representative. For the sword he finds a counterpart in the sword of Rhydderch Hael, one of the lightning weapons of Welsh mythology.[106]

The Grail Castle, called Palace Adventurous and Corbenic, provided Gawain with a series of breathtaking adventures. Gawain, arriving at night at the moated castle, was hospitably received by the king. A dove and then a fair damsel with a rich vessel came from a chamber. All kneeled before the holy vessel, which replenished the dishes on the table. Gawain asked no questions, and all departed except Gawain, who found the doors shut fast. An encounter with a dwarf, armed repose upon a rich bed, a wound by a fiery lance, a fight to the death between a dragon and a lion, tumultuous noise of windows clapping to, the entrance of twelve weeping damsels, a fight to exhaustion with a knight, a damsel placing the Holy Grail on a silver table, the departure of the damsels, and Gawain's expulsion from the castle[107]—these events occurred in sequence in the hall in the midst of which lay the Fisher King. Before him was a fire on the hearth. This castle, with its three fires and one hundred couches, was quite different from medieval castles, but it was similar to ancient Welsh structures. The source for this castle may be the Welsh Otherworld fortress of Curoi. It is also identifiable with the abode of other Welsh gods, Manawyddan, Bran, and Beli, who were imagined as dwelling especially in Happy Isles beyond the sunset; it may be a composite of Celtic conceptions of the dwellings of the gods.[108] Lewis finds the original of this castle in the palace of the Atridae. Such a palace had the hearth in the middle of the hall, with an opening in the roof for the smoke to escape. The hearth was surrounded by four columns which supported the roof.[109]

In the Grail legend appears the Siege Perilous, an empty seat at the Round Table which was reserved for the best knight in the world. Those unworthy ones who were bold enough to try the chair were swallowed up in the fissure which suddenly yawned beneath the quivering chair. A deafening noise accompanied each trial.[110] The incidents connected with the Siege Perilous have been drawn from various sources. There is a hint of the seat of watch in the castle of Curoi, as well as of the king's seat at Nuada's court, which the youthful Lug occupied at the opening of his career. There is also a prototype in the Lia Fail, which roared and broke under Conn. The Throne of Narberth, where Pryderi and Manawyddan sat, after their feast, with disastrous consequences to the land, is a garbled form of the Siege Perilous.[111]

The Marvelous Bed in the Chateau Marvelous had bells attached to it, in order to provide the noise while arrows and swords rained upon the shield of any knight bold enough to attempt to lie in it.[112] This bed without question goes back to the perilous seat of watch; for example, the perilous seat, the Stone of Fal, roared under the king of Ireland when he tried it. Protoyptes of this bed are discovered in *Bricriu's Feast* and in the *Ecstasy of the Champion*.[113]

The fabulous, which plays such an important role in the French romances, is of equal importance in a number of English romances, because this particular group were more or less close translations of the French accounts. Such, for example, is the case of the romances dealing with the adventures of Alexander and of Cheuelere

Assigne. Let me be more specific and cite from the French *Chevelier au Cygne* a passage dealing with the fabulous chains about the children's necks:

Au maistre des enfans VII fees y avoit/ Qui les enfans distenent que cascun avenroit,/ Ensi que li uns enfens apres l'autre naissoit,/ Au col une caine de fin argent avoit,[114]

which was translated thus into English:

Whenne God wolde þey were borne, þenne browzte she to honde/ Sex semelye sonnes; & a dowzter þe seventh,/ Alle safe & alle sounde: & a selver cheyne/ Eche on of hem hadde aboute his swete swyre.[115]

But some of the redactors evidently found the material too unreal in places, so that they rationalized parts of the fabulous material; others were eclectic; still others eliminated almost all of the unreal.

In the main, the English version of Benoit's *Troie* is a fairly close translation. For example, the fabulous ring given to Jason by Medea defended him from all perils, because it rendered invulnerable the man who wore it. Moreover, it had the virtue of making the wearer invisible whenever he turned the stone toward the palm of the hand.[116] The English versions are almost literal translations:

Than ho raught hym a ring with a riche stone,/ þat no poison enpaire might, þe power is soche:/ And if it borne were in batell on his bare flesshe,/ He shulde slyde forth sleghly & unslayn worthe/ Achates it calde is with clene men of wit.[117]

Another translator says of this ring that if a man "coude it bere a-rizt,/ With-Inne his honde next þe skyn enclosed,/ þe strengþe of sizt schulde be deposed."[118] Other parts of the same romance show some change. The fabulous tomb of Hector stood on four statues, all of precious stones, according to the French version. One of the statues was made of "pedoire" which was characterized thus:

*Dedenz le flun de Paradis/ A uns arbes d'estranges pris;/ **Pomes** chargent que al fonz vont:/ Celes qui set anz i estont/ Pieres devienent forz e dures,/ Teus vertuz ont e teus natures/ Qu'ome desve senz escient,/ Qui riens ne set ne rien n'entent,/ Rameinent tot en son memorie.*[119]

The English translator has rationalized the material: "Thei set it all In foure pilers/ Off pure gold at foure correres,/ The pilers alle of red gold/ From a-boue to the mold;/ On eche a pilere stod an ymage."[120]

More significant as showing this rationalizing process is the romance of Floris and Blanchefleur. In the French account there is a long description of two statues placed on the tomb of Blanchefleur; they represented two children carrying some roses and lilies. When the wind blew, the statues swung around, met, and kissed:

Si disoient par nigremance/ Trestout lor bon et lor enfance./ Ce dist Floires a Blanceflor:/ "Baissiez moi, bele, par amor";/ Blanceflor respont en baisant:/ "Je vous aim plus que riens vivant."/ Tant com li vent les atouchoient,/ Et li enfant s' entrebaisoient,/ Et quant il laisse de venter,/ Dont se prenent a reposer./ Tant doucement s'entregardoient,/ Qu'il ert a vis que il rioient.[121]

No reference is made to these figures in the English account. Also the tower of the Emir in the French account was surmounted by a sixty-foot "needle" or spire as well as by a carbuncle in the tower's summit; this gem had been placed there *"par enchantment."*[122] The rationalized English version refers to the carbuncle stone but omits the other elements:

Stondeþ a toure, y the plyzt,/ An hundryd fathum it is hye,—/ Who-soo beholdeþ hit, fer or nere,/ An hundred fathum it is y-fere;—/ It is made withouten pere,/ of lyme and of Marbulstone;/ In al þis world is suche noone,/ Now is þe morter made so wele,/ Ne may it breke, iren ne steele./ Þe Pomel þat aboue is leide,/ It is made with muche pride;/ Þat man ne þar in þe Tour berne/ Nouther torcher ne lanterne;/ Suche a pomel was þer bygone,/ Hit shyned a nyzt so doþ þe soone.[123]

The Emir's orchard, surrounded by a wall on which birds were singing, was depicted in both the French and English versions. In the French account, these birds, *"Quant il vente, si font dous cri/ Qu'onques nus home tel n'oi;/ Si ne fu aine beste tant fiere,/ Se de lor chant ot la maniere,/ Lupars, ne tygre, ne lion,/ Qu'il n'en soient en soupecon."*[124] The English version merely states: "an Orchard/ þe feirest of al mydlerd:/ þeryn is mony fowles song;/ Man myzt leue þeryn ful long."[125] Other features of the garden and the marvelous virtue-detecting tree and stream are similar in both.[126]

It would seem that reality was more akin to the temperament of the English than extravaganza, so that when the English translator chose to depart from his French original he allowed his mind to suppress entirely or subdue the play of illogical imagination found in the original. It is very likely that the English romancer, working without foreign models, would have eliminated almost entirely all reference to the strictly fabulous.

notes

FOREWORD

[1] Elizabeth Harris, *The Mural as a Decorative Device in Medieval Literature*, Vanderbilt University Dissertation (1935).
[2] W. P. Ker, *Epic and Romance* (London, 1931), pp. 4, 325.

CHAPTER ONE

[1] E. L. Cutts, *Scenes and Characters of the Middle Ages* (London, 1872), p. 530.
[2] H. Pirenne, *Medieval Cities* (Princeton, 1925), p. 140; Sidney Toy, *Castles* (London, 1939), pp. 1-15, 21-50.
[3] *Wars of Alexander*, ed. W. W. Skeat, *EETS, ES*, No. 47, ll. 1148 ff. Also, *Prose Life of Alexander*, ed. J. S. Westlake, *EETS, OS*, No. 143, p. 18.
[4] *The Seege or Batayle of Troye*, ed. M. E. Barnicle, *EETS, OS*, No. 172, ll. 309 ff. See also *Partonope of Blois*, ed. A. T. Bodtker, *EETS, ES*, No. 109, l. 837; *Godeffroy of Bologne*, ed. M. N. Colvin, *EETS, ES*, No. 64, pp. 73-4; *Romance of the Emperor Octavian*, ed. J. O. Halliwell, Percy Society, XIV, ll. 407 ff.
[5] *Libeaus Desconus*, ed. M. Kaluza, *Altenglische Bibliothek*, V, p. 73.
[6] *Godeffroy of Bologne*, p. 62. See *Merlin*, ed. E. A. Kock, *EETS, OS*, No. 185, ll. 17334 ff.
[7] *Kyng Alisaunder*, ed. H. Weber, *Metrical Romances*, I, ll. 7145. See *Partonope of Blois*, ll. 901 ff.
[8] *Melusine*, ed. A. K. Donald, *EETS, ES*, No. 68, p. 88; *Richard Coer de Lion*, ed. H. Weber, *Metrical Romances*, II, ll. 14285 ff.; *Duke Huon of Burdeux*, ed. S. L. Lee, *EETS, ES*, No. 43, 50, p. 596; *William of Palerne*, ed. W. W. Skeat, *EETS, ES*, No. 1, ll. 2835 ff.
[9] Pirenne, *op. cit.*, p. 148.
[10] *Partonope of Blois*, ll. 837 ff. *See Sir Ysumbras*, ed. J. Zupitza, *Palaestra*, XV, 44, ll. 553-4; Pirenne, *op cit.*, pp. 73-4; *Sir Isumbras*, ed. J. O. Halliwell, *Thornton Romances*, Camden Society, st. xlvii, ll. 547-8; *The Bruce*, ed. W. W. Skeat, *EETS, ES*, No. 55, p. 414; *ES*, No. 11, p. 33, pp. 108-9; *Amis and Amiloun*, ed. H. Weber, *Metrical Romances*, II, ll. 1891 ff.; Lydgate's *Siege of Thebes*, ed. A. Erdmann,

EETS, ES, No. 108, ll. 3572 ff. Others refer to the defense unit within as a palace: *Merlin*, ll. 9304 ff.; *Caxton's Blanchardyn and Eglantine*, ed. L. Kellner, *EETS, ES*, No. 58, pp. 208-9, 159-60; *Destruction of Troy*, ed. G. A. Panton, *EETS, OS*, No. 39, ll. 316 ff.

[11] *Melusine*, pp. 88, 206.

[12] *Huon of Burdeux*, p. 674.

[13] *Romance of Tristram and Ysolt*, ed. R. S. Loomis (New York, 1931), pp. 154-55.

[14] *Lydgate's Siege of Thebes*, ll. 4088 ff., 1242 ff.; *Kyng Alisaunder, op. cit.*, ll. 2643 ff.; *Godeffroy of Bologne*, pp. 73-4.

[15] *Generydes*, ed. W. A. Wright, *EETS, OS*, No. 55, 70, ll. 5988 ff.; *Huon of Burdeux*, p. 596; *Sir Eger, Sir Grahame, and Sir Gray-Steel*, ed. Ellis, *English Metrical Romances*, III, 321.

[16] K. Lamprecht, *Deutsche Geschichte* (Berlin, 1895-1909), IV, 211-17.

[17] For details see A. Blanchet, *Les Enceintes romaines de la Gaule*.

[18] *Lydgate's Troy Book*, ed. H. Bergen, *EETS, ES*, No. 97, ll. 535 ff.

[19] *Huon of Burdeux*, No. 40, 41, p. 122.

[20] R. Escholier, "La Fleur Des Manuscrits" in *L'Illustration*, No. 4840, Christmas, 1935.

[21] *Caxton's Eneydos*, ed. W. T. Culley and F. J. Furnivall, *EETS, ES*, No. 57, p. 48; *Sir Ferumbras*, ed. S. J. Herrtage, *EETS, ES*, No. 34, ll. 4308 ff.

[22] *Merlin*, l. 17343; *Lydgate's Siege of Thebes*, l. 239.

[23] *Sir Ferumbras*, ll. 4308 ff.; *Le Roman de Troie*, ed. L. Constans, Société des anciens textes francais (Paris, 1904-1912), I, ll. 3006-7.

[24] *Huon of Burdeux*, No. 43, 50, p. 596.

[25] *Partonope of Blois*, l. 880.

[26] W. Besant, *Mediaeval London* (London, 1906), p. 159.

[27] *Lydgate's Siege of Troy*, l. 642.

[28] *The Knightly Tale of Golagros and Gawane*, ed. F. J. Amours, *Scottish Alliterative Poems*, l. 43; *Laud Troy Book*, ed. J. E. Wulfing, *EETS, OS*, No. 121, ll. 530 ff.; *The Seege or Batayle of Troye*, ed. M. E. Barnicle, *EETS, OS*, No. 172, p. 171, l. 309.

[29] *Destruction of Troy*, ed. G. A. Panton and D. Donaldson, *EETS, OS*, No. 39, pp. 52 ff.

[30] *Romance of Emperor Octavian*, l. 826 ff.

[31] *The Bruce*, p. 420, ll. 377 ff.

[32] Besant, *op. cit.*, p. 160-1.

[33] *Kyng Alisaunder*, I, ll. 7145 ff; *Lydgate's Troy Book*, ll. 571-2.

[34] *Book of Fayttes of Armes and of Chyualrye*, ed. A. T. Byles, *EETS, ES*, No. 189, p. 136. Also *Knyghthode and Bataile*, ed. Dyboski and Arend, *EETS, OS*, No. 201, ll. 2259 ff.

[35] *Ibid.*

Notes

36 *Melusine*, p. 88. See also *Wars of Alexander*, p. 60.
37 *British Museum Reproductions from Illuminated Manuscripts* (London, 1923), Series IV, No. xlvi.
38 Toy, *op. cit.*, p. 204; *Caxton's Book of Fayttes of Armes; op. cit.*, p. 136.
39 *William of Palerne*, ll. 2219-20, 2857-3000.
40 Lamprecht, *op. cit.*, pp. 211 ff.
41 Besant, *op. cit.*, pp. 160-61.
42 *Knyghthode & Bataile*, pp. 647-48.
43 *Merlin*, ll. 1863 ff. *Arthour & Merlin*, ed. E. Kolbing, *Altenglische Bibliothek*, 4, l. 5813.
44 Besant, *op. cit.*, p. 159.
45 *Charles the Grete*, p. 205; also *The Bruce*, p .33.
46 Besant, *op. cit.*, p. 159.
47 *The Three Kings Sons*, ed. F. J. Furnivall, *EETS, ES*, No. 67, pp. 52-3; (also see *Destruction of Troy*, ed. G. A. Panton & D. Donaldson, *EETS, OS*, No. 39, p. 30).
48 *Ibid.*
49 Toy, *op. cit.*, pp. 170-71.
50 *Alexander & Soredamour*, ed. W. W. Newell, *King Arthur & Table Round*, p. 137; see *The Three Kings Sons*, p. 52.
51 *Illuminated Manuscripts, op. cit.*, Series IV, plate xxxviii.
52 Toy, *op. cit.*, pp. 170-71.
53 *Valentine & Orson*, ed. A. Dickson, *EETS, OS, No.* 204, p. 219; also see *Godeffroy of Bologne*, p. 142.
54 Toy, *op. cit.*, pp. 110-11.
55 *Romance of Partenay*, ll. 1170 ff.
56 *Knyghthode & Bataile*, pp. 647-48.
57 *The Seege or Batayle of Troye*, p. 171.
58 *The Sowdone of Babylone*, ed. E. Hausknecht, *EETS, ES*, No. 38, l. 264; see Lydgate's *Siege of Thebes*, l. 2771; *Merlin*, p. 464.
59 *Huon of Burdeux*, No. 43, 50, p. 338.
60 *The Bruce*, p. 211.
61 Toy, *op. cit.*, pp. 172-3.
62 *Sir Ferumbras*, ll. 4308 ff.; see *Valentine & Orson*, p. 239.
63 *Libeaus Desconus, loc. cit.*, l. 1361.
64 Toy, *op. cit.*, p. 191.
65 *The Seege or Batayle of Troy*, p. 171. See *Merlin*, p. 498.
66 The gates were often given names which characterized their position of service, such as water gate—one opening on the water—and land gate —one opening on the land. Berwick had one called the cowport. See *Bruce*, p. 407.

[67] Besant, *op. cit.,* p. 159.

[68] *Huon of Burdeux,* No. 40, 41, p. 141; *Siege of Jerusalem,* l. 644; *Kyng Alisaunder,* l. 2647; *Destruction of Troy,* pp. 52-54.

[69] Lamprecht, *op. cit.,* pp. 211-17.

[70] Toy, *op. cit.,* pp. 103-9.

[71] *Romance of Partenay,* p. 46.

[72] *Richard Coer de Lion,* ed. H. Weber, *Metrical Romances,* II, l. 4747.

[73] *Lydgate's Troy Book,* pp. 162-3.

[74] *Richard Coer de Lion, loc. cit.,* l. 4314. Also *Valentine & Orson,* p. 61.

[75] *Sir Ferumbras,* ll. 4628 ff. See *Destruction of Troy,* ll. 6017-19.

[76] *Merlin,* p. 464.

[77] *Troy Book,* No. 97, pp. 161-2.

[78] W. W. McKenzie, *The Mediaeval Castle in Scotland* (London, 1927), p. 97.

[79] *The Bruce,* p. 434.

[80] Toy, *op. cit.,* pp. 189-90.

[81] Besant, *op. cit.,* p. 162.

[82] *Siege of Jerusalem,* ed. E. Kolbing and Mabel Day, *EETS, OS,* No. 188, ll. 613 ff. Also *The Sowdone of Babylone,* l. 429; *Richard Coer de Lion,* ll. 1929, 4318.

[83] Toy, *op. cit.,* pp. 106-9; Besant, *op. cit.,* p. 162.

[84] *Godeffroy of Bologne,* pp. 181-3.

[85] Besant, *op. cit.,* pp. 227-8.

[86] *Richard Coer de Lion,* ll. 4233-4.

[87] *Huon of Burdeux,* No. 40, 41, p. 99.

[88] Cutts, *op. cit.,* pp. 532-3; Toy, *op. cit.,* p. 170.

[89] Besant, *op. cit.,* pp. 236-7.

[90] *Troy Book,* p. 162.

[91] *Kyng Alisaunder,* ll. 2653 ff.

[92] *Richard Coer de Lion,* l. 1931; *Horn Childe & Maiden Rimnild,* ed. J. Caro, *Englische Studien,* XII, p. 353, l. 173; *Huon of Burdeux,* No. 40, 41, p. 232.

[93] Besant, *op. cit.,* p. 232.

[94] H. T. Riley, *Munimenta Gildhallae Londoniensis, Liber Albus* in *Rolls Series* vol. I, pp. xl-xliv. Also E. L. Sabine, "City Cleaning in Medieval England" in *Speculum,* 12 (1937), 19-43; "Latrines and Cesspools in Medieval London" in *Speculum,* 9 (1934), 303-21.

[95] *Partonope of Blois,* ll. 1004 ff.; *Wars of Alexander,* p. 52; *Troy Book,* pp. 163-4.

[96] Besant, *op. cit.,* pp. 172, 248.

[97] *Illuminated Manuscripts, op. cit.,* Series III, No. liii.

[98] Cutts, *op. cit.,* p. 172.

[99] *Coronet,* January, 1938, p. 24.

Notes

100 *Perceval*, ed. W. W. Newell, *King Arthur & Table Round*, p. 34.

101 *Morte Arthure*, ed. E. Brock, *EETS, OS,* No. 8, ll. 3038 ff. See *Amoryas & Cleopes*, ed. H. Craig, *EETS, OS,* No. 132, ll. 1398 ff.

102 Besant, *op. cit.*, p. 250.

103 *The Seven Sages*, ed. T. Wright, Percy Society, XVI, ll. 1381 ff.; *Caxton's Blanchardyn & Eglantine*, p. 50; *Lays of Marie*, ed. Geo. Ellis, *English Metrical Romances*, I, 175.

104 Riley, *op. cit.*, p. xxxv.

105 Cutts, *op. cit.*, p. 105.

106 *Ibid.*, p. 106.

107 *Destruction of Troy*, p. 107.

108 *Troy Book*, p. 163.

109 J. Grant, *Old Edinburgh* (London, 1881), p. 258.

110 *Destruction of Troy*, l. 1598.

111 Besant, *op. cit.*, p. 251.

112 Grant, *op. cit.*, I, p. 270; II, p. 28.

113 *Destruction of Troy*, ll. 1600-01.

114 Cutts, *op. cit.*, pp. 542-3.

115 *Valentine & Orson*, ed. A. Dickson, *EETS, OS,* No. 204, pp. 70-1; 293; *Kyng Alisaunder*, ll. 1025 ff.; *Sir Beues of Hamtoun*, ed. E. Kolbing, *EETS, ES,* No. 46, 48, 65, p. 176.

116 *Sir Beues of Hamtoun*, p. 50.

117 Besant, *op. cit.*, pp. 163-4.

118 *The Knight of the Lion*, ed. W. W. Newell, *King Arthur & Table Round*, p. 216. See *Huon of Burdeux*, No. 43, p. 764.

119 Cutts, *op. cit.*, pp. 544-5; Toy, *op. cit.*, p. 170.

120 H. W. C. Davis, *Mediaeval England*, (Oxford, 1928), p. 311.

121 *Three Kings Sons*, *EETS, ES,* No. 67, pp. 52-3; also *Huon of Burdeux*, p. 674; *Three Kings of Cologne*, ed. C. Horstmann, *EETS, OS,* No. 85, p. 25.

122 *The Pistill of Susan*, ed. F. J. Amours, Scottish Text Society, l. 293.

123 *Lydgate's Siege of Thebes*, ll. 242 ff. See *Valentine & Orson*, p. 239.

124 Davis, *op. cit.*, frontispiece.

125 E. L. Sabinee, "City Cleaning in Mediaeval London" in *Speculum,* 12 (1937), 32; Besant, *op. cit.*, pp. 230-3.

126 *Siege of Jerusalem*, ll. 670 ff.

127 *Troy Book*, No. 97, ll. 1603 ff.

128 *Ibid.*, ll. 744 ff.

129 *Ibid.*, l. 700.

CHAPTER TWO

[1] William Mackenzie, *The Mediaeval Castles in Scotland* (London, 1927), p. 4.

[2] H. W. C. Davis, *Mediaeval England* (Oxford, 1928), pp. 96-7.

[3] Mackenzie, *op. cit.*, p. 33.

[4] Sidney Toy, *Castles* (London, 1939), pp. 52-65.

[5] *Roman von Guillaume le Clerc* (Ashtord, 1936), ll. 304-13; see Mackenzie, *op. cit.*, p. 34.

[6] *Richard Coer de Lion*, ll. 2683 ff.

[7] *Arthour & Merlin, loc. cit.*, ll. 523-33.

[8] Toy, *op. cit.*, pp. 66-80.

[9] *Merlin*, ll. 26058 ff. See *Anonymous Short English Metrical Chronicle*, ed. E. Zettl, *EETS, OS*, No. 196, l. 1075.

[10] *Firumbras & Otuel & Roland*, ed. Mary O'Sullivan, *EETS, OS*, No. 198, ll. 37 ff.

[11] Toy, *op. cit.*, pp. 90-99; Davis, *op. cit.*, p. 102.

[12] *Godeffroy of Bologne*, pp. 184-5.

[13] *Romans of Partenay*, ed. W. W. Skeat, *EETS, OS*, No. 22, ll. 1121 ff. See also *Knight of the Lion*, ed. W. W. Newell, *King Arthur & Table Round*, p. 202.

[14] Toy, *op. cit.*, pp. 116-40.

[15] *Ibid.*, p. 119.

[16] *Perceval*, ed. W. W. Newell, *King Arthur & Table Round*, II, p. 26.

[17] *Melusine, op. cit.*, pp. 62-3.

[18] *Ibid.*, p. 300.

[19] Toy, *op. cit.*, pp. 153-9; Davis, *op. cit.*, pp. 103-8.

[20] *Romance of Morien*, ed. J. L. Weston (London, 1910), pp. 62 ff.

[21] *Torrent of Portyngale*, ll. 705 ff.

[22] *Lyfe of Ipomydon*, ed. H. Weber, *Metrical Romances*, II, ll. 104 ff.

[23] *Charles the Grete*, p. 142; also see *Romance of Morien*, p. 133; *Huon of Burdeux*, No. 40, 41, p. 68, 203; *Sir Beues of Hamtoun*, p. 85; *The Knightly Tale of Golagros & Gawane*, ll. 493, 525, 235; *Richard Coer de Lion*, l, 4889.

[24] *Sir Degrevant*, ed. J. O. Halliwell, *Thornton Romances*, st. LVII, ll. 901 ff.

[25] Toy, *op. cit.*, pp. 153-5.

[26] Mackenzie, *op. cit.*, pp. 149-64.

27 *Huon of Burdeux*, No. 43, p. 642.
28 *Reinbrun*, ed. J. Zupita, *EETS, ES*, No. 42, 49. 59, st. 79.
29 *Wars of Alexander*, ll. 3217 ff.
30 *Libeaus Desconus*, ed. M. Kaluza, *Altenglische Bibliothek*, V, p. 91, l. 1861.
31 *Guy of Warwick*, ed. J. Zupitza, *EETS, ES*, No. 25, 26, ll. 11441-5; see *Di Romanze von Athelston*, ed. J. Zupitza, *Englische Studien*, XIII, p. 333, ll. 357-9.
32 Mackenzie, *op. cit.*, pp. 180-213; Toy, *op. cit.*, pp. 222-5.
33 *Valentine & Orson*, p. 151.
34 *Romans of Partenay*, ll. 4661 ff.
35 *Melusine*, pp. 328-9.
36 *Huon of Burdeux*, No. 40, 41, p. 96.
37 *Perceval*, pp. 56; see *Morte Arthure*, ll. 562 ff.; *Merlin*, ed. E. A. Kock, *EETS, ES*, No. 93, ll. 1927 ff.
38 Toy, *op. cit.*, pp. 120, 130, 155, 177, 127, 116, 136, 163, 157, 161, 154, 157; Mackenzie, *op. cit.*, p. 12.
39 *The Knightly Tale of Golagros & Gawane*, ll. 235 ff.
40 *Huon of Burdeux*, No. 40, 41, p. 203.
41 *Perceval, loc. cit.*, p. 26.
42 *Huon of Burdeux*, No. 43, 50, p. 368; *Lydgate's Siege of Thebes*, l. 2268; see *Arthour & Merlin, loc. cit.*, ll. 6636 ff.
43 *Godeffroy of Bologne*, p. 184; *Pistill of Susan*, l. 5.
44 *Seuyn Sages*, ed. H. Weber, *Metrical Romances*, III, ll. 166 ff. *Huon of Burdeux*, No. 40, 41, p. 68.
45 *Alexander & Sordeamour*, ed. W. W. Newell, *King Arthur & Table Round*, p. 125.
46 *Kyng Alisaunder*, l. 4089.
47 *Valentine & Orson*, p. 133.
48 *The Seven Sages*, ed. T. Wright, Percy Society, XVI, l. 137.
49 Mackenzie, *op. cit.*, pp. 31, 33, 44-5; Toy, *op. cit.*, p. 205.
50 Mackenzie, *op. cit.*, pp. 32-3. Nowadays, most of this ashlar would be called course rubble, ashlar being reserved for stones with a finer surface.
51 *Ibid.*, pp. 135-6.
52 *Ibid.*, p. 131.
53 *Arthour & Merlin, loc. cit.*, ll. 513 ff.
54 *Sir Tristram*, ed. G. P. McNeill, Scottish Text Society, ll. 2964 ff., p. 144.
55 *Seven Sages of Rome*, ed. K. Brunner, *EETS, OS*, No. 191, p. 6; *The History of the Holy Grail*, ed. Robt. de Borron, *EETS, ES*, No. 28, l. 512.

[56] *Godeffroy of Bologne*, pp. 184-5.

[57] *Destruction of Troy*, pp. 272-3; *Sir Eglamour*, ed. G. Schleich, *Palaestra*, LIII, p. 19, l. 334, p. 7, l. 181 ff.; *Sir Eglamour*, ed. J. O. Halliwell, *Thornton Romances*, st. xxix, ll. 334 ff.; *Richard Coer de Lion*, l. 6019.

[58] *Perceval, loc. cit.*, p. 26.

[59] *Alexander & Sordeamour*, p. 125; *Romance of Morien,,* p. 133.

[60] *The Tale of Beryn*, ed. W. G. Stone, *EETS, ES*, No. 105, ll. 2711 ff.

[61] Philo of Byzantium, ca. 120 B. C., says, "The curtain wall should be at least fifteen feet thick, built in gypsum and well bonded. They should be thirty feet high to prevent escalade. The part of a fortification most exposed to attack is sometimes protected by two walls, spaced from twelve to eighteen feet apart, and joined at the top by a vault or timber roof. Some curtain walls are embattled, but have no wall walk. In time of siege temporary platforms of timber may be put behind these battlements, and removed when necessary." A. de Roche, "Aiglum et C Graux," *Revue de Philologue*, 1897; Toy, *op. cit.*, p. 21.

[62] Mackenzie, *op. cit.*, p. 93; Toy, *op. cit.*, pp. 59, 119, 135-7, 160, 202.

[63] *Merlin*, ll. 26058 ff.; *Sir Ferumbras*, l. 2401.

[64] *Knightly Tale of Golagros & Gawane*, ll. 493 ff.

[65] *Godeffroy of Bologne*, pp. 184-5.

[66] *The Knightly Tale of Golagros & Gawane*, ll. 235 ff.

[67] Mackenzie, *op. cit.*, p. 93.

[68] *Melusine*, pp. 62-3; *Alexander & Sordeamour*, p. 125.

[69] Mackenzie, *op. cit.*, p. 101; Toy, *op. cit.*, pp. 100, 126-36, 159-62.

[70] *Perceval*, p. 26; *Huon of Burdeux*. No. 40, 41, p. 68; *Knightly Tale of Golagros & Gawane*, l. 248.

[71] *Valentine & Orson*, p. 230; *Sir Gawayne & the Green Knight*, ed. Richard Morris, *EETS, OS*, No. 4, ll. 795 ff.

[72] *Godeffroy of Bologne*, p. 102.

[73] *Huon of Burdeux*, No. 40, 41, p. 203.

[74] *Richard Coer de Lion*, ll. 6077 ff.

[75] *Sir Ferumbras*, ll. 2321 ff.; 3226 ff.; see *The Sowdone of Babylone*, ll. 331 ff.

[76] Toy, *op. cit.*, pp. 173-6.

[77] *Romans of Partenay*, ll. 1122 ff.

[78] *The Bruce*, p. 244.

[79] Mackenzie, *op. cit.*, pp. 92-3.

[80] Toy, *op. cit.*, pp. 157-63.

[81] *Richard Coer de Lion*, ll. 3844 ff.

[82] *Arthour & Merlin, loc. cit.*, ll. 8309, 6660, 1373.

[83] *The Bruce*, pp. 80-2.

[84] Mackenzie, *op. cit.*, p. 92.

85 *Destruction of Troy*, ll, 861-3; *Richard Coer de Lion*, l. 3845.
86 Toy, *op. cit.*, p. 204; Mackenzie, *op. cit.*, p. 88.
87 *Romans of Partenay*, ll. 1128 ff.
88 *Sir Ferumbras*, ll. 3226 ff.
89 *Sir Gawayne & The Green Knight*, l. 801; see *Romance of Duke Rowland & Of Sir Ottuel of Spayne*, ed. S. J. H. Herrtage, *EETS, ES*, No. 35, ll. 444 ff.; *Richard Coer de Lion*, l. 3845.
90 Toy, *op. cit.*, pp. 204-6; Mackenzie, *op. cit.*, pp. 88-9.
91 *Melusine*, p. 62; *Perceval, loc. cit.*, p. 56.
92 Toy, *op. cit.*, pp. 100, 162, 139; Mackenzie, *op. cit.*, pp. 55, 65, 95.
93 *Morien*, pp. 62 ff.
94 *Richard Coer de Lion*, l. 6021.
95 *Romans of Partenay*, l. 1115.
96 *The Pistill of Susan, loc. cit.*, ll. 5 ff. *History of the Holy Grail*, l. 103.
97 *Knightly Tale of Golagros & Gawayne, loc. cit.*, l. 239; *Alexander & Soredamour*, p. 125.
98 *Valentine & Orson*, p. 230; see *Charles the Grete*, p. 123.
99 Toy, *op. cit.*, pp. 154-60, 192, 202, 217; Mackenzie, *op. cit.*, p. 96.
100 *The Sowdone of Babylone*, ed. Emil Hausknecht, *EETS, ES*, No. 38, ll. 2548, 2053.
101 *Arthour & Merlin, loc. cit.*, l. 7255; see *Firumbras & Otuel & Roland*, ll. 44 ff.
102 *Ywain and Gawain*, ed. G. Schleich, l. 2214; *Sir Ferumbras*, ll. 3752 ff.
103 *Melusine*, p. 253.
104 *Richard Coer de Lion*, ll. 4079 ff.
105 *Alexander & Soredamour, loc. cit.*, p. 125.
106 *Perceval, loc. cit.*, p. 26.
107 *Valentine & Orson*, p. 230.
108 Toy, *op. cit.*, pp. 106, 153-7; Mackenzie, *op. cit.*, p. 97.
109 *Perceval, loc. cit.*, p. 26; *The Knight of the Lion*, ed. W. W. Newell, *King Arthur & the Table Round*, p. 202.
110 *Kyng Alisaunder*, H. Weber, *Metrical Romances*, I, ll. 1589 ff.
111 *Godeffroy of Bologne*, p. 264.
112 *Beues of Hamtoun*, l. 2094.
113 *Morte Arthure*, l. 2470.
114 *Richard Coer de Lion*, l. 2687.
115 Toy, *op. cit.*, pp. 189-98, 103-9; Mackenzie, *op. cit.*, p. 98.
116 *Huon of Burdeux*, No. 43, 50, p. 338; No. 40, 41, pp. 113-6.
117 *Morien*, pp. 62-71.
118 *The History of the Holy Grail*, p. 112, ll. 349 ff.
119 *The Knight of the Lion*, p. 155.
120 *Ywain & Gawain*, ll. 671 ff., 696-809.
121 Mackenzie, *op. cit.*, p. 100.

[122] *Alexander & Soredamour, loc. cit.*, p. 125; *Melusine*, p. 253.

[123] *Sir Gawayne & the Green Knight*, ll. 2069 ff.

[124] *The Bruce*, ll. 238 ff.

[125] *Arthour & Merlin, loc. cit.*, l. 1886.

[126] T. H. Turner, *Domestic Architecture* (London, 1877), p. 91.

[127] *Godeffroy of Bologne*, p. 182.

[128] *Pistill of Susan, loc. cit.*, l. 227.

[129] *Richard Coer de Lion*, l. 4211.

[130] *Ywain & Gawain*, ll. 2978 ff.

[131] *Rauf Coilzear*, ed. F. J. Amours, Scottish Text Society, l. 628; p. 325.

[132] *Toy, op. cit.*, pp. 198-202; *Mackenziie, op. cit.*, p. 100.

[133] *Torrent of Portyngale*, ll. 229, 1526 ff.

[134] *Firumbras & Otuel & Roland*, ll. 1353 ff.

[135] Mackenzie, *op. cit.*, p. 100.

[136] *Ywain & Gawain*, ll. 849, 2996; *Huon of Burdeux*, No. 40, 41, pp. 99, 109; *Firumbras & Otuel & Roland*, l. 1353.

[137] Mackenzie, *op. cit.*, p. 100; *Toy, op. cit.*, p. 122.

[138] *Pistill of Susan, loc. cit.*, ll. 118 ff.; *William of Palerne*, ed. W. W. Skeat, *EETS, ES*, No. 1, ll. 1751 ff.

[139] *Sowdone of Babylone*, ll. 379 ff.

[140] *The Maid with the Narrow Sleeves*, W. W. Newell, *King Arthur & Table Round*, pp. 103, 109; *Tale of Beryn*, ll. 2715 ff.

[141] *Toy, op. cit.*, pp. 112-4; Mackenzie, *op. cit.*, pp. 103-5.

[142] *Huon of Burdeux*, No. 43, p. 652.

[143] *Sir Eger, Sir Grahame, & Sir Gray-Steel*, ed. G. Ellis, *Metrical Romances*, III, pp. 318-19.

[144] *Merlin*, ll. 6775, 9752 ff.

[145] *Sir Gawayne & The Green Knight*, ll. 1742 ff.

[146] *Arthour & Merlin, loc. cit.*, ll. 1129 ff.

[147] *Firumbras & Otuel & Roland*, ll. 37, 987.

[148] *Charles the Grete*, p. 120.

[149] *Sir Ferumbras*, ll. 2298 ff.; *Huon of Burdeux*, No. 40, 41, p. 92; see *Seege of Troye*, ed. A. Zietsch, *Herrig's Archiv*, 72, p. 33, l. 1645.

[150] *Huon of Burdeux*, No. 43, 50, p. 384.

[151] *Kyng Alisaunder*, H. Weber, *Metrical Romances*, I, l. 7665.

[152] *Sir Beues of Hamtoun*, ll. 1130 ff.

[153] *Castell of Pleasure*, ed. R. Cornelius, *EETS, OS*, No. 179, l. 235.

[154] *Morte Arthure, loc. cit.*, p. 320.

[155] *William of Palerne*, ll. 3672-3.

[156] *Ywain & Gawain*, ll. 799 ff., 849 ff.

[157] *Toy, op. cit.*, pp. 100-2, 225-6; Mackenzie, *op. cit.*, pp. 111-5; Turner, *op. cit.*, p 3.

[158] *Morien*, p. 20; see *Erec & Enide*, ed. W. W. Newell, *King Arthur &*

Table Round, p. 11; *Romance of Sir Perceval of Galles*, ed. J. O. Halliwell, *Thornton Romances*, st. LXXXIII, ll. 1316 ff.

[159] *Partonope of Blois*, l. 951.

[160] *William of Palerne*, ll. 4563 ff.

[161] *Huon of Burdeux*, No. 40, 41, p. 57.

[162] *History of the Holy Grail*, ll. 444 ff.

[163] *Partonope of Blois*, ll. 944 ff.

[164] *Sir Eger, Sir Grahame, & Sir Gray-Steel, loc. cit.*, pp. 333-4.

[165] *Romance of Partenay*, ll. 916 ff.

[166] *Caxton's Blanchardyn & Eglantine*, ed. L. Kellner, *EETS, ES*, No. 58, p. 76.

[167] *Sir Gawayne & The Green Knight*, ll. 850 ff.

[168] *Huon of Burdeux*, No. 43, 50, p. 383.

[169] Mackenzie, *op. cit.*, pp. 111-6; Turner, *op. cit.*, p. 5.

[170] *Romance of Tristram and Ysolt, loc. cit.*, chap. XII.

[171] *Lyfe of Ipomydon*, ed. H. Weber, *Metrical Romances*, II, ll. 871 ff.

[172] *Ywain & Gawain*, ll. 3115 ff.

[173] *Melusine*, p. 205; see *Generydes*, ed. W. A. Wright, *EETS, OS*, No. 55, 70, p. 146.

[174] *Merlin*, ll. 9752 ff.

[175] *Huon of Burdeux*, No. 40, 41, pp. 138-9.

[176] *Sir Eger, Sir Grahame, & Sir Gray-Steel, loc. cit.*, p. 310.

[177] *Seven Sages of Rome*, p. 6.

[178] *Lydgate's Siege of Thebes*, ll. 2382 ff.

[179] *Sir Eger, Sir Grahame, & Sir Gray-Steel*, pp. 318-9.

[180] *Eric & Enide*, p. 61.

[181] *The Destruction of Troy*, ll. 690 ff.

[182] *Ibid.*, ll. 683-4.

[183] *Sir Eglamour*, ed. G. Schleich, *Palaestra*, LIII, p. 7, ll. 109 ff.

[184] *Sir Tristram*, ed. G. P. McNeill, Scottish Text Society, ll. 1929 ff. The ease of access to the queen's chamber shows the primitiveness of domestic architecture at that time. Scott says that the chamber of the queen was constructed of wooden boards or shingles which could be easily removed. It was probably called a bower because of its resemblance to an arbor. The hall was a separate building, and the art of partitioning was probably unknown. *Ibid.*, p. 123.

[185] Mackenzie, *op. cit.*, pp. 91, 101-2; Toy, *op. cit.*, pp. 173-5.

[186] *Sir Ferumbras*, ll. 2024 ff.

[187] *Beues of Hamtoun*, ll. 1657 ff.

[188] *Torrent of Portyngale*, l. 1634.

[189] *Valentine & Orson*, l. 291.

[190] *Ibid.*, p. 189.

[191] *Morte Arthure*, pp. 320-1.

[192] *Destruction of Troy*, ll. 749 ff.

[193] *Prose Life of Alexander*, ed. J. S. Westlake, *EETS, OS*, No. 143, p. 100.

[194] *Quest of the Holy Grail*, p. 161.

[195] *Sowdone of Babylone*, ll. 1647 ff.

[196] *Huon of Burdeux*, No. 43, 50, p. 412.

[197] *Sir Cleges*, ed. H. Weber, *Metrical Romances*, I, l. 469; *Legend of Dido*, ed. J. O. Halliwell, *Thornton Romances*, ll. 185 ff.; *Huon of Burdeux*, No. 34, p. 779.

[198] *Huon of Burdeux*, No. 40, 41, p. 90.

[199] Mackenzie, *op. cit.*, p. 119; Toy, *op. cit.*, p. 97.

[200] *Morte Arthure*, l. 231.

[201] *Amis & Amiloun*, H. Weber, *Metrical Romances*, II, ll. 2257 ff.

[202] Toy, *op. cit.*, p. 74.

[203] *Amis & Amiloun*, ll. 724 ff.

[204] *Lay of Havelock the Dane*, ed. W. W. Skeat, *EETS, ES*, No. 4, ll. 2071 ff.

[205] Toy, *op. cit.*, pp. 72, 102, 162, 226; Mackenzie, *op. cit.*, pp. 119-20; see G. Rouches, *L'Architecture Italienne* (Paris, 1928), plate XIII.

[206] *Melusine*, pp. 98 ff.

[207] *Sir Gawayne & The Green Knight*, ll. 930 ff.

[208] *Romans of Partenay*, ll. 926 ff.

[209] Mackenzie, *op. cit.*, pp. 120-1, 162.

[210] *Eric and Enide*, pp. 47, 22.

[211] *Liberate Roll*, 35 Henry III; Turner, *op. cit.*, pp. 233-4.

[212] *Coronet*, March, 1937, p. 148.

[213] *Ibid.*, January, 1938, p. 22.

[214] *Assembly of the Gods*, ed. O. L. Triggs, *EETS, ES*, No. 69, ll. 1478 ff.

[215] *Pistill of Susan*, *loc. cit.*, ll. 118 ff.

[216] *Huon of Burdeux*, No. 43, 50, pp. 434, 384.

[217] *Sir Degrevant*, ed. J. O. Halliwell, *Thornton Romances*, st. 39, ll. 609 ff.

[218] *William of Palerne*, ll. 1751-3.

[219] *Sir Degrevant*, *loc. cit.*, ll. 657 ff.

[220] Mackenzie, *op. cit.*, p. 349; Turner, *op. cit.*, p. 3.

[221] Toy, *op. cit.*, p. 95; Mackenzie, *op. cit.*, pp. 122-4; Turner, *op. cit.*, pp. 14, 65.

[222] Mackenzie, *op. cit.*, pp. 122-5; Turner, *op. cit.*, pp. 14, 68; Toy, *op. cit.*, pp. 217, 226; S. O. Addy, *Evolution of the English House* (London, 1933), p 140.

[223] *William of Palerne*, ll. 1681 ff.

[224] *Huon of Burdeux*, No. 43, 50, p. 407.

[225] *Valentine & Orson*, pp. 70-1.

[226] *The Bruce*, ll. 119 ff.

227 *Floriz & Blancheflur*, ed. G. D. McKnight, *EETS, OS*, No. 14, p. 73, ll. 171 ff.

228 *Anonymous Short English Metrical Chronicle*, l. 1075.

229 *Lyfe of Ipomydon*, l. 313.

230 *Sir Degrevant, loc. cit.*, ll. 1393 ff.

231 Toy, *op. cit.*, pp. 71, 136, 154, 156, 160, 165; Turner, *op. cit.*, p. 93.

232 *Perceval*, p. 18; *Sir Gawayne & The Green Knight*, ll. 221-2.

233 *Romance of the Emperor Octavian*, ed. J. O. Halliwell, Percy Society, XIV, ll. 739 ff.

234 *Romance of Sir Perceval of Galles, loc. cit.*, ll. 491 ff.

235 *Partonope of Blois*, ll. 944 ff.

236 *Huon of Burdeux*, No. 43, 50, p. 380.

237 *Romans of Partenay*, ll. 4890 ff.; Turner, *op. cit.*, p. 5.

238 Toy, *op. cit.*, pp. 120, 208; Mackenzie, *op. cit.*, pp. 128-30.

239 *Romans of Partenay*, ll. 4904 ff.; *Caxton's Eneydos*, ed. W. T. Culley and F. J. Furnivall, *EETS, ES*, No. 57, p. 104; *William of Palerne*, ll. 809 ff.

240 *Eric & Enide*, p. 30.

241 Turner, *op. cit.*, pp. 14, 147.

242 *Sir Perceval of Galles, loc. cit.*, ll. 944-5, 1313.

243 *Merlin*, ll. 13771 ff.

244 *Beues of Hamtoun*, p. 85.

245 Toy, *op. cit.*, pp. 226-9; Mackenzie, *op. cit.*, pp. 106-9.

246 *Lyfe of Joseph Aramathia*, ed. W. W. Skeat, *EETS, OS*, 44, ll. 49 ff.

247 *Pistill of Susan*, l. 170; *Torrent of Portyngale*, l. 307.

248 *Huon of Burdeux*, No. 43, 50, p. 406.

249 *Guy of Warwick*, ll. 6188 ff.; *Beues of Hamtoun*, p. 73.

250 *Huon of Burdeux*, No. 43, 50, ll. 3518-20.

251 *Valentine & Orson*, p. 230.

252 *Huon of Burdeux*, No. 40, 41, p. 134.

253 *Charles the Grete*, pp. 89, 92-3.

254 *Huon of Burdeux*, No. 40, 41, p. 125.

255 *Charles the Grete*, pp. 89, 91.

256 *Beues of Hamtoun*, ll. 1297 ff.

257 *Guy of Warwick*, ll. 6199 ff.

258 *The Bruce*, p. 561.

259 *Torrent of Portyngale*, pp. 307 ff.; *Melusine*, pp. 328-9.

260 Toy, *op. cit.*, pp. 77, 79, 94, 182; Mackenzie, *op. cit.*, pp. 129-30; Turner, *op. cit.*, p. 94.

261 *The Bruce*, p. 119.

262 *Pistill of Susan, loc. cit.*, ll. 118 ff.

263 *King Horn*, ed. G. H. McKnight, *EETS, OS*, No. 14, p. 88, ll. 219 ff.

264 Toy, *op. cit.*, pp. 148-9.

265 Turner, *op. cit.*, p. 93.

266 *Sir Tristrem, loc. cit.*, ll. 1558 ff.; *Merlin*, ll. 15257 ff.; *Sowdone of Babylone*, ll. 1647 ff.; *Sir Eglamour*, ed. G. Schleich, *Palaestra*, LIII, p. 19, ll. 524 ff.

267 *Melusine*, p. 296.

268 Toy, *op. cit.*, pp. 114-8; Turner, *op. cit.*, pp. 83, 147 ff.; Mackenzie, *op. cit.*, pp. 117-9.

269 *Libeaus Desconus*, ed. M. Kaluza, *Altenglische Bibliothek*, IV, p. 91, ll. 1865 ff.; *Gawain & The Green Knight*, ll. 1648 ff.

270 *Golagros & Gawane, loc. cit.*, l. 76; *Gawain & The Green Knight*, l. 875.

271 *Sowdone of Babylone*, p. 209.

272 *Huon of Burdeux*, No. 43, 50, p. 383.

273 *Sir Degrevant, loc. cit.*, ll. 1377 ff.

274 *Sowdone of Babylone*, ll. 2347 ff.

275 J. C. Wall, *Mediaeval Wall Painting* (London, n.d.), pp. 27-31, 53, 74-82; Mackenzie, *op. cit.*, pp. 15, 71, 85, 90, 185; Addy, *op. cit.*, pp. 119-20, 133-4, 151; M. D. Anderson, *The Medieval Carver*, (Cambridge, 1935), p. 64; see E. Harris, *The Mural as a Decorative Device in Medieval Literature*, Vanderbilt University Dissertation (1935).

276 *Prose Life of Alexander*, ed. J. S. Westlake, EETS, OS, No. 143, pp. 64, 100, 54; *Huon of Burdeux*, No. 43, 50, pp. 407, 412.

277 *Partonope of Blois*, ll. 1132 ff.; *Troy Book*, No. 97, ll. 962-4.

278 *Huon of Burdeux*, No. 43, 50, p. 589; *Troy Book*, No. 121, ll. 1497 ff.; *Prose Life of Alexander*, p. 99.

279 *Sir Degrevant, loc. cit.*, ll. 1457 ff.

280 *Kyng Alisaunder*, ll. 7760 ff.; *Melusine*, p. 364; *Partonope of Blois*, ll. 213-4; *Charles the Grete*, p. 94; *Romans of Partenay*, l. 5743.

281 *Troy Book*, No. 97, pp. 55-6.

282 *Blanchardyn & Eglantine*, pp. 14-15; *Merlin*, l. 25735; *Huon of Burdeux*, No. 43, 50, p. 590, No. 40, 41, p. 102; *Rauf Coilzear*, ed. F. J. Amours, Scottish Text Society, ll. 628 ff.; *Valentine & Orson*, p. 207.

283 *Traill of Rauf Coilyear*, ll. 667 ff.

284 *Reinburn*, st. 80.

285 Turner, *op. cit.*, pp. 92, 98; Addy, *op. cit.*, p. 134.

286 *Lancelot of the Lake*, ed. W. W. Newell, *King Arthur & Table Round*, p. 148; *Merlin*, ll. 25734 ff.

287 *Sir Degrevant, loc. cit.*, ll. 1469 ff.; *Ywain & Gawain*, ll. 1131-2; *Gawain*, ll. 1131-2; *Gawain & The Green Knight*, l. 568; *Eric & Enide*, p. 47.

288 *Prose Life of Alexander*, p. 54; *Wars of Alexander*, l. 3220.

289 Turner, *op. cit.*, pp. 8, 72-3, 30 ff.

290 *The Castell of Pleasure*, ll. 226 ff.; see Anderson, *op. cit.*, pp. 122-40.

[291] Turner, *op. cit.*, pp. 10-12, 91.

[292] *Joseph of Arimathie*, ll. 204 ff.; *Sir Ferumbras*, ll. 2172 ff.; *Charles the Grete*, p. 117.

CHAPTER THREE

[1] S. O. Addy, *Evolution of the English House*, (London, 1933), pp. 23-5; *Our English Home*, (Oxford, 1876), p. 2. Hereafter referred to as *Home*.

[2] *Lay of Havelock the Dane*, ll. 735 ff.

[3] Addy, *op. cit.*, pp. 32-7.

[4] *Tristram & Ysolt*, LXIV, p. 178, LXXVIII, pp. 215 ff.; *Sir Tristrem*, ll. 2465 ff.

[5] Addy, *op. cit.*, pp. 43-96.

[6] *Rauf Coilzear*, ll. 92-145.

[7] Addy, *op. cit.*, pp. 81-3, 94, 140-1.

[8] *The Bruce*, p. 77.

[9] *Lovelich Merlin*, ll. 211 ff.

[10] Addy, *op. cit.*, pp. 138-53; T. H. Turner, *Domestic Architecture* (London, 1877), pp. 58-61; M. Viollet-le-Duc, *Dictionaire de l'Architecture Francaise du XI au XVI Siècle* (Paris, 1868), VI, 300-16.

[11] *The Bruce*, pp. 158-9.

[12] *History of the Holy Grail*, ll. 293 ff.

[13] *Ibid.*, ll. 569 ff.

[14] *Ibid.*, ll. 397 ff.; *Seven Sages of Rome*, ll. 3063 ff.; *Morien*, p. 57.

[15] *Liberate Roll*, 10 Henry III; Turner, *op. cit.*, p. 100.

[16] *Home*, *op. cit.*, pp. 100-10.

[17] Turner, *op. cit.*, pp. 14 ff.

[18] *Coronet*, December, 1937, p. 21.

[19] Addy, *op. cit.*, p. 102.

[20] E. L. Cutts, *Scenes and Characters of the Middle Ages* (London, 1872), pp. 541-2.

[21] Turner, *op. cit.*, pp. 14 ff.

[22] *Ibid.*, p. 100; *Home*, *op. cit.*, pp. 108-10; Viollet-le-Duc, *Dictionaire Raisonne du Mobilier Francais* (Paris, 1868), I, 156-62. Hereafter referred to as *Mobilier*.

[23] Addy, *op. cit.*, p. 151.

24 *History of the Holy Grail,* p. 396.
25 *King of Tars, loc. cit.,* l. 398; *Sir Eglamour, loc. cit.,* ll. 98 ff.
26) *Melusine,* p. 37.
27 *Beues of Hamtoun,* l. 3796.
28 *Huon of Burdeux,* No. 43, 50, p. 384.
29 *Prose Life of Alexander,* p. 106.
30 *Caxton's Eneydos,* p. 74.
31 *Eric & Enide, loc. cit.,* p. 93.
32 *History of the Holy Grail,* p. 186.
33 *Seven Sages of Rome, loc. cit.,* p. 177.
34 *Siege of Thebes,* l. 2384.
85 *Sir Degrevant, loc. cit.,* st. XCIII, ll. 1472 ff.; *Huon of Burdeux,* No. 43, 50, p. 384.
36) *Sir Gawayne & Green Knight,* ll. 1179-81.
37 *Ibid.,* ll. 853-7.
38 *Sir Degrevant, loc. cit.,* st. XCIV, ll. 1488 ff.
39 *Beues of Hamtoun,* l. 3214.
40 *Generydes,* ll. 69 ff.
41 *Huon of Burdeux,* No. 40, 41, p. 102; *Melusine,* pp. 56 ff.; *William of Palerne,* ll. 2054 ff.
42 *Generydes,* p. 173; *Sir Degrevant, loc. cit.,* st. XCIV, l. 1488; *Eric & Enide,* p. 16.
43 *Ywain & Gawain,* l. 751; *Sir Degrevant, loc. cit.,* st. XCIV, l. 1489; *Beues of Hamtoun,* l. 3996.
44 *Ywain & Gawain,* ll. 1131-2; *Siege of Thebes,* ll. 2382 ff.; *Morte Arthur, loc. cit.,* p. 337; *Launfal, loc. cit.,* l. 94; *Launfal Miles, loc. cit.,* ll. 283-4; *King of Tars, loc. cit.,* ll. 780 ff.; *Kyng Alisaunder, loc, cit.,* p. 37; *Emperor Octavian, loc. cit.,* l. 141; *The Maid of Ascolat, loc. cit.,* p. 216; *Romans of Partenay,* l. 1006.
45 *Sir Ferumbras,* l. 1341.
46) *Horn Childe & Maid Rimnild, loc. cit.,* ll. 370 ff.
47 *Beues of Hamtoun,* ll. 857 ff.; *Blanchardyn & Eglantine,* p. 77.
48 *Quest of the Holy Grail, loc. cit.,* p. 168.
49 *Valentine & Orson,* p. 207.
50 *Seven Sages of Rome,* l. 754; *Lovelich Merlin,* l. 20482.
51 *Home, op. cit.,* p. 29 ff.; Turner, *op. cit.,* pp. 16 ff.; Viollet-le-Duc, *Mobilier,* I, 254-64.
52 Turner, *op. cit.,* pp. 96 ff.; Addy, *op. cit.,* pp. 76-9, 151.
53 *Sir Gawain & the Green Knight,* l. 884.
54 *The Antur of Arthur at Tarnewathelan, loc. cit.,* ll. 439ff.;
55 *Melusine,* p. 54; *Lyfe of Ipomydon, loc. cit.,* ll. 313 ff.
56 *Richard Coer de Lion, loc. cit.,* l. 102; *Le Morte Arthur,* l. 1504.
57 *The Bruce,* p. 118; *Huon of Burdeux,* No. 40, 41, p. 75.

[58] *Amis & Amiloun*, ll. 1576 ff.; *Melusine*, p. 364.
[59] *King of Tars, loc. cit.*, ll. 85 ff.; *Richard Coer de Lion, loc. cit.*, l. 3421; *Torrent of Portyngale*, ll. 816 ff.
[60] *Percival, loc. cit.*, p. 59; *Wars of Alexander*, l. 2926.
[61] *The Awntyrs off Arthure, loc. cit.*, p. 353, l. 400.
[62] Addy, *op. cit.*, pp. 71 ff.; *Liberate Roll*, 35 Henry III; Turner, *op. cit.*, pp. 232, 97-8; *Home, op. cit.*, pp. 113-4, 161-2.
[63] Turner, *op. cit.*, pp. 16 ff.; 96-8, 103-4.
[64] *Wars of Alexander*, ll. 2926 ff.; *Emperor Octavian, loc. cit.*, l. 1084.
[65] *Huon of Burdeux*, No. 43, 50, p. 384; No. 40, 41, p. 75.
[66] *The Bruce*, p. 162.
[67] *William of Palerne*, ll. 4563 ff.
[68] *Amis & Amiloun, loc. cit.*, ll. 1899 ff.; *Romance of Otuel*, ll. 90, 1897 ff.; *Siege of Jerusalem*, ll. 587 ff.
[69] *Richard Coer de Lion, loc cit.*, p. 179.
[70] *Sir Perceval of Gallois, loc. cit.*, ll. 1321 ff.; *Huon of Burdeux*, No. 40, 41, p. 131.
[71] *Sir Ysumbras, loc. cit.*, l. 592; *Valentine & Orson*, p. 196.
[72] *Huon of Burdeux*, No. 43, 50, p. 407.
[73] *Sir Gawayne & The Green Knight*, ll. 1875 ff.
[74] *Seuyen Sages, loc. cit.*, l. 434; *Horn Childe & Maiden Rimnild, loc. cit.*, ll. 327 ff.
[75] *Eric & Enide, loc. cit.*, p. 59.
[76] *Huon of Burdeux*, No. 40, 41, pp. 190, 47.
[77] *Eric & Enide, loc. cit.*, p. 102.
[78] *Assembly of the Gods*, p. 67 n., l. 186.
[79] *Sir Ysumbras, loc. cit.*, ll. 592 ff.
[80] *Wars of Alexander*, l. 236; *Eneydos*, p. 48; *Horn Childe & Maiden Rimnild, loc. cit.*, l. 331.
[81] *Eric & Enide, loc. cit.*, p. 11; *Awntyrs off Arthure, loc. cit.*, l. 341.
[82] *Home, op. cit.*, pp. 30-1.
[83] *Partonope of Blois*, ll. 955 ff.
[84] *Sir Gawayne & The Green Knight*, ll. 113 ff.; *Morte Arthure*, ll. 204 ff.
[85] Addy, *op. cit.*, p. 151; *Home, op. cit.*, pp. 114-5.
[86] *Huon of Burdeux*, No. 43, 50, p. 384.
[87] *Richard Coer de Lion, loc. cit.*, ll. 2064, 5115 ff.
[88] *Huon of Burdeux*, No. 43, p. 770.
[89] *Sir Tristrem, loc. cit.*, ll. 1565 ff.
[90] *Sir Amadace, loc. cit.*, st. XLIV.
[91] *Morte Arthure*, ll. 2282 ff.
[92] *Lancelot of the Lake, loc. cit.*, p. 146.

[93] *Eric & Enide, loc. cit.,* p. 93.

[94] Turner, *op. cit.,* pp. 100-1; *Home, op. cit.,* pp. 29 ff., 36.

[95] Cutts, *op cit.,* pp. 277-8.

[96] *Beues of Hamtoun,* l. 860.

[97] *Emperor Octavian, loc. ct.,* l. 11306.

[98] *Percival, loc. cit.,* p. 59.

[99] *Sir Gawayne & the Green Knight,* l. 885; *Huon of Burdeux,* No. 43, 50, p. 313.

[100] *The Anturs of Arther at the Tarnewathelan, loc. cit.,* st. xxxv.

[101] *Launfal Miles, loc. cit.,* ll. 243-4; *Sir Degrevant, loc. cit.,* ll. 1385 ff.

[102] *Lovelich Merlin,* l. 15266; *Huon of Burdeux,* No. 43, 50, pp. 142, 589.

[103] *Home, op. cit.,* pp. 40-1, 50-1, 45-8; Turner, *op. ct.,* pp. 102-3; Viollet-le-Duc, *Mobilier,* II, 70-87, 108-12.

[104] Turner, *op. cit.,* pp. 102-3.

[105] *Ibid.,* pp. 64-5.

[106] *Ywain & Gawain, loc. cit.,* ll. 758 ff.; *Beues of Hamtoun,* l. 3998.

[107] *Richard Coer de Lion, loc. cit.,* l. 2068.

[108] *Arthour & Merlin, loc. cit.,* ll. 2269-719; *Amis & Amiloun,* ll. 241 ff.

[109] *Cheuelere Assigne,* ll. 154 ff.

[110] *Sir Tristrem, loc. cit.,* ll. 1662 ff., p. 121.

[111] *Seege of Troye, loc. cit.,* ll. 941 ff.; *Wars of Alexander,* ll. 3141 ff.

[112] *Tale of Beryn,* ll. 3922 ff.

[113] *Alexander & Soredamour, loc. cit.,* p. 131.

[114] *Floriz and Blanchefleur,* ll. 163-76.

[115] *Partonope of Blois,* ll. 944 ff.; *Gawayne & Green Knight,* l. 868.

[116] *Sir Degrevant, loc. cit.,* l. 1389; *Awntyrs off Arthure, loc. cit.,* l. 450.

[117] *Beues of Hamtoun,* l. 2742.

[118] *Generides,* ll. 1347 ff.

[119] *History of the Holy Grail,* l. 601.

[120] *Eneydos,* p. 64.

[121] *Arthour & Merlin, loc. cit.,* l. 6944; *Richard Coer de Lion, loc. cit.,* ll. 2067 ff.

[122] *Melusine,* p. 54; *Life of Alexander,* p. 47; *Arthour & Merlin, loc. cit.,* ll. 2257 ff.; *Huon of Burdeux,* No. 43, 50, pp. 410, 413; *Morte Arthure,* l. 1026; *Ywain & Gawain, loc. cit.,* l. 759.

[123] *Morte Arthure,* ll. 176 ff.

[124] *Sir Degrevant, loc. cit.,* l. 1390.

[125] *Launfal,* l. 63; *Partonope of Blois,* ll. 1009 ff.

[126] *Huon of Burdeux,* No. 40, 41, p. 75, No. 43, 50, pp. 413, 589.

[127] *Seven Sages of Rome,* l. 2450; *Mabinogion,* trans. C. Guest (London, 1910), p. 44.

Notes

[128] Turner, *op. cit.*, p. 101; *Home, op. cit.*, pp. 89-91; Addy, *op. cit.*, p. 151; *Coronet*, January, 1938, p. 20.

[129] *Huon of Burdeux*, No. 40, 41, p. 125; *Valentine & Orson*, p. 295.

[130] *Ibid.*, p. 119; *Lydgate's Troy Book*, ll. 2837 ff.

[131] *Siege of Jerusalem*, l. 590; *Melusine*, pp. 17, 327-8.

[132] *The Awntyrs off Arthure, loc. cit.*, l. 451.

[133] *Sir Eglamour, loc. cit.*, ll. 670 ff.; *Kyng Alisaunder, loc. cit.*, l. 5253; *Sowdone of Babylone*, ll. 2347 ff.

[134] *Haus und Hof*, p. 27; *Englischen Leben, op. cit.*, p. 14.

[135] *Seven Sages*, ll. 1580 ff.

[136] H. H. Parkhurst, *Cathedral* (Princeton, 1925), p. 23.

[137] Parkhurst, *op. cit.*, pp. 10, 25-7; D. Rock, *Church of Our Fathers* (London, 1905), I, 150, 228, 246-7, IV, 242; Wall, *op. cit.*, pp. 38, 59, 109, 129-33; Cutts, *op. cit.*, pp. 135-6; T. G. Bonney, *Cathedrals, Abbeys and Churches of England and Wales* (London, 1891), I, 1-15; H. Adams, *Mont St. Michel and Chartres* (Boston, 1905), pp. 10-41.

[138] *Kyng Alisaunder, loc. cit.*, l. 1515.

[139] *Lovelich Merlin*, l. 14466; *Sir Perceval of Galles, loc. cit.*, ll. 36 ff.; *Sir Degrevant, loc. cit.*, ll. 1833 ff.

[140] *William of Palerne*, ll. 1954 ff.; *Huon of Burdeux*, No. 40, 41, p. 38.

[141] *Three Kings of Cologne*, pp. 86, 104.

[142] *The Death of Arthur, loc. cit.*, p. 235.

[143] *Kyng Alisaunder, loc. cit.*, ll. 758 ff.

[144] *Huon of Burdeux*, No. 43, 50, p. 590.

[145] *Three Kings of Cologne*, p. 133.

[146] *Huon of Burdeux*, No. 43, 50, p. 591.

[147] *Athelston, loc. cit.*, ll. 429 ff.

[148] *Gest Hystoriale of Destruction of Troy*, ll. 5614-5.

[149] *Charles the Grete*, ll. 207-8.

[150] *Joseph of Arimathie*, ll. 285 ff.

[151] *Melusine*, pp. 53-4.

[152] *Three Kings of Cologne*, p. 152.

[153] *Sir Amadace, loc. cit.*, p. 18; *Roland & Vernagu*, l. 360.

[154] *Three Kings of Cologne*, p. 18.

[155] *Sir Amadace, loc. cit.*, pp. 50-1.

[156] *Melusine*, pp. 50-1.

[157] *Seven Sages, loc. cit.*, ll. 2518 ff.

[158] Cutts, *op. cit.*, pp. 70-91; Viollet-le-Duc, *op. cit.*, pp. 308-9.

[159] *Huon of Burdeux*, No. 43, 50, p. 546.

[160] *Ibid.*, p. 220.

[161] *Lay le Freine, loc. cit.*, ll. 257 ff.

162 *Roland & Vernagu*, ll. 353 ff.

163 *Athelston, loc. cit.*, ll. 429 ff.; see *Guy of Warwick*, ll. 11089 ff.; *Percival, loc. cit.*, p. 34.

164 *Melusine*, pp. 336-44.

165 *Ibid.*, p. 442.

166 Cutts, *op. cit.*, pp. 93-119.

167 *History of the Holy Grail*, pp. 114 ff.

168 *Ywain & Gawain, loc. cit.*, ll. 1671 ff.

169 *Morien, loc. cit.*, p. 114.

170 *Ibid.*, pp. 112, 151; see *Le Morte Arthure*, ll. 3526 ff.

171 Cutts, *op. cit.*, pp. 120-51.

172 *Ibid.*, p. 134; Malory's *Prince Arthur*, ed. H. O. Sommer (London, 1889).

173 *Ibid.*, p. 124.

174 Davis, *op. cit.*, pp. 6, 29, 497-9, 505-8; Viollet-le-Duc, *op. cit.*, IX, 21-58.

175 *Siege of Thebes*, l. 3408.

176 *Le Morte Arthur*, ll. 3526 ff.

177 *The Bruce*, ll. 584 ff.

178 *Charles the Grete*, p. 248.

179 *Romans of Partenay*, ll. 4493 ff.; see *Melusine*, pp. 17, 327-8.

180 *Laud Troy Book*, ll. 11129-206, 15505-16, 15881-8.

181 Cutts, *op. cit.*, p. 76.

182 *Melusine*, pp. 17, 327-8.

183 *Le Morte Arthur*, ll. 3526 ff.; see *The Death of Arthur, loc. cit.*, p. 230.

184 Cutts, *op. cit.*, p. 476.

185 *Ibid.*, pp. 461-86; Davis, *op. cit.*, pp. 245-79.

186 *Three Kings Sons*, p. 45.

187 *Sir Isumbras, loc. cit.*, l. 221.

188 *Blanchardyn & Eglantine*, p. 154.

189 *Melusine*, p. 108.

190 *Wars of Alexander*, ll. 1291 ff.

191 *Richard Coer de Lion, loc. cit.*, l. 2458.

192 *The Bruce*, l. 87.

193 *Richard Coer de Lion, loc. cit.*, l. 2043.

194 *Blanchardyn & Eglantine*, p. 154.

195 *Tristram & Ysolte, loc. cit.*, pp. 23, 46.

196 *Gest Hystoriale of Destruction of Troye*, l. 1077.

197 *Lay of Havelock the Dane*, ll. 706 ff.

198 *Idem.*

199 *Seege of Troye, loc. cit.*, p. 11, l. 54.

200 *Richard Coer de Lion, loc. cit.*, l. 2046.

[201] *Eneydos*, p. 74.

[202] *Partonope of Blois*, ll. 723 ff.

[203] *Sir Eglemour, loc. cit., l.* 1042; *Sir Ysumbras, loc. cit.,* l. 208; *Melusine,* pp. 114-15.

[204] *History of the Holy Grail*, pp. 299, 357, 396.

[205] *The Maid of Ascolat, loc. cit.,* p. 25.

[206] *Gest Hystoriale of Destruction of Troye*, ll. 5667-69.

[207] *Seege of Troye*, p. 6; *Sir Ysumbras, loc. cit.,* ll. 208-09.

[208] *Seege of Troye*, p. 52.

[209] *Sowdone of Babylone*, ll. 129 ff.

[210] *Richard Coer de Lion, loc. cit.,* l. 2643.

[211] *Sir Tristram, loc. cit.,* ll. 1279 ff.

[212] *Tristram & Ysolt, loc. cit.,* p. 46.

[213] *Morte Arthure,* ll. 729 ff., 3602 ff., 3655 ff.

[214] *Richard Coer de Lion, loc. cit.,* ll. 2597 ff.

[215] Davis, *op. cit.,* pp. 277-78.

[216] *Ibid.,* p. 341.

[217] *Ibid.,* p. 613.

[218] Cutts, *op. cit.,* p. 539.

[219] *Froissart's Chronicles*, p. 71; Besant, *op. ct.,* pp. 94 ff.

[220] *Coronet* (March, 1937), p. 144.

[221] Cutts, *op. cit.,* p. 426; Violet-le-Duc, *Mobilier,* I, 56-63, 509-13.

[222] Turner, *op. cit.,* p. 122.

[223] Cutts, *op. cit.,* p. 425.

[224] *Sir Ferumbras,* l. 2692.

[225] *Percival, loc. cit.,* p. 76.

[226] *Lancelot of the Laik,* ll. 729 ff.

[227] *Sowdone of Babylone,* l. 2699; *Merlin,* l. 13092.

[228] *Syr Tryamoure, loc. cit.,* ll. 946 ff.

[229] *Beues of Hamtoun,* l. 1415.

[230] *King of Tars, loc. cit.,* l. 351.

[231] *Laud Troy Book,* l. 4811.

[232] *Gest Hystoriale of Destruction of Troy,* ll. 6201-08.

[233] *Eric & Enide, loc. cit.,* p. 85.

[234] *Lovelich Merlin,* ll. 6594-96.

[235] *Amis & Amiloun,* l. 1858; Davis, *op. cit.,* p. 341.

[236] Cutts, *op. cit.,* pp. 276, 279, 414.

[237] F. W. Galpin, *Old English Musical Instruments* (London, 1910).

[238] *Blanchardyn & Eglantine,* p. 56.

[239] *Siege of Jerusalem,* l. 1178.

[240] *Fragment of Song of Roland,* l. 53.

[241] *Siege of Thebes,* l. 3578.

242 *The Awntyrs off Arthure, loc. cit.,* l. 343.

243 *Huon of Burdeux,* Nos. 40, 41, p. 170.

244 *Gest Hystoriale of Destruction of Troy,* ll. 1535-37.

245 *Sir Tristrem, loc. cit.,* ll. 1809 ff.

246 *Huon of Burdeux,* Nos. 43, 50, p. 590; *Guy of Warwick,* l. 6855; *Merlin,* l. 13364; *Torrent of Portyngale,* l. 2449 ff.

247 *Sir Gawayne & the Green Knight,* l. 116.

248 See G. G. Coulton, *The Chronicler of European Chivalry* (London, 1930); Cutts, *op. cit.,* pp. 363, 372, 434; *Mobilier,* VI, 340-51.

249 *Richard Coer de Lion, loc. cit.,* ll. 5117, 1664.

250 *Kyng Alisaunder, loc. cit.,* l. 5235; *Golagros & Gawane, loc. cit.,* ll. 312 ff.

251 *Sir Ferumbras,* l. 78; *Tristram & Ysolt, loc. cit.,* p. 3; *Alexander & Soredamour, loc. cit.,* p. 125; *Percival, loc. cit.,* p. 13.

252 *Romans of Partenay,* l. 1003.

253 *Kyng Alisaunder, loc. cit.,* l. 4301.

254 *Morte Arthure,* l. 1294.

255 *Launfal Miles, loc. cit.,* l. 268.

256 *Golagros & Gawane, loc. cit.,* ll. 312 ff.

257 *Siege of Jerusalem.* ll. 322 ff.

258 *Richard Coer de Lion, op. cit.,* l. 5118; *Blanchardyn & Eglantine,* p. 57.

259 *Romans of Partenay,* l. 1005; *Melusine,* pp. 35, 56, 282; *Emperor Octavian, loc. cit.,* l. 1084; *Richard Coer de Lion, loc. cit.,* l. 1523; *Morte Arthure, l.* 3192.

260 *Melusine,* p. 53.

261 *Ibid.,* p. 54.

262 *The Awntyrs off Arthure, loc. cit.,* ll. 439 ff.

263 *Wars of Alexander,* ll. 2922 ff.

264 Cutts, *op. cit.,* pp. 380-93, 439-51; Davis, *op. cit.,* pp. 117-42. *Fayttes of Armes & Of Chyualrye,* pp. 154-90; *Mobilier,* VI, 333-39.

265 *The Bruce,* p. 432.

266 *Siege of Jerusalem,* ll. 670 ff.

267 *Huon of Burdeux,* No. 43, p. 664; *Siege of Thebes,* l. 4314.

268 *Destruction of Troy,* p. 154.

269 *Sir Ferumbras,* l. 3312; *Wars of Alexander,* l. 1419.

270 *Short English Metrical Romance,* l. 2086.

271 *Lancelot of the Laik,* l. 730.

272 *Siege of Jerusalem,* ll. 612 ff.

273 *Lydgate's Troy Book,* l. 8128.

274 *Siege of Thebes,* l. 4312.

275 *Siege of Jerusalem,* ll. 670-1.

276 *Ibid.,* l. 653; *Sir Ferumbras,* ll. 3279 ff.

277 *Three Kings Sons,* pp. 40, 45.
278 *Godeffroy of Bologne,* p. 102.
279 *The Bruce, op. cit.,* p. 432.
280 *Siege of Jerusalem, op. cit.,* ll. 647 ff.
281 *Richard Coer de Lion, loc. cit.,* l. 1841.
282 *Godeffroy of Bologne, op. cit.,* p. 264.
283 *Sir Ferumbras, op. cit.,* ll. 3252 ff.
284 *The Bruce, op. cit.,* pp. 428-9.

CHAPTER FOUR

1 *Lydgate's Troy Book,* ll. 4770 ff.
2 *Laud Troy Book,* ll. 9451 ff.
3 *Prose Life of Alexander,* p. 99.
4 *Ibid.,* p. 47; *Wars of Alexander,* ll. 3220 ff., 2922 ff.
5 *Tristram & Ysolt,* p. 176.
6 *Sir Gawain and the Grail Castle,* pp. 33-34.
7 R. S. Loomis, *Celtic Myth and Arthurian Romance* (New York, 1927), p. 212.
8 *Reinbrun,* st. 79, ll. 7 ff.
9 E. Faral, *Recherches sur les sources latines des contes et romans courtois du moyen age* (Paris, 1913), pp. 320-25; M. Otto Sohring, "Werke bildender Kunst in altfranzosischen Epen," in *Romanische Forschungen,* XII (1900), 491 ff.
10 *Floriz and Blanchfleur,* ll. 568 ff.
11 Faral, *op. cit.,* pp. 322-25.
12 M. G. Paris, "Le Pelerinage de Charlemagne," *Romania,* IX (1880), 6 ff.
13 *Prose Life of Alexander,* p. 92.
14 C. B. Lewis, *Classical Mythology and Arthurian Romance* (New York, 1932), p. 185.
15 *Caxton's Eneydos,* p. 117.
16 Lewis, *op. cit.,* pp. 161-63.
17 *Tale of Beryn,* ll. 2711 ff.
18 F. J. Furnivall and W. G. Stone, *The Tale of Beryn,* p. 135; F. J. Furnivall, E. Brock, and W. A. Clouston, *Originals and Analogues of Some of Chaucer' Tales* (London, 1888), p. 336.

[19] *Neville's Castell of Pleasure*, ll. 234-35, 291-94.

[20] Faral, *op. cit.*, p. 355.

[21] *Huon of Burdeux*, pp. 370-71.

[22] *Mandeville's Travels*, pp. 109, 180.

[23] *Huon of Burdeux*, p. 798.

[24] *Life of Alexander*, p. 64.

[25] *Wars of Alexander*, ll. 3662 ff.

[26] G. F. Kunz, *The Curious Lore of Precious Stones* (Philadelphia, 1913), pp. 300-15; Faral, op. cit., pp. 379-80.

[27] *Troy Book*, ll. 962-1030.

[28] *Laud Troy Book*, ll. 9451 ff.

[29] *Floriz and Blanchefleur*, ll. 583 ff.

[30] *Reinbrun*, st. 80, ll. 8 ff.

[31] *Huon of Burdeux*, No. 43, pp. 770 ff.

[32] *Troy Book*, ll. 4770 ff.

[33] *Prose Life of Alexander*, p. 108.

[34] *Huon of Burdeux*, Nos. 43, 50, pp. 440, 589-90.

[35] *Richard Coer de Lion*, *loc. cit.*, II, ll. 77 ff.

[36] *Launfal Miles*, *loc. cit.*, l. 265; *Siege of Jerusalem*, ll. 322 ff.; *Guy Of Warwick*, ll. 3640 ff.

[37] Faral, *op. cit.*, pp. 352-54; Kunz, *op. cit.*, pp. 143-75; D. B. Easter, *A Study of the Magic Elements in the Romans d'Aventure and the Romans Breton* (Johns Hopkins University Dissertation, 1906), p. 96.

[38] *Prose Life of Alexander*, p. 100.

[39] *Three Kings of Cologne*, p. 18.

[40] *Perceval*, pp., 195-96.

[41] Edited by E. Koschwitz (Strassburg, 1875).

[42] E. Rhys, *Arthurian Legend* (Oxford, 1891), p. 332; W. O. Sypherd, *Studies in Chaucer's House of Fame*, pp. 144 ff.; W. A. Nitze, "The Castle of the Grail—An Irish Analogue," *Studies in Honor of A. Marshall Elliott*, p. 26; Loomis, *op. cit.*, p. 173; Faral, *op. cit.*, p. 323; J. D. Bruce, "Human Automata in Classical Tradition and in Mediaeval Romance," *Modern Philology*, 10 (1913), 511-26.

[43] *The Seven Sages of Rome*, ll. 1987 ff.

[44] Faral, *op. cit.*, pp. 80-82.

[45] *Huon of Burdeux*, Nos. 40, 41, pp. 98-99.

[46] H. O. Sommer, *Vulgate Version of Arthurian Romances*, IV, 144, 151, 191.

[47] Faral, *op. cit.*, p. 352.

[48] *Lydgate's Troy Book*, No. 97, ll. 6757 ff.

[49] *Destruction of Troy*, ll. 4951 ff.

[50] *Tale of Beryn*, ll. 2760 ff.

[51] *Huon of Burdeux*, Nos. 43, 50, p. 412.

[52] *Reinbrun*, st. 80, ll. 1 ff.

[53] *Guy of Warwick*, ll. 11384 ff.

[54] *Tale of Beryn*, ll. 2711 ff.

[55] *Wars of Alexander*, ll. 3662 ff.

[56] *Prose Life of Alexander*, p. 64.

[57] F. J. Furnivall, Edmund Brock, *Originals and Analogues of Chaucer's Canterbury Tales*, p. 336; *Tale of Beryn*, p. 135.

[58] Faral, *op. cit.*, pp. 328-29; Lewis, *op. cit.*, pp. 78-79.

[59] *Huon of Burdeux*, Nos. 43, 50, pp. 434, 442.

[60] *Floriz and Blanchefleur*, ll. 273 ff.

[61] *Mandeville's Travels*, I, 202-31; Faral, *op. cit.*, p. 353.

[62] *Huon of Burdeux*, Nos. 40, 41, p. 260.

[63] *Ibid.*, No. 43, pp. 304-05.

[64] *History of Holy Grail*, ll. 531 ff.

[65] *Huon of Burdeux*, No. 40, 41, pp. 454-57.

[66] *Ibid.*, No. 43, pp. 808-09.

[67] *Melusine*, pp. 110, 119,319, 25.

[68] *Ibid.*, p. 376. See note to passage.

[69] *Huon of Burdeux*, Nos. 40, 41, p. 76.

[70] *Ibid.*, No. 43, pp. 807-8 (see note to passage); S. Baring-Gould, *Curious Myths of the Middle Ages* (New York, 1901), p. 431.

[71] *Prose Life of Alexander*, p. 105.

[72] *Huon of Burdeux*, No. 43, p. 806 (see note on passage).

[73] *Beues of Hamtoun*, p. 66, ll. 175 ff.

[74] *Prose Life of Alexander*, p. 96.

[75] Faral, *op. cit.*, p. 338.

[76] *Siege of Jerusalem*, ll. 1249 ff.

[77] Kunz, *op. cit.*, p. 237; Faral, *op. cit.*, p. 81.

[78] *Partonope of Blois*, ll. 840 ff.

[79] Faral, *op. cit.*, pp. 79 ff., 321.

[80] *Lydgate's Troy Book*, ll. 5469 ff.

[81] *Valentine & Orson*, p. 133.

[82] *Siege of Thebes*, ll. 534 ff.

[83] *Gest Hystoriale of Destruction of Troy*, ll. 776-80.

[84] *Charles the Grete*, p. 206.

[85] *Roland & Vernagu*, ll. 329 ff.

[86] *One Hundred and One Nights*, trans. G. Demombynes (Paris, 1883), p. 302; Bruce, *op. cit.*, pp. 511-26.

[87] *Anonymous Short English Metrical Chronicle*, ll. 736 ff.

[88] Dickman, *op. cit.*, pp. 136-37.

[89] *Laud Troy Book*, ll. 11129 ff.

[90] *Lydgate's Troy Book*, ll. 5613 ff.

[91] Guido delle Colonne, *Historia Destructionis Troiae*, ed., N. D. Griffin (Cambridge: The Mediaeval Academy of America, 1936), pp. 177-78.

[92] Faral, *op. cit.*, pp. 326-28.

[93] *War of Alexander*, ll. 3141 ff. (See *Prose Life of Alexander*, p. 51.)

[94] *Ibid.* (See note to passage.)

[95] *Ibid.*, ll. 530 ff.

[96] Kunz, *op. cit.*, pp. 230-1; *Wars of Alexander*, p. 290.

[97] *Partonope of Blois*, ll. 868 ff.

[98] *Huon of Burdeux*, p. 810.

[99] *Lovelich History of Holy Grail*, pp. 257, 409.

[100] A. C. L. Brown, "The Irish Element in King Arthur and the Grail," in *Mediaeval Studies in Memory of Gertrude Schoepperle Loomis*, p. 100; Sommer, *op. cit.*, VI, 143, 163, 192; Loomis, *op. cit.*, pp. 258-59.

[101] *Ywain* & *Gawain*, ll. 327 ff.; *Knight of the Lion, loc. cit.*, p. 150.

[102] Lewis, *op. cit.*, pp. 47-127.

[103] *Lovelich History of Holy Grail*, p. 79.

[104] Lewis, *op. cit.*, pp. 257, 266, 75.

[105] *Ibid.*, pp. 268-75.

[106] Loomis, *op. cit.*, pp. 237-49.

[107] *Gawain at the Grail Castle*, pp. 54 ff.

[108] Loomis, *op. cit.*, pp. 158-76; Nitze, *op. cit.*, pp. 19-52.

[109] Lewis, *op. cit.*. pp. 269-72.

[110] Loomis, *op. cit.*, pp. 218-19.

[111] Loomis, *op. cit.*, pp. 215-26.

[112] *Parzival*, sec. 567.

[113] Loomis, *op. cit.*, pp. 223-24.

[114] *Chevalier au Cygne*, ed, Baron de Reiffenberg (Bruxells, 1841), I, 58.

[115] *Cheuelere Assigne*, ll. 40 ff.

[116] *Troie, op. cit.*, V, 1681 ff.

[117] *Gest Hystoriale of Destruction of Troye*, ll. 786 ff.

[118] *Lydgate's Troy Book*, ll. 3019 ff.

[119] *Troie*, V, 16683-91.

[120] *Laud Troy Book*, ll. 11129 ff.

[121] *Floire et Blanceflor*, ed. M. Edelstand du Meril (Paris. 1856), V, 585 ff.

[122] *Ibid.*, V, 1607 ff.

[123] *Floriz and Blanceflur*, ll. 568 ff.

[124] *Floire et Blanceflor*, V, 1731 ff.

[125] *Floriz and Blancheflur*, ll. 605 ff.

[126] *Ibid.*, ll. 618 ff.; *Floire et Blanceflor*, V, 597 ff.

BIBLIOGRAPHY

Alexander & *Dindimus*, ed. W. W. Skeat, *EETS, ES*, No. 31 (London: N. Trubner & Co., 1867).

Alexander & *Soredamour*, ed. W. W. Newell, *King Arthur* & *Table Round* (New York: Hougton, Mifflin & Co., 1897).

Amis & *Amiloun*, ed. MacEdward Leach, *EETS, OS*, No. 203 (London: Oxford Press, 1937).

Amoryas & *Cleopes*, ed. H. Craig, *EETS, OS*, No. 132 (London: Paul, Trench, Trubner & Co., 1916).

Anonymous Short English Metrical Chronicles, ed. E. Zettl, *EETS, OS*, No. 196 (London: Oxford Press, 1935).

The Anturs of Arthur at the Tarnewathelan, ed. J. Robson, *Three Early English Metrical Romances* (London: J. B. Nichols & Son, 1842).

Arthour & *Merlin*, ed. E. Kolbing, *Altenglische Bibliothek*, IV (1889), 1-72.

Arthur, ed. F. J. Furnivall, *EETS, OS*, No. 2 (London: N. Trubner & Co., 1869).

The Assembly of the Gods, ed. O. L. Triggs, *EETS, ES*, No. 69, (London: Paul, Trench, Trubner, 1886).

The Assumption of Our Lady, ed. G. H. McKnight, *EETS, OS*, No. 14 (London: Paul, Trench, Trubner, 1901).

The Avowynge of King Arther, Sir Gawan, ed. J. Robson, *Three Early English Metrical Romances* (London: J. B. Nichols & Son, 1842).

The Awntyrs off Arthure at the Terne Wathelyne, ed. F. J. Amours, *Scottish Text Society* (London: W. Blackwood & Sons, 1897).

Book of the Fayttes of Armes & *of Chualrye*, ed. A. T. P. Byles, *EETS, OS*, No. 189 (London: Oxford Press, 1932).

The Bruce, ed. W. W. Skeat, *EETS, ES*, No. 11 (London: Paul, Trench, Trubner, 1890).

The Castell of Pleasure, ed. R. Cornelius, *EETS, OS*, No. 179 (London: Oxford Press, 1930).

Caxton, William, *Blanchardyn* & *Eglantine*, ed. L. Kellner, *EETS, ES*, No. 57 (London: N. Trubner & Co., 1890).

Charles the Grete, ed. S. J. H. Herrtage, *EETS, ES*, Nos. 36, 37 (London: N. Tubner & Co., 1880).

Chevalier au Cygne, ed. Baron de Reiffenburg (Bruxelles: M. Hayes, 1841).

The Death of Arthur, ed. W. W. Newell, *King Arthur & Table Round* (New York: Houghton, Mifflin Co., 1897).

Duke Huon of Burdeux, ed. S. L. Lee, *EETS, ES,* Nos. 40, 41, 43, 50 (London: N. Trubner & Co., 1882, 1883).

Ellis, George, *Specimens of Early English Metrical Romances* (London: Longman, Hurst, Rees, Orme, & Browne, 1811).

Erec & Enide, ed. W. W. Newell, *King Arthur & Table Round* (New York: Houghton, Mifflin & Co., 1897).

The Fire of Love, ed. R. Harvey, *EETS, OS,* No. 106 (London: Paul, Trench, Trubner, 1896).

Firumbras & Otuel & Roland, ed. M. O'Sullivan, *EETS, OS,* No. 198 (London: Oxford Press, 1935).

Floire et Blancheflor, ed. M. E. du Meril (Paris: P. Jannet, 1856).

Floriz and Blancheflur, ed. G. H. McKnight, *EETS, OS,* No. 14 (London: Paul, Trench, Trubner, 1901).

Four Lays of Marie de France, trans. J. L. Weston (London: David Nutt, 1910).

Four Sonnes of Aymon, ed. O. Richardson, *EETS, ES,* Nos. 44, 45 (London: N. Trubner & Co., 1874).

Froissart, John, *Chronicles,* trans. J. Bourchier (New York: Macmillan Co., 1908).

Gawain & the Green Knight, ed. I. Gollancz, *EETS, OS,* No. 162 (London: Oxford Press, 1923).

Generydes, ed. W. A. Wright, *EETS, OS,* Nos. 55, 70 (London: N. Trubner & Co., 1878).

Gest Hystoriale of Destruction of Troy, ed. G. A. Panton and Donaldson, *EETS, OS,* No. 39 (London: N. Trubner & Co., 1869).

Geste of the Worthie King & Emperour Alisaunder of Macedoine, ed. W. W. Skeat, *EETS, ES,* No. 1 (London: Paul, Trench, Trubner, 1894).

Godeffroy of Bologne, ed. M. Colvin, *EETS, ES,* No. 64 (London: Paul, Trench, Trubner, 1894).

Guido delle Colonne, *Historia Destruction Troiae,* ed. N. D. Griffin (Cambridge: The Mediaeval Academy of America, 1936).

Guy of Warwick, ed. J. Zupitza, *EETS, ES,* Nos. 25, 26, 42, 49, 59 (London: N. Trubner & Co., 1875).

Halliwell, J. O., *Thornton Romances* (London: J. B. Nichols, 1844).

History of the Holy Rood Tree, ed. A. S. Napier, *EETS, OS,* Nos. 103, 106 (London: Paul, Trench, Trubner, 1894).

Horn Childe & Maiden Rimnild, ed. J. Caro, *Englische Studien,* XII (1889), 351-66.

Hunttyng of the Hare, ed. H. Weber, *Metrical Romances of the 13th, 14th, and 15th Centuries* (Edinburgh: A. Constable & Co., 1810).

Bibliography

Joseph of Arimathie, ed. W. W. Skeat, *EETS, OS,* No. 44 (London: N. Trubner & Co., 1871).

Karls des Grossen Reise Jerusalem und Constantinople, ed. E. Koschwitz (Strassburg: K. J. Trubner, 1875).

King Horn, ed. G. H. McKnight, *EETS, OS,* No. 14 (London: Paul, Trench, Trubner, 1901).

The King of Tars, ed. F. Krause, *Englische Studien,* XI (1888), 1-63.

The Knight of the Lion, ed. W. W. Newell, *King Arthur & Table Round* (New York: Hougton, Mifflin Co., 1897).

The Knightly Tale of Golagros & Gawane, ed. F. J. Amours, *Scottish Alliterative Poems* (London: W. Blackwood & Sons, 1897).

Knyghthode & Bataile, ed. R. Dyboski and Z. M. Arend, *EETS, OS,* No. 201 (London: Oxford Press, 1938).

Kyng Alisaunder, ed. H. W. Weber, *Metrical Romances of the 13th, 14th, and 15th Centuries* (Edinburg: A. Constable & Co., 1810).

Lancelot of the Laik, ed. W. W. Skeat (London: N. Trubner & Co., 1865).

Lancelot of the Lake, ed. W. W. Newell, *King Arthur & Table Round* (New York: Houghton, Mifflin & Co., 1897).

Laud Troy Book, ed. J. E. Wulfing, *EETS, OS,* Nos. 121, 122 (London: Paul, Trench, Trubner, 1902).

Launfal, ed. G. L. Kittredge, *American Journal of Philology,* X (1889), 1-34.

Launfal Miles, ed. M. Kaluza, *Englische Studien,* XVIII (1893), 165-184.

Lay of Gugemar, trans. E. Mason, *French Metrical Romances,* Everyman Library (London: J. M. Dent & Sons, 1924).

The Lay of Havelock the Dane, ed. W. W. Skeat, *EETS, ES,* No. 4 (London: Paul, Trench, Trubner, 1869).

Lay of the Dolorous Knight, trans. E. Mason, *French Metrical Romances,* Everyman Library (London: J. M. Dent & Sons, 1924).

Marie le Fraine, ed. H. W. Weber, *Metrical Romances of the 13th, 14th, and 15th Centuries* (Edinburgh: A. Constable, 1810).

Lays of Marie, ed. George Ellis, *Specimens of Early English Metrical Romances* (London: Longman, Hurst, Rees, Orme, & Browne, 1811).

The Legend of Dido, ed. J. O. Halliwell, *Thornton Romances* (London: J. B. Nichols, 1884).

Lestoire de Merlin, ed. H. O. Sommer, *Vulgate Version of Arthurian Romances* (Washington: Riverside Press, 1911).

Libeaus Desconus, ed. M. Kaluza, *Altenglische Bibliothek,* V (1890), 25-117.

Liberate Rolls, 10 Henry III, ed. W. H. Stevison (London: Longman, Green, Longman, and Roberts, 1916).

The Lovelich History of the Holy Grail, ed. F. J. Furnivall, *EETS, ES,* Nos. 20, 24, 28, 30 (London: N. Trubner & Co., 1874).

Lydgate, John, *Minor Poems*, ed. H. N. MacCracken, *EETS, ES,* No. 107 (London: Oxford Press, 1911).

Siege of Thebes, ed. A. Erdmann, *EETS, ES,* No. 108 (London: Oxford Press, 1911).

Troy Book, ed. H. Bergen, *EETS, ES,* Nos. 97, 103, 106 (London: Oxford Press, 1906).

Lyfe of Ipomydon, ed. H. W. Weber, *Metrical Romances of the 13th, 14th, and 15th Centuries* (Edinburgh: A. Constable & Co., 1810).

Lyfe fo Joseph of Armathy, ed. W. W. Skeat, *EETS, OS,* No. 44 (London: N. Trubner & Co., 1871).

Lyfe of Joseph of Armathy, ed. W. W. Skeat, *EETS, OS,* No. 44 (London: N. Trubner & Co., 1871).

Mabinogion, trans. Lady C. Guest, Everyman Library (London: J. M. Dent & Sons, 1910).

The Maid of Ascolat, ed. W. W. Newell, *King Arthur & Table Round* (New York: Houghton, Mifflin & Co., 1897).

The Maid with the Narrow Sleeve, ed. W. W. Newell, *King Arthur & Table Round* (New York: Houghton, Mifflin & Co., 1897).

Malory, Thomas, *La Morte D'Arthur*, ed. H. O. Sommer (London: David Nutt, 1889).

Mandeville, John, *Travels*, ed. P. Hamilius, *EETS, OS,* No. 154 (London: Oxford Press, 1923).

Melusine, ed. A. K. Donald, *EETS, ES,* No. 68 (London: Paul, Trench, Trubner, 1895).

Merlin, ed. E. K. Kock, *EETS, ES,* Nos. 93, 112; *OS,* No. 185 (London: N. Trubner & Co., 1904).

Merlin, ed. W. W. Newell, *King Arthur & Table Round* (New York: Houghton, Mifflin & Co., 1897).

Merlin, ed. H. B. Wheatley, *EETS, OS,* Nos. 10, 21 (London: Paul, Trench, Trubner, 1899).

Le Morte Arthur, ed. J. D. Bruce, *EETS, ES,* No. 88 (London: Paul, Trench, Trubner, 1903).

Morte Arthure, ed. E. Brock, *EETS, OS,* No. 8 (London: Paul, Trench, Trubner, 1865).

Morte Arthure, ed. G. Ellis, *Specimens of Early English Metrical Romances* (London: Longman, Hurst, Rees, Orme, & Browne, 1811).

Newell, W. W., *King Arthur & Table Round* (New York: Houghton, Mifflin & Co., 1897).

Octuian Imperator, ed. H. W. Weber, *Metrical Romances of the 13th, 14th, and 15th Centuries* (Edinburgh: A. Constable & Co., 1810).

One Hundred and One Nights, trans. G. Demombynes (Paris: L. Baros
& Forcel, 1883).

Otuel & Roland, ed. M. O'Sullivan, *EETS, OS,* No. 198 (London: Oxford Press, 1935).

Partonope of Blois, ed. A. T. Bodtker, *EETS, ES,* No. 109 (London:
N. Trubner & Co., 1911).

Le Pelerinage de Charlemagne, ed. M. G. Paris, *Romania,* IX (1880),
6 ff.

Perceval, ed. W. W. Newell, *King Arthur & Table Round* (New York:
Houghton, Mifflin & Co., 1897).

The Pistill of Susan, ed. F. J. Amours, Scottish Text Society (London:
W. Blackwood & Son, 1897).

Prose Life of Alexander, ed. J. S. Westlake, *EETS, OS,* No. 143 (London: Oxford Press, 1904).

Quest of the Holy Grail, ed. W. W. Newell, *King Arthur & Table
Round* (New York: Houghton, Mifflin & Co., 1897).

Rauf Coilyear, ed. S. J. H. Herrtage, *EETS, ES,* No. 36 (London: N.
Trubner & Co., 1882).

Rauf Coilzear, ed. F. J. Amours, Scottish Text Society (London: W.
Blackwood & Son, 1897).

Reinbrun, ed. J. Zupitza, *EETS, ES,* Nos. 42, 49, 59 (London: N. Trubner & Co., 1883).

Richard Coer de Lion, ed. H. W. Weber, *Metrical Romances of the 13th,
14th, and 15th Centuries* (Edinburgh: A. Constable & Co., 1810).

Riley, H. T., *Munimenta Gildhallas Londoniensis, Liber Albus,* Rolls
Series, I, xl (London: Longman, Green, Longman, & Roberts,
1859-62).

Roman de Troie, ed. L. Constans, Société des Anciens Textes Francais
(Paris: F. Didot & Co., 1904-12).

Roman von Guillaume de Clerc, trans. G. C. Druce (Ashford, Kent:
Headley Bros., 1936).

Romance of Amoryas & Cleopes, ed. H. Craig, *EETS, OS,* No. 132
(London: Oxford Press, 1916).

Romance of Cheulere Assigne, ed. H. H. Gibbs, *EETS, ES,* No. 6 (London: Paul, Trench, Trubner, 1898).

Romance of Duke Rowland & of Sir Ottuell of Spayne, ed. S. J. H. Herrtage, *EETS, ES,* No. 35 (London: N. Tubner & Co., 1880).

Romance of Emare, ed. E. Rickert, *EETS, ES,* No. 99 (London: N.
Trubner & Co., 1908).

Romance of Emperor Octavian, ed. J. O. Halliwell, Percy Society (London: T. Richards, 1844).

Romance of Morien, ed. J. L. Weston (London: David Nutt, 1910).

Romance of Otuel, ed. S. J. H. Herrtage, *EETS, ES,* No. 39 (London: N. Trubner & Co., 1882).

Romance of Sir Perceval of Galles, ed. J. O. Halliwell, *Thornton Romances* (London: J. B. Nichols, 1844).

Romance of Syr Traymore, ed. T. Wright, Percy Society (London: T. Richards, 1845).

Romance of Tristram and Ysolt, trans. R. S. Loomis (New York: Columbia University Press, 1931).

Romans of Partenay, ed. W. W. Skeat, *EETS, OS,* No. 22 (London: Paul, Trench, Trubner, 1866).

Die Romanze von Athelston, ed. J. Zupitza, *Englische Studien,* XIII (1889), 331-43.

Rouland & Vernagu, ed. S. J. H. Herrtage, *EETS, ES,* No. 39 (London: N. Trubner & Co., 1882).

De Sancto Joseph ab Armathy, ed. W. W. Skeat, *EETS, OS,* No. 44 (London: N. Trubner & Co., 1871).

The Seege of Troye, ed. A. Zietsch, *Herrig's Archiv,* 72 (1885), 1-58.

The Seege or Batayle of Troye, ed. M. E. Barnicle, *EETS, OS,* No. 172 (London: Oxford Press, 1927).

Sege of Melayne, ed. S. J. H. Herrtage, *EETS, ES,* No. 35 (London: N. Trubner & Co., 1880).

Seuyn Sages, ed. H. W. Weber, *Metrical Romances of the 13th, 14th, and 15th Centuries* (Edinburgh: A. Constable & Co., 1810).

The Seven Sages, ed. T. Wright, Percy Society (London: T. Richards, 1845).

Seven Sages of Rome, ed. K. Brunner, *EETS, OS,* No. 191 (London: Oxford Press, 1933).

Siege of Jerusalem, ed. E. Kolbing and M. Day, *EETS, OS,* No. 188 (London: Oxford Press, 1932).

Sir Amadace, ed. J. Robson, *Three Early English Metrical Romances* (London: J. B. Nichols & Son, 1842).

Sir Amadas, ed. H. W. Weber, *Metrical Romances of the 13th, 14th, and 15th Centuries* (Edinburgh: A. Constable & Co., 1810).

Sir Beues of Hamtoun, ed. E. Kolbing, *EETS, ES,* Nos. 46, 48, 65 (London: Paul, Trench, Trubner, 1885).

Sir Cleges, ed. H. W. Weber, *Metrical Romances of the 13th, 14th, and 15th Centuries* (Edinburgh: A. Constable & Co., 1810).

Sir Degrevant, ed. J. O. Halliwell, *Thornton Romances* (London: J. B. Nichols, 1844).

Sir Eger, Sir Grahame, & Sir Gray-Steel, ed. G. Ellis, *Specimens of Early English Metrical Romances* (London: Longman, Hurst, Rees, Orme, & Browne, 1811).

Bibliography

Sir Eglamour, ed. G. Schleich, *Palaestra*, LIII (1906), 1-60.

Sir Eglamour, ed. J. O. Halliwell, *Thornton Romances* (London: J. B. Nichols, 1844).

Sir Ferumbras, ed. S. J. H. Herrtage, *EETS, ES*, No. 34 (London: Paul, Trench, Trubner, 1903).

Sir Gawayne & the Green Knight, ed. R. Morris, *EETS, OS*, No. 4 (London: Paul, Trench, Trubner, 1864).

Sir Gawain & the Green Knight, ed. J. L. Weston (London: David Nutt, 1912).

Sir Gawain at the Grail Castle, trans. J. L. Weston (London: David Nutt, 1903).

Sir Isumbras, ed. J. O. Halliwell, *Thornton Romances* (London: J. B. Nichols, 1844).

Sir Tristrem, ed. G. P. McNeill, Scottish Text Society (London: W. Blackwood & Sons, 1886).

Sir Ysumbras, ed. J. Zupitza, *Palaestra*, XV (1868), 1 ff.

Song of Roland, ed. S. J. H. Herrtage, *EETS, ES*, No. 35 (London: N. Trubner & Co., 1880).

The Sowdone of Babylone, ed. E. Hausknecht, *EETS, ES*, No. 38 (London: N. Trubner & Co., 1879).

The Story of Tristram & Iseult, ed. J. L. Weston (London: David Nutt, 1910).

Taill of Rauf Coilyear, ed. S. J. H. Herrtage, *EETS, ES*, No. 39 (London: N. Trubner & Co., 1882).

The Tale of Beryn, ed. W. G. Stone, *EETS, ES*, No. 105 (London: N. Trubner & Co., 1909).

Thomas of Ercldoune, ed. J. A. H. Murray, *EETS, OS*, No. 61 (London: N. Trubner & Co., 1875).

Three Kings of Cologne, ed. G Horstmann, *EETS, OS*, No. 85 (London: N. Trubner & Co., 1886).

Three Kings Sons, ed. F. J. Furnivall, *EETS, ES*, No. 67 (London: N. Trubner & Co., 1895).

Torrent of Portyngale, ed. E. Adam, *EETS, ES*, No. 51 (London: N. Trubner & Co., 1887).

Valentine & Orson, ed. A. Dickson, *EET, OS*, No. 204 (London: Oxford Press, 1937).

Vulgate Version of the Arthurian Romances, ed. H. O. Sommer (Washington: Riverside Press, 1911).

The Wars of Alexander, ed. W. W. Skeat, *EETS, ES*, No. 47 (London: N. Trubner & Co., 1886).

Weber, H. W., *Metrical Romances of the 13th, 14th, and 15th Centuries* (Edinburgh: A. Constable & Co., 1810).

William of Palerne, ed. W. W. Skeat, *EETS, ES,* No. 1 (London: Paul, Trench, Trubner, 1867).

Ywain and Gawain, ed. G. Schleich (Leipzig: Geo. Maske, 1887).

SECONDARY MATERIALS

Adams, Henry, *Mont St. Michel and Chartres* (Boston: Houghton, Mifflin & Co., 1905).

Addy, S. O., *Evolution of the English House* (London: George Allen & Unwin, 1933).

Anderson, M. D., *The Mediaeval Carver* (Cambridge: University Press, 1935).

Baring-Gould, S., *Curious Myths of the Middle Ages* (New York: Longmans, Green & Co., 1901).

Besant, Walter, *Mediaeval London* (London: Adams and Charles Black, 1906).

Blanchet, A., *Les Enceintes Romaines de la Gaule* (Paris: E. Leroux, 1907).

Bonney, T. G., *Cathedrals, Abbeys, and Churches of England and Wales* (London: Cassel & Co., 1891).

British Museum Reproductions from Illuminated Manuscripts (London: Oxford Press, 1923).

Brown, A. C. L., "The Irish Element in King Arthur and the Grail," *Mediaeval Studies in Honor of A. Marshall Elliott* (Baltimore: Johns Hopkins Press, n.d.).

Bruce, J. B., "Human Automata in Classical Tradition and in Mediaeval Romance," *Modern Philology,* 10 (1913), 511-26.

The Evolution of the English Romances from the Beginning Down to the Year 1300 (Baltimore: Johns Hopkins Press, 1923).

Coronet (December, 1937), p. 21, (January, 1938), p. 24.

Coulton, G. G., *The Chronicler of European Chivalry* (London: H. Reiach, 1930).

Cutts, E. L., *Scenes and Characters of the Middle Ages* (London: Virtue & Co., 1872).

Davis, H. W. C., *Mediaeval England* (Oxford: Clarendon Press, 1928).

Dickman, A. J., *Le Role du surnaturel dans les chansons de geste* (University of Iowa Dissertation, 1925).

Bibliography

Doerks, Henry, *Haus und Hof in den Epopoen des Crestien von Troies* (Griefswald: J. Abel, 1885).

Easter, D. B., *A Study of the Magic Elements in the Romans d' Adventure and the Romans Breton* (Johns Hopkins University Dissertation, 1906).

Escholier, R., 'La Fleur des manuscrits," *L'Illustration,* No. 4840 (Christmas, 1935).

Faral, Edmond, *Recherches sur les sources latines des contes et romans courtois* (Paris: E. Champion, 1913).

Furnivall, F. J., Brock, E., and Clouston, W. A., *Originals and Analogues of Some of Chaucer's Canterbury Tales* (London: N. Trubner & Co., 1888).

Galpin, F. W., *Old English Instruments of Music* (London: Methuen & Co., 1910).

Gobel, Heinrich, *Tapestries of the Lowlands* (New York: Brentano's, Inc., 1924).

Grant, J., *Old Edinburgh* (London: Cassell, Petter, and Galpin Co., 1881).

Gunther, E. C., *Englische Leben in vierzehnten Jahrhundert* (Leipzig: Druck von Hesse und Becker, 1889).

Harris, Elizabeth L., *The Mural as a Decorative Device in Mediaeval Literature* (Vanderbilt University Dissertation, 1935).

Herbert, J. A., *Illuminated Manuscripts* (New York: G. P. Putnam Sons, 1911).

Johnston, O. M., "The Description of the Emir's Orchard in Floire & Blancheflor," *Zeitschrift fur romanische Philologie,* 32 (1908), 705 ff.

Ker, W. P., *Epic and Romance* (London: Macmillan & Co., 1931).

Kunz, G. F., *The Curious Lore of Precious Stones* (Philadelphia: J. B. Lippincott Co., 1913).

Lamprecht, K. G., *Deutsche Geschichte* (Berlin: R. Gaertners, 1895-1909).

Lewis, C. B., *Classical Mythology and Arthurian Romance* (New York: Oxford Press, 1932).

Loomis, R. S., *Celtic Myth and Arthurian Romance* (New York: Columbia University Press, 1927).

Mackenzie, William, *The Mediaeval Castles in Scotland* (London: Methuen & Co., 1927).

Munro, D. C., and Sellery, G. C., *Mediaeval Civilization* (New York: Century Co., 1907).

Munro, D. C., and Sontag, R. J., *The Middle Ages* (New York: Century Co., 1921).

Nitze, W. A., "The Castle of the Grail—An Irish Analogue," *Studies in Honor of A. Marshall Elliott* (Baltimore: Johns Hopkins Press, n.d.).

Our English Home, Its Early History and Progress, with Notes on the Introduction of Domestic Inventions (Oxford: Jas. Parker & Co., 1876).

Parkhurst, H. H., *Cathedral* (Boston: Houghton, Mifflin & Co., 1936).

Pirenne, Henri, *Mediaeval Cities* (Princeton: Princeton University Press, 1925).

Roche, A. de, "Aiglum et C Graux," *Revue de Philologie,* 20 (1897), 64-75.

Rock, D., *The Church of Our Fathers* (London: John Murray, 1905).

Rouches, Gabriel, *L'Architecture italienne* (Paris: G. V. Oest, 1928).

Rhys, E., *Arthurian Legend* (Oxford: Clarendon Press, 1891).

Sabine, E. L., "City Cleaning in Mediaeval England," *Speculum,* 12 (1937), 19-34.

Sypherd, W. O., *Studies in Chaucer's House of Fame* (London: Paul, Trench, Trubner, 1907).

Toy, Sidney, *Castles* (London: William Hinemann, 1939).

Turner, T. H., *Some Accounts of Domestic Architecture in England from the Conquest to the End of the 13th Century* (London: J. H. Parker, 1877).

Viollet-le-Duce, M., *Dictionaire de l'architecture francaise du XI au XVI siecle* (Paris: V. A. Morel, 1868).

Dictionaire raisonné du mobilier francais de l'epique a la renaissance (Paris: V. A. Morel, 1868).

Wall, J. C., *Mediaeval Wall Painting* (London: Talbot & Co., n.d.).

Withington, Robert, *English Pageantry* (Cambridge: Harvard University Press, 1918).

index

Bailey, 40, 41, 43-46, 48, 56, 62-64, 72, 80
Bakery, 74, 82, 83
Bankets. *See* Cushions
Barber shop, 36
Barbican, 28, 47, 49, 62, 63
Barges, 27, 127, 128
Barn, 99, 100-102
Barras, 30, 67
Bartizan, 26
Basins for bathing, 91, 111, 114
Baths, 91
Battlement, 23-25, 29, 45, 51, 58, 59, 68, 87
Beds, 36, 48, 66, 70, 76, 77, 78, 103, 104, 105, 115, 120, 134
Benches, 74, 100, 102, 105, 107, 108, 134
Boats, 112, 128, 129
Bolt, 30, 31, 63, 67, 68, 96
Bower, 101, 102, 107, 110, 115
Brewery, 82, 83, 101
Bridges, 26-31, 41, 45-48, 53, 58, 60, 61, 62, 64
Buffet. *See* Cupboard
Building site: marshland, 19, 52; eminence, 19, 52, 60; river, 18, 19, 22, 27, 52, 60, 62, 64, 91; seashore, 18, 52, 90
Burg or suburb, 19, 20, 47
Buttery or winehouse, 72, 82, 83, 85, 99, 100

Cabriolet, 130
Candles, 114, 115, 120, 124, 125, 134
Candlesticks, 114, 115, 126, 134
Canopy, 103-105
Carpets and rugs, 80, 96, 104, 108, 109

Carriages, 130
Carts, 129, 130
Castles, 18-20, 40, 45, 98;
  types: mote bailey, 40-43, 44, 60, 62, 70; square keep, 44, 45, 48, 90; cylindrical keep, 45-47, 90; keepless castle, 47-49; palace, 50; tower, 50, 51;
  battlement, 45, 51, 58, 59, 68, 87; caphouse, 87; chapel, 43, 76, 79, 80; decoration, 93, 94, 95; doors, 44, 45, 47, 48, 60, 67, 70, 83, 86, 88, 89, 96; living room, 43, 50; loopholes, 44, 45, 62; materials, 52, 53; postern, 44, 47, 80, 81; stairs, 44, 47, 51, 56, 58, 73, 82, 83, 85-88; turrets, 45, 47, 50, 51, 78
Castle wall, 40-43, 44, 45, 46, 47, 48, 50, 54, 62, 63, 67, 70, 71, 72, 81
Cellar, 37, 43, 73, 82, 83, 85, 87
Chairs, 92, 107, 108
Chambers, 43, 44, 50, 72, 75-79, 81, 82, 85, 87, 93, 94
Chantry chapel, 124
Chapels, 43, 76, 79, 80, 102, 119, 122, 123, 125, 134
Chariots, 130, 131
Chests, 110
Chimneys, 34, 82, 92, 93, 98, 99, 100, 102
China, 111-113
Churches, 18, 33, 114-119, 123-125
Church furnishings and vessels, 118, 119
Cistern, 90, 91
Cities, 18-24, 29, 33

201

Index

City walls, 18-24, 29, 33;
   battlement, 23-25, 29; curtain, 24-26, 32; embrasures, 23; gates, 21; loopholes, 23, 26, 29; materials, 21, 24, 28, 29; merlons, 23; parapet, 23, 28; sally port, 29; stairs, 24, 25; towers, 24-26; turrets, 25, 26; wall walk, 23-26
Conduits, 38, 39, 90, 91, 96
Couches, 103, 104, 105, 123
Cradles, 103-105
Cupboard or buffet, 109
Cups, 109, 112, 113, 114, 134
Curtain, 24-26, 32, 53, 54
Curtains, 103-105
Cushions and bankets, 107-109, 130

Disarming room, 79
Domestic houses, 33, 34, 36, 95, 103, 108;
   types: huts, 98; manor house, 101, 104; pit dwelling, 99; rectangular house, 99;
   apartments, 36; barns, 99-102; bower, 101, 102, 107, 110, 115; brewery, 101; buttery, 99, 100; chapel, 102; doors, 98, 100, 101; fireplace, 100, 108; floor, 100, 102; gate, 102; hall, 101, 102, 106, 108, 109, 131; latrine, 39, 101; pigcote, 101; roof, 33; screens, 99, 100, 107, 108; stairs, 36, 100; washhouse, 101
Donjon, 20, 44, 46, 47, 56, 71, 79, 89
Doors, 24-26, 29, 44, 45, 47, 48, 60, 63, 64, 66, 67, 70, 72, 82, 83, 86-88, 96, 98, 100, 101

Embrasures, 23
Engines of war, 30, 135-137

Fireplace, 91, 92, 100, 102, **108**
Floors, 95, 96, 100, 102, **108**
Forks, 112, 113
Fortress, 19, 20
Fountain, 81

Gallery, 80, 88
Galley, 126-128
Garden, 80, 81, 87, **91, 133**

Gates, 21, 28, 29, 37, 51, 58, 62, 63, 66, 67, 68, 69, 75, 81, 86, 102, 119, 121, 123
Gateways, 28, 29, 30, 32, 34, 46, 47, 48, 55, 58, 59, 61, 62, 63, 64, 66, 68, 71, 121
Guild hall, 37, 38

Halls, 44, 48, 50, 51, 56, 72-74, 75-79, 81, 85-87, 92, 95;
   bakery, 74, 82, 83; brewhouse, 82, 83; buttery, 72, 82, 85; chambers, 75-78, 81, 82, 85, 87, 93, 94; dining room, 72, 74, 78; disarming room, 79; doorway, 72, 81; fountain, 81; gallery, 80, 88; garden, 80, 81, 87, 91, 133; kitchen, 72, 81; living room, 72, 76, 77; pantry, 72, 82, 85; parlor, 74, 94; screens, 72, 82
Harbor chains, 129
Henhouse, 101
Hermitages, 122, 123
Hoards, 59

Inns, 34, 36, 37, 88, 103

Keep, 41-47, 54, 55, 62, 70, 75, 77, 79, 86, 90
Kitchen, 37, 72, 82, 83, 85, 120, **122**
Kitchen utensils, 112, 114
Knives, 112, 113, 134

Ladders, 25, 54, 135, 136
Lamps, 115, 126
Larder, 82, 83
Latrines, 39, 88, 90, 91, 101
Lighting, 89, 114, 115, 120, **124-126,** 134
Linen, 103, 104, 106, 110, 111, 134
Litters, 130, 131
Locks, 30, 67, 81, 89, 96
Loopholes or meurtrieres, 23, 26, **29,** 44, 45, 62, 63, 64, 88

Machicolations, 28, 29, 47, 59, 63, **64,** 68
Manor house, 18, 91, 101, 102, **104,** 110
Market, 37, 38, 117

Index

Mattresses, 103, 104

Merlons, 23, 58, 59

Meurtrieres. *See* Loopholes

Mills, 34

Moat, 21, 27, 28, 31, 39, 40, 41, 43, 46, 48, 58, 59, 60, 62, 63

Monasteries, 34, 79, 119, 120, 121, 122

Murals, 94, 95

Musical instruments, 131-133

Out buildings, 82, 83, 99-102

Ovens, 82, 83

Palaces, 18, 32, 33, 38, 50, 86, 87

Palisades, 21

Pantry, 72, 82, 85

Parapet, 23, 28

Parlor, 74, 94

Pavement, 32, 33

Pavilion or tent, 106, 128, 131, 133, 134

Pigcote, 101

Pillows, 103, 104

Places: Alexander, 22; Alnwick, 58, 78; Amisfield, 53; Angers, 54; Arques, 79, 90; Auchences, 52; Avignon, 24, 25, 26; Aydon, 87, 92; Beaumaris, 48, 52, 55, 56, 57, 60, 80; Beaurepaire, 94, 110; Beeston, 60; Berwick, 22; Bodiam, 61; Bolleit, 99; Bolsterstone, 100; Borthwick, 79, 80, 82, 92; Bothwell, 54, 56, 58, 60, 68, 73, 74; Burg Ez-Zefer, 60, 64; Caerlaverock, 54, 56, 58, 60, 74, 76; Caernarvon, 52, 55, 56, 58, 61, 64, 87; Caerphilly, 28, 48, 49, 52, 61, 62, 86, 87; Cahors, 28; Cairo, 29, 31; Canterbury, 69, 70, 120; Cardross, 76; Chapel Uny, 99; C h a r n e y, 102; Chateau de Bologne, 60; Chateau Gaillard, 46, 91; Chepstow, 70, 72; Chester, 24; Clarendon, 93; Clermont, 121; Colchester, 69, 86; Comlongon, 51, 82; Constantinople, 140, 144, 146, 148; Conway, 24, 52, 56, 59, 60, 61, 62, 86, 87; Corfe, 70, 79; Cornwall, 99; Crichton, 88; Dalhouse, 60; Denbigh, 63, 64; **Derbyshire, 94; Dinant, 62; Dirle-**ton, 53, 54, 89, 92; Doune, 50, 56, 67, 68, 74, 83; Dover, 44, 85, 90; Dumfriesshire, 92; Dunnottar, 60, 68, 82, 87; Dunscaith, 61; Duntulm, 68; Durham, 41, 52, 80, 103, 106; Edinburgh, 19, 82; Elstow, 32; Etampes, 46; Exeter, 63; Flint, 52; Foix, 56, 70; Fountains, 120; Geddington, 91; Gisors, 80; Gloucester, 119; Gunthwaite, 1 0 1 ; Halforest Tower, 85; Harlech, 54, 61, 86; Houdan, 45, 69; Huntley, 50; Invernochty, 52; Kenilworth, 27, 70; Kensworth, 101; Kildrummy, 80; Kinmont, 52; La Roche Guyon, 54, 91; Laval, 52; Ledes, 91; Leicester, 72; Le K r a k des Chevaliers, 54, 55, 86; Leominster, 38; Lincoln, 37; Linlithgow, 50, 77; Loches, 44, 69; Lochleven, 83; London, 19, 22, 23, 24, 25, 29, 31, 32, 33, 34, 35, 38, 44, 107, 119, 121, 125; Longtown, 69; Ludgershall, 93; Marleybone, 38; Midhope, 106; Monserrat, 122; Morton, 50, 53, 60; Najac, 55; Newark-on-Trent, 63; Newcastle, 85, 90; Oakham, 96; Oxford, 90, 119; Paris, 117; Parthenay, 31, 63; Peirrefonds, 88, 89; Pembroke, 47, 52, 63, 68; Pensitone, 99; Perth, 27; Peterborough, 119; Provins, 46; Ravenscraig, 50, 53; Richmond, 55, 80; Rising, 85; Rochester, 85, 129; Rome, 117; Rothesay, 53; Rowsley, 122; Rushy Lee, 101; Salisbury, 99, 106; Saltcoats, 53; Sandon, 101; Sherborne, 58, 72; Skenfrith, 41, 55, 60, 70, 88; Southampton, 37; Spedlins Tower, 88; St. Andrews, 88; Stonypath T o w e r, 53; Tantallon, 53, 54, 58, 60, 88; Threaves, 51, 53, 85, 90; Totnes, 42, 54; Tulliallan, 53, 85; Upnor, 129; Visby, 24, 26; Walton, 101; Warwick, 52, 56, 88; Wilton, 110; Winchester, 86, 106; Windsor, 52, 62; Yester, 55; York, 24, 103, 124; Yorkshire, 122

Index

Portcullises, 30, 31, 63, 64, 66, 68, 69
Postern, 31, 44, 47, 68, 69, 80, 81
Prison, 87, 88, 89, 90, 121

Reclusorium, 123
Roofs, 24, 26, 33, 44, 45, 51, 56, 63, 72, 74, 82, 92, 94, 96, 101, 120
Rugs. *See* Carpets

Sails, 127, 128, 129
Sally port, 29
Screen, 72, 82, 99, 100, 107, 108
Sewerage, 38, 39
Sewery, 82
Shackles, 90
Ships, 28, 110, 126-129
Shops, 34, 35, 36
Shutters, 34, 35, 58, 69, 70, 123
Silverware, 78, 109, 110, 111, 112, 113, 114
Sink, 82
Spoons, 109, 112, 113
Stables, 37, 48, 87, 88, 100, 121, 123
Stairs, 24, 25, 36, 44, 47, 51, 56, 58, 73, 82, 83, 85, 86, 87, 88, 100
Statutes, 124, 125, 126
Streets, 32, 34-36, 38, 39, 130
Supernatural:
  architecture, 138-149, 1 5 2 , 153; Duke Isope's castle, 141, 142; Grail castle, 160, 161; house of Dedalus, 141; Illium, 138-140; magnetized castles, 142; palace of the sun god, 140, 141; Porus' palace, 142, 143; turning castle, 144, 145;
  automata, 145, 146, 163; bed, 161; carbuncle stone, 143, 144, 163; chains, 162; fabulous fountains, 149, 158, 159; fabulous jewels, 139, 140, 150; fabulous stones, 139-141; flying chair, 152; glass walls, 140; horn, 151; lance, 159, 160; magic cups and vessels, 150, 159, 160; magic mirror, 145; magnetized stones, 142; mechanical birds, 147-149; metal tree,

146, 147; musical instruments, 151; rings, 150, 151, 162; ships, 157, 158; Siege Perilous, 161; talismen or oracles, 149, 150, 153, 154, 159, 162, 164; thrones, 156, 157

Table linen, 106, 110, 111, 134
Tables, 72, 74, 75, 100, 102, 105-107, 110, 111, 115, 134
Tapestry, 94, 95, 109, 119, 126
Tent. *See* Pavilion
Tiles, 96, 118
Tombs, 124, 125, 126
Torches, 89, 115
Towers, 20, 21, 24-26, 28, 33, 41, 43, 44, 46-48, 50, 51, 54-56, 58, 59, 62-64, 70, 71, 77, 78, 82, 83, 87, 88, 89, 91
Town hall, 37, 38
Towns and villages, 18-21, 46
Turrets, 25, 26, 45, 47, 50, 51, 78

Utensils, 85, 91, 111, 112, 114, 118, 119

Villages. *See* Towns

Wagons, 110, 129-131
Walls, 41-54, 59, 63-64. *See also* bailey, castle walls, churches, city walls, c u r t a i n , gateways, halls, screen, and towers
Wall walk, 23-26, 46, 56, 58
Wardrobes, 76, 102, 103
Washhouse, 101
Washroom, 79, 90
Water supply 38, 39, 44, 45, 74, 81, 90, 91
Wells, 44, 45, 74, 81, 90, 91
Wicket, 31, 68, 123
Windows, 34, 44, 45, 50, 69, 70-74, 77, 87-89, 94, 98, 102, 119, 123, 134
Winehouse. *See* Buttery

Yetts, 67, 68